For
Marion Stewart

Thank you, Uncle Sam.
Proud to have flown with you.
Thank you for the loan of the beautiful big airplanes.
Squadron Leader John Crompton RAF

(The North American RB-45C Tornado)

Clydeside Aviation

Sabres from the North

By

Charles E. Mac Kay

Publisher: A. MacKay (Publisher) Ltd

ISBN: 9781838056735 Editor: C. Barrowman
Layout picture sourcing & design: GM

Printed and bound in Scotland
by Merchant City Print
High Street, Glasgow
Scotland

CONTENTS

1.

Introduction

You used to see them over the city, small dots in the sky. Sometimes they would climb contrailing and then came down screaming and roaring, they crossed the shipyards, came over the River Clyde and landed at Renfrew airport. They were the symbol of the perfect jet fighter, it looked right, it sounded right, it was right – the Canadair Sabre.

This is an account of my personal encounter with the Sabrejet. My Dad had a shop in Renfrew and during his lunch hours we were taken to Renfrew Airport as a treat. This would be about 1957-58 when the post-war world was new and the world was being rebuilt, made new after the World War. Every day was new, something new was being said and some new invention was being displayed, we even had radio and television. Yet we had coal fires, horses and carts in the street and moved around Glasgow in trams and went on holiday with trains pulled by steam engines. Then there were the pictures, the moving pictures, Tuesday, Thursday and Saturday mornings. John Wayne made a film with the Sabre, *"Jet Pilot,"* with Janet Leigh then there was Robert Mitchum in the 1958 film, *"The Hunters."* Were they the stars? No! It was the North American F-86 Sabre.

But there was one Sabre, with one star and that was Jacqueline Cochran. She had managed to procure the Canadair Sabre Mk3 for her pioneering flight in May 1953. In a blaze of publicity she flew across Rogers Dry Lake, California at the speed of sound becoming the first woman to break the sound barrier.

As we crossed the River Clyde from Yoker to Renfrew, on the ferry, we were met by the sound of riveting from Yarrows and Simon Lobnitz and we had to wait till the Burns & Laird steamer for Ireland crossed the chains. When we moved the chains would spring up from the Clyde and make a rattling sound with the vibration going right through the whole ferry.

When we got to the airport there was the sound of jets mixed with the sound of piston engined air liners. If we were lucky we could get on the apron and move around the Dakotas, Elizabethans and Yorks and then the treat - a helicopter. But more so in the background you could hear and see the jets. They were not British but Canadian – Canadair Sabres and Avro CF-100s of the Royal Canadian Air Force. They lived in the Lockheed hangars and it seemed as if there were hundreds of them. As they took off clouds of smoke would drift over the airfield then they would be gone. Going back we went down a lane which had a huge wire fence and in the grass there were plastic tubes filled with red hydraulic fluid –"Don't touch they're poisonous." Needless to say they were touched! With just one more look round we would then return to Renfrew town centre.

Renfrew Airport designed by W.H. Kininmonth for the Ministry of Civil Aviation, contractors A.A. Stewart and Sons (Glasgow) Ltd. Civil Engineers, Blyth and Blyth Edinburgh

The completed Renfrew Airport Terminal about 1954

Renfrew Airport Control Tower and flight apron

Other times we would stand at the Arklestone Cemetery gate and watch the aeroplanes land and take off. I could remember this camouflaged Canadair Sabre with a black tail marked with the *"Cutty Sark"* in white, take-off in a trail of exhaust smoke. The pilot held the Sabre low over the runway, he accelerated, pulled up and then he was a speck in the clouds, a small dot climbing the distant blue, then, coming down from the sky, it grew larger and larger till the Sabrejet landed gracefully.

But leaving Renfrew was not the end. Always in the minds' eye were the pairs of Sabres and CF-100s taking off, heading for altitude over Glasgow. Sometimes they would dive and the sound barrier would be broken. Bitten with the aviation bug we went back and back often. Life was the Royal Air Force Flying Review, Flight, Air Pictorial, The Dumpy Book of Flight and the Observers Book of

Aircraft, the Wonder Book of the Royal Air Force and cuttings of aeroplanes from the newspapers glued into exercise books. Time was further spent on making Airfix, Revell and Monogram models, the latter, the ultimate aeroplane model kit in 1/48 scale.

British European Airways at Renfrew 15 June 1962 as Dakota Pionair "C.G. Grey," G-ALTT makes its final departure. To the rear Viscount and Vanguard, (foreground) Herald and Heron for the Western Isles.

There was a downside to aviation. As they came into land at Renfrew the television screen would be covered in lines and become distorted and it would make strange noises. When the aircraft passed further on and landed the television screen returned to normal.

One day my elder brother took me Renfrew, a treat on the tram and ferry. We were sitting in the cafeteria on Morris Contract chairs. As they talked, the Spotters swapped registrations, photographs and negatives. I think there were five of us when this god approached us. He was a Royal Canadian Air Force pilot from Scottish Aviation. He wore a flying jacket over his uniform, a smooth blue number two; he had a crew cut and wore a forage cap. He established if we were Spotters, he quickly disappeared and reappeared, carrying brown tubes. I was ignored but he gave the others a tube each. Inside was a rolled up coloured picture of a Sabre or a CF-100. We were astonished at such kindness – he was Flying Officer Tony Gunter-Smith. A year later he did impressive low-level aerobatics at the Abbotsinch air display in a CF-100.

The reception area, this was where the Spotters gathered to the right of the stair. Here Flying Officer A. Gunter-Smith presented them with coloured images of Sabres and CF-100s

The Canadair Sabre was delivered to Europe via Canada, Iceland, Greenland then Great Britain. They were flown over the North Atlantic hence the title, "Sabres from the North." Later the United States Air Force flew the North American Sabre across the North Atlantic to Prestwick in Ayrshire over the same route. These aircraft flew with four external wing tanks to extend the aircraft's range. Other Sabres arrived to be refurbished by Scottish Aviation for MDAP or Spain. (Every spare piece of ground at the time at Prestwick seemed to be occupied by Sabres). Later, in the early Sixties, the nuclear capable F-86H arrived to build up NATO forces in Europe during the Berlin Wall crisis.

Sabre Mark 5s for the West German Air Force refurbished by Scottish Aviation at Renfrew 1957

West German Sabre Mark 5 landing at Renfrew

Preparing Mk 5 Sabre 921at Renfrew, formerly RCAF 23131

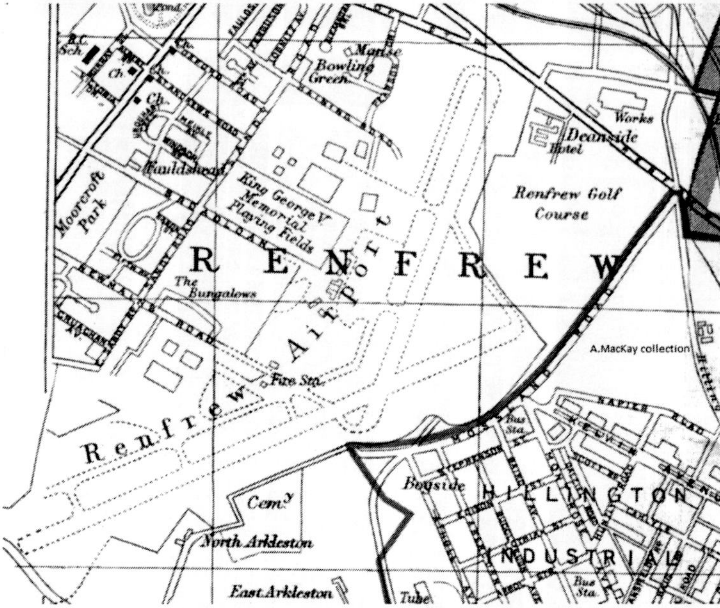

Renfrew Airport at about 1961, the Spotters stood at the gate of Arkleston Cemetery

Royal Canadian Air Force Canadair Sabre 6

Royal Canadian Air Force Avro CF-100 Mark 4, 18389

Prestwick Airport Hotel and Control Tower

Sabre Mark 5, BB-108 ex RCAF 23027at Prestwick 1957

USAF North American F-86 Sabre FU-347 at Prestwick with four underwing fuel tanks

In 1958 the Spotters went to RAF Kinloss on an annual camp. Air experience was provided by an Anson and from the air they saw naval aircraft in open storage at Lossiemouth. One treat was to be taken round the aircraft hangars at Kinloss. There were two hangars set aside which no-one went to but the cadets were taken there. Inside, to their surprise, the two hangars were filled with F-86 Sabres. No cameras or notes were allowed and all they did was leave to speculate.

USAF Boeing WB-50D 0-80105, landing at Prestwick, 12 September 1962 after an operation over the North Atlantic

Years later spotting had expanded and there was Leuchars and Turnhouse, but it was Prestwick we headed for. Scottish Aviation had moved its operations from Renfrew to Prestwick in 1960, Renfrew was just too small and the Lockheed Hangars had been lost to British European Airways. There the Sabres and CF-100s were serviced and repaired but now was added the American aircraft of the United States Air Force with Grumman Albatross seaplanes, Globemasters, Constellations, C-54s, C-118s, B-57 jets and later rescue SC-54s. But now, because Prestwick had more room for storage there were many more cocooned Canadair Sabres. Time had moved and we were now in the nineteen sixties, a different age. Wandering through the lines of aircraft we realised it was the twilight of the gods, Canadair Sabre and the CF-100 both types now being reduced to scrap at Prestwick. Spotters from the continent were now in abundance and one caused controversy by logging the Sabres as CF-100s and the CF-100s as Sabres. No more was the sky to be filled with powered dots – it was the end of the era.

USAF North American F-86 Sabre in Korea

The Canadair Sabre has its genesis in the North American F-86 Sabre which itself was heavily influenced by German aeronautical research particularly the swept wing Messerschmitt ME-262 fighter. The Sabre was mass produced after World War Two in the political climate of the Cold War. To achieve a balance of power the western powers formed NATO to halt the aggressive expansion of the Soviet Union. It was the time of the "Iron Curtain," the Korean War, the Atom Bomb, the Hungarian uprising, the Congo and the MiG-15, with "Reds under the Beds."

In addition to MDAP contract work Scottish Aviation produced the Twin Pioneer STOL airliner Left Twin Pioneer in production at Prestwick

A civilian Twin Pioneer produced for Swissair

Royal Air Force Twin Pioneer XL966 of 152 Squadron

As a means of defence, free armament to Europe was supplied by the United States of America, which had the finance introduced into its defence budget as the Mutual Defense Aid Program (MDAP) this was when America supplied her allies with modern munitions and equipment. Part of that aid was the Canadair Sabre, funded by MDAP for the Royal Air Force. MDAP also operated within the NATO powers with each nation supplying each other, free of charge, military equipment. This was to counter the expansion of the Soviet Union (USSR); the perceived threat from the USSR was 200 divisions, over 9000 aircraft, with airfields being built all over Eastern Europe and the dogma of Soviet world domination. The Cold War could get "Hot" in places such as Korea and Vietnam with the USSR funding nationalist movements in the countries of the European Empires. One such hot–spot was the former Belgian Congo, another was Malaya.

1947 USAF B-29 Superfortress in formation with Bomber Command Avro Lancaster Mk VIIs

With the Soviet Union blockading Berlin in 1948 the Americans returned to the United Kingdom in some force; the United States Air Force (USAF) brought to these shores bombers and fighters and quickly re-established its wartime relationship with the Royal Air Force (RAF). The first movement we are aware of was the American vessel *U.S.A.T. Barney Kirschbaum* carrying thirteen Shooting Stars, then the carrier vessel *USS Sicily* coming into King George V Dock with the 36th Fighter Wing of F-80 Shooting Stars, though sixteen F-80s were flown to Europe at first, through Stornoway, 81 were due in total.

Avro CF-100s on extended maintenance in the Lockheed Hanger at Renfrew

Avro CF-100 on engine test at Prestwick

Avro CF-100 at Prestwick undergoing maintenance tests by Scottish Aviation

Avro CF-100 18320 at Aldergrove for the 1961 Battle of Britain display. This aircraft was tested by the RAF but the design combination of airframe and armament did not meet the RAF requirements

General LeMay, had requested the Pentagon to permit him to station B–29s either on continental Europe or in Britain. Their response was positive and quick. The two squadrons of the 301st that remained at Salinas Air Force Base (AFB) were immediately put on alert and then deployed to West Germany in early July. At the same time, the 28th Bomb Group, based at Rapid City, South Dakota, and the 307th Bomb Group, based at MacDill AFB, Tampa, Florida, went on alert and were ordered to deploy within 12 and 3 hours, respectively, after receiving the warning notice.

The rest of SAC went on 24-hour alert. Later in the month the 28th and 307th each consisting of 30 B–29 aircraft and crews were deployed to the United Kingdom. The 28th Group deployed to Royal Air Force Station Scampton, Lincolnshire, while the 307th Group deployed one squadron of ten planes to RAF Station Waddington, Lincolnshire, and two squadrons of B-29s to RAF Station Marham, Norfolkshire. (The 307th flew to England via Kindley Airfield, Bermuda). These B-29s were not nuclear capable and none had been converted to Silverplate status.

By 1952 the RAF had taken on some of the responsibility of the reconnaissance functions of the USAF by flying missions over the Soviet Union from RAF Sculthorpe. Spotters had seen American reconnaissance aircraft marked with British markings at Prestwick and Spotters promptly had their film and notebooks confiscated. Later the RAF became much more involved with other types of missions overflying the Soviet Union; this was part of American policy, so much so the integration of the USAF and the RAF was called, "Kissing Cousins." Roughly translated this means that they are so close they may as well be related. This later extended to Lockheed U-2 flights in a word called "Jackson." RB-36 strategic reconnaissance aircraft flew out of Britain at extreme high altitude over Norway and photographed the submarine pens at Murmansk, flying so high they were impervious to interception by Soviet aircraft.

Canadair Sabre Mk.6s cocooned at Prestwick

23018 Mark 5 Sabre cocooned then broken up

Preserved Canadair Sabre Mark 6 23562 in storage 15 March 1958

Sabre Mark 6 on external maintenance by Scottish Aviation at Prestwick

Soviet Yak-9 fighter intercepting a transport near Berlin

Short Sunderland of 201Squadron during the Berlin airlift

Douglas C-54 Skymaster landing at Templehof Berlin

A B-29 of the 28th Bombardment Group,
718th Bombardment Squadron at RAF Scampton 1948

The shape of the book was projected differently; it was to be just a section on the North American/Canadair Sabre. Due to circumstances the chief researcher dropped out and was unable to complete the relevant sections. With more research and investigation it was felt important to include joint British and American co-operation. The first aeroplane the RAF used was the North American RB-45C Tornado which was from the same stable as the F-86 Sabre and powered by the same engine, the General Electric J-47. More research had to be done on this aircraft and its successors which still fly today. Some obscure details are included in this publication, "*…lest it perish*."

Today Renfrew Airport is now but a fading memory: the spirits of Spotters, aeroplanes, Canadair Sabres and CF-100s replaced by the motorway to Greenock which follows the course of the old runway. The control tower with all the hangars and buildings are now demolished; houses are on the site together with a huge grocery store, and the streets named after aeroplanes: here and there on the site, will be found memorials to the aeronautical exploits of the aviation pioneers of Renfrew Airport. The sound of jets and propellers has been replaced by the sound of the motor car, the bus and the truck, all witnessed by the ghosts at Arklestone Cemetery gate.

Ex-Royal Navy MDAP Douglas Skyraider AEW-1, WT952, SE-EBA at Prestwick, August 1962. Refurbished by Scottish Aviation for target tug duties in Sweden for the Swedish company Svensk Flygtjanst AB

2.

Acknowledgements

Grateful thanks to The Mitchell Library, five stars to level four which was a ready primary source of aeronautical material, the late Neil B. Morris, Chaz Bowyer, Jack Bruce, the Central Intelligence Agency, National Security Archive, United States Department of Energy, Renfrew Spotters Club, Defense Technical Information Center, AERADE, NASA Technical Server: the Royal Canadian Air Force provided key documents and anecdotes, many members of Air Britain gave me their personal accounts and access to key sources including images: my family and friends for their encouragement to complete the project and access to their archive papers and pictures, Iain c. MacKay collection, the members of Rolls-Royce Heritage Trust for their interest and encouragement, the Spicer family, the National Collection of Aeronautical Photography, camera work-Scott McCallum of Max Spielmann, Bearsden, The Science Museum, The Smithsonian Institute, Scran and the Aviation Bookshop, Tunbridge Wells for supplying information, data and books. The Operational Readiness Books (ORBs) of the Royal Canadian Air Force and the Royal Air Force have been published by the relevant national archives and these were consulted in-depth for this book, for these I am deeply grateful. The ORBs are tablets of stone giving names, dates, deployments and aircraft identities. Through the ORBs the publisher was made aware of certain aspects of the intelligence gathering activities of the NATO countries. Other facts and conclusions have been published and have made their way to the public domain but have not been included due to the accuracy of that information, those details being in conflict with the ORBs, these are not complete. This has meant that certain public domain details have not been included or been modified, this includes, aircraft, names, dates and places etc. This book has been originally researched from source material at the relevant national archives. I have been given fullest access to source material which was made available at the time and the views and conclusions expressed are mine and mine alone.

Netherton *18 June 2021*

3.

Evolution of the F.86 Sabre

Germany had lost the Great War and had agreed to an Armistice in 1918. Later in 1919 Germany signed the Versailles Peace Treaty to ensure a permanent peace and an end to war, the war to end all wars. Part V of the Versailles Treaty, which was signed 28 June 1919 and put into effect on 10 January 1920, prohibited Germany from undertaking any activity whatsoever in the field of military aviation and in the manufacture of military aeroplanes, including aero-engines, weapons and equipment. Following the disbandment of the German Air Force, a small number of pilots were transferred to the Reichswehr (National Army) which was established on 6 March 1919 and whose nucleus consisted of volunteer units.

Germany could produce no high performance aeroplanes that could be used for war-like purposes. It also meant that Germany could have no air force with which to defend the Reich or to wage war. Generaloberst Hans von Seeckt, Chief of the Troop Office and later Chief of the Reichswehr and founder of the 100000 Man Army, recommended that an air branch be established as part of the armed services. On 1 March 1920, the following agencies were established by Generaloberst von Seekt:

a) An Air Organization and Training Office within the Troop Office of the Reich's Ministry of Defence.

b) The "Foreign Air Office" (one officer), within the T-3 Department of the Troop Office to monitor foreign air forces.

c) The "Air Technical Office," within the Office for Weapons and Equipment in the Army Ordnance Office. The officer in charge of this office was Captain Kurt Student who monitored foreign air force technical developments.

d) The "Air Armament Economics Office" whose task was to compile and evaluate information pertaining to developments in the sector of armament economy abroad. This office was under the direction of Captain Wilhelm Vogt.

e) An air procurement department was planned but never came into existence.

Generaloberst Hans von Seeckt

To get round the Versailles Treaty Germany invested heavily in gliding schools and gliding competitions. Gliding presented the perfect discipline to develop air consciousness in Germany. It was also the perfect cover to form a professional air force. The Gliding and Soaring movement was established in Germany resulting in the Rhon sailplane contests. Gliding was a sport, which was not subject to the restrictions of the Versailles Treaty and Captain Kurt Student did everything in his power to support that sport in Germany. In the summer of 1921 some of Germany's former pilot officers organized the first glider courses on the Wasserkuppe, a high point in the Rhon Mountains in Hessen, located north of Gersfeld, where gliding contests had traditionally been held. Sport Fliers Ltd (Sportflug GMBh) was then founded in Berlin by director Fritz Siebel with the help and backing of the Reich Defence Ministry. With the signing of the Paris Agreement on 21 May 1926, Sport Fliers Ltd was wound up. Germany had regained its ability to produce aeroplanes and aero-engines.

In the Wasserkuppe district the best slopes for gliding practice face from S.E. by S. to N.W., while the prevailing winds are westerly. The slopes facing N. and E. are also good, so that the general lie of the ground is almost ideal. One reported glide at Rhon was on 5 September 1921, just at the close of the competition. Arthur Martens on the Hannover H.1 Vampyr monoplane glider, which was designed by G. Madelung made a flight lasting 15 minutes 40 seconds.

Starting from Wasserkuppe he alighted at Batten, near Hilders at a point 500 meters below where he started. Martens covered a distance of 7.5 kilometres (over 4.5 miles) at an average gliding angle of 1 in 15. In the Vampyr design were, for the first time, the essential lines worked out in the design of a popular glider. The problem was to build an aircraft with a low sinking speed, a good gliding angle, with sufficient strength and good manoeuvrability. The Vampyr was a cantilever high-wing type with a thick highly cambered wing section with large span and aspect ratio. In this type of glider a single-spar wing was used for the first time in which the torsional forces were taken up by the leading edge. This was built up as a thin-walled tube, closed at the rear by spar proper. This "torsion-nose" allowed at the same time the possibility of keeping the most sensitive part of the wing section, the leading edge, at exactly the correct shape and angle. Plywood was the essential material which made this construction possible. Further notable characteristics of the Vampyr were the three-part wing of the fuselage, completely built of plywood and with a landing gear consisting of three football wheels and the pendulum-type elevator. At Wasserkuppe it was possible to get eight gliders in the air at one time. The site of the Rhon Flying School was selected on a gentle eastward slope about midway between the southern slope of the "Wasserkuppe" and the western slope of the "Weltensegler," a ridge running at right angles to the former, the slopes of which were the most used for training glides. The beginners' course included pupils holding only the A certificate for glider pilots. Pupils who had passed the B glider test or who held full pilots' certificates were classed as advanced. A gliding course lasted for four weeks and concluded with the B test for pupils of moderate skill. Approved pupils would then take the advanced course of four weeks' further training for the C test and for all types.

The first training glider used at Rhon was of the suspension type which was used by Pelzner in 1920-1921. It was similar to the Chanute glider. In 1921 the Nuerberger Club developed a small biplane single seat-type glider out of the above type which became the first training glider. By this time the biplane was favoured as better

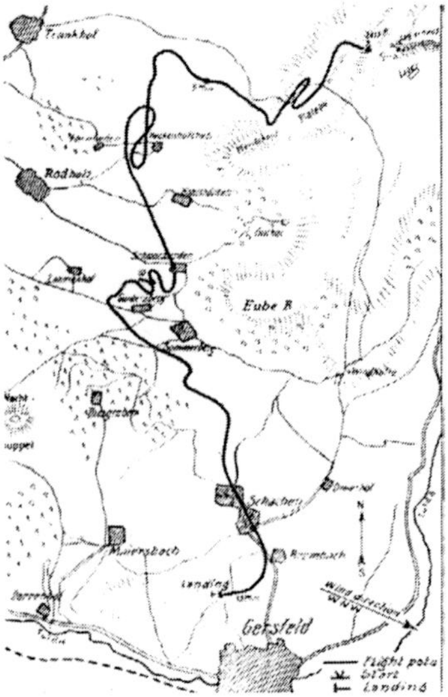

The Rhon Mountain gliding course. The competitions started here from 1920

Pelzner Glider

Djavlar Annam

Zoeglin

Pegasus

flying characteristics were expected from this type. This glider flew like a parachute. Then came a notable step forward, this was the primary training biplane "Frohe Welt" (Happy World) designed by F. Stamer. Its construction was simple and the flying characteristics were very pleasant and at the same time the gliding angle and sinking speed were quite suitable for the passing of the glider pilot's examination of the time (the A Licence). There was much trouble caused by damage to the lower wing due to wing-down landings and later it was also found difficult to pass the tests for B Licence in this machine.

For these reasons the monoplane type glider came into favour with the German gliding clubs. The development began with the Munich glider of 1921. This machine was, however, not designed as a training glider and had a special control system. Then came the Schulz glider of 1922 which was built of broomsticks and tin cans and in which Schulz flew for eight hours. On the basis of this glider Alexander Lippisch built the training glider "Djavlar Annama" in 1923 with the idea of building the simplest and cheapest glider possible. As the years went by this glider was modified annually for each Rohn competition and was built by Schleicher and Peppenhausen. It became the beginner's glider and was built in large numbers. Another example of this glider was the Pegasus built by the Martens Flying School whose simple structure meant it also could be built in large numbers. From the Pegasus was developed the Zoegling (Beginner) which was developed into the Stamer-Lippisch glider and was known in Great Britain as the RFD Dagling. The Zoegling due to its very low C.G. and low speed it was found very difficult to make

The first Lippisch glider on the Wasserkuppe

the ailerons and rudder sensitive. The most important control for the "ab initio" student was the elevator and this was made very sensitive.

By 1929 Alexander Lippisch had designed the Wien which was one of the first gliders built to exploit thermals. In 1928 Robert Kronfeld had won the Rhon competition in the glider, Professor. Lippisch had designed the Professor as a glider training machine and Kronfeld asked him to redesign it further with more aerodynamic refinements. This further development of the Professor consisted of increasing the span, using a higher cambered wing section, a more rounded fuselage cross section and faired fittings. This glider became the Wien which Kronfeld used to cross the English Channel and fly over London.

In 1923 the celebrated German ace Udet founded the firm of Udet Flugzeugbau G.m.b.H., Munich, for the development and construction of training and transport planes. Due to financial liquidity problems of the firm, in July 1926, negotiations were carried out by Udet with the Reich's Transportation Ministry, Bavarian Trade Ministry and Merck, Fink & Co. (Banking firm), Munich, for financial support which resulted in the creation of a new company, namely, Bayerische Flugzeugwerke A.G. and the dissolution of Udet-Flugzeugbau. At the same time there existed another aircraft enterprise in the State of Bavaria, namely, Messerschmitt Flugzeugbau, G.m.b.H. of Bamberg. This firm was operated by Professor Willy Messerschmitt, celebrated aeronautical engineer, but the firm was confined to building gliders and prototype aeroplanes. Its capital structure was financed entirely on a 50-50 basis by Professor Willy Messerschmitt and the Baroness Raulino of Bamberg. Both the BFW, A.G. and the Messerschmitt concern were being heavily subsidized at this time by the German Reich which was reluctant, however, to continue to give support to two aircraft companies in Bavaria. A merger of BFW, A.G. and Messerschmitt was therefore initiated and completed by the autumn of 1927. This meant BFW confined itself to the production of new types of aeroplanes developed by Messerschmitt. Willi Messerschmitt's skill was in simplifying and changing the metal aircraft structure in aircraft. Messerschmitt introduced simple metal spars connected by riveting. He also introduced single spar wings with metal panels structurally connected to the spar giving the wing a smooth metal finish. In addition to wings he designed the undercarriage and all metal, monococque fuselages in aircraft. He backed up his designs with patents and by 1944 he had published thirty European patents.

By the contract of 8 September 1927, these firms, although once existing individually, agreed to operate as one economic unit with Messerschmitt confining its operations to the design and development of new models and BFW, A. G. restricting itself to the manufacture of Messerschmitt aeroplanes. On 11 July 1938 the BFW A.G. was officially called Messerschmitt A.G, "bf" being dropped from aircraft designations after this date.

In November 1925 Alexander Lippisch had become technical director of the Rhon Rositten Company; this was the research institute for gliding at Wasserkuppe. There Lippisch designed the tailless glider with swept wings, the Storche. By 1929 the Storche had become a powered glider with a maximum speed of 78 mph and a flying weight of 551 pounds.

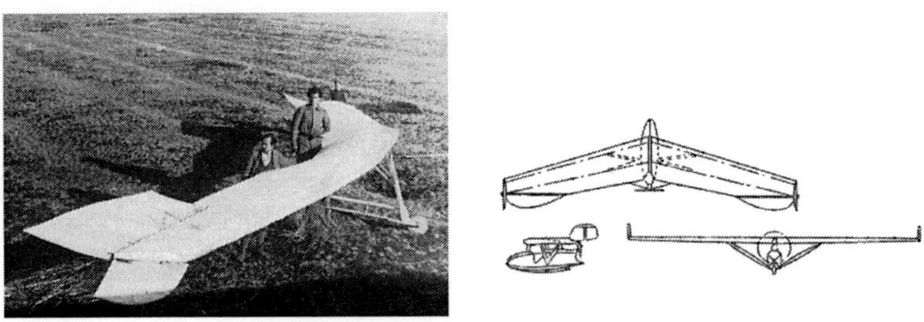

The first Storch and powered Storch

In the Storch the wings were swept back with normal ailerons which also served as elevators. Beneath the tips of the wings, placed obliquely and in front, were the rudders. Stability was obtained by the inversion of the wing profile. An aeroplane was built at first with a dihedral wing with rudders extending downward but since this arrangement gave poor manoeuvrability, the dihedral was completely eliminated and the lateral rudders were transferred to the upper surface of the wing. After a series of flights the Storch had its fuselage modified but it did prove the concept of the swept wing.

The success of this glider meant that the airframe could be modified to take an aero-engine; this was in the autumn of 1929. The engine chosen was as low-powered as possible - 500 cm3 (30.5 cu.in). DKW air-cooled engine. The engine, placed behind the wing necessitated moving the pilot's seat forward. The fuselage was then reconstructed and the lateral rudders replaced by stronger ones. The Storch was flown first as a glider with the propeller locked and then with the engine running. The Storch demonstrated its complete aptitude for flight although, due to the excessive dimensions of the propeller, the difficulty of cooling necessitated reducing the revolutions to 2800 r.p.m. (the maximum power corresponding to 3300 r.p.m).. Under these conditions, however, the climbing and speed performances of the airplane were very satisfactory, with a maximum speed of 78 m.p.h. and a flying weight of 551 pounds. No official order was received for the Storch because there was hostility to its tailless configuration.

In December 1934, following an invitation by Colonel Dinort, Lippisch gave a talk to the Richthofen squadron at the Air Base Doberitz near Berlin on the military application of tailless and delta aircraft. By this time the Storch had evolved into a Delta wing aircraft. At this presentation Lippisch showed an Illustration of a low-wing monoplane Delta fighter squadron and the project drawing of a high-wing reconnaissance plane. The Delta now had an engine set as a tractor not as a pusher configuration. Heini Dittmar became test pilot for the rebuilt and modified airplane which now had the designation Delta IVb. In 1939 a follow on from this design was the D.F.S.39 which was tested at Rechlin. The swept wing design had now evolved into a pure Delta wing aircraft.

The DFS 194 was built in 1937 at the DFS as an experimental prototype of a tailless fighter, under contract from the Research Department of the RLM. The DFS 194 was a shoulder wing design with swept-back wings with positive dihedral and downward deflected wing-tip control surfaces. It was designed for a pusher propeller and a 100 h.p. Argus engine. The Argus engine was

DFS-194

Me -163

replaced with a Walther rocket motor. The rocket-propelled DFS194 made its first flight in August 1940 on the airfield at Peenemunde West with Heini Dittmar at the controls.

By now the Lippisch design series was taken over by Messerschmitt concern and developed into an aerodynamic prototype, this was the Messerschmitt 163 which attained flight when it was towed engineless by a Me-110. The success of the Walther rocket motor powered delta meant an order for 79 Me-163s from the Reich Air Ministry. By now the rocket engines were proving to be very unreliable and dangerous, the remaining fuel would explode on landing. On 28 April 1943, Department "L" at Messerschmitt was dissolved and Lippisch left the company. Further development of the Me 163 B was entrusted to the Messerschmitt Project Bureau under the direction of Dr. Voigt. They designed the Me-163C with an additional cruise engine and the Me-163D with greater range and a retractable nose wheel undercarriage. For a short time a simplified series version was studied by Professor Hertel at Junkers under the designation Ju-248. For promotional purposes it was renamed Me-263 when this number became available again. A few experimental aircraft were built of each of these versions but none of them was produced in series nor did they reach military service.

In addition to the work of Lippisch on early swept wing and delta configuration, the work of Dr Albert Betz on aerofoil theory was published in 1935. The basic theory for swept and yawed wings as developed by Betz is based on, "*…the concept that only the component of velocity normal to the wing leading edge determines the chord wise pressure distribution. Thus, by increasing the sweep angle, the normal component of flow is reduced and the critical Mach number at which the drag rise due to compressibility is increased.*" In 1926, Dr Betz had been appointed professor at Gottingen. By 1936 he succeeded Ludwig Prandtl as director of the Aerodynamische Versuchsanstalt (AVA, aerodynamics laboratory), a position he held until 1956. (source NACA) Dr Betz then went onto the Messerschmitt Company where he developed the Messerschmitt swept wing. He recognised the importance of experimental work in the wind tunnel at Göttingen. By 1936 Betz succeeded Ludwig Prandtl as director of the Aerodynamische Versuchsanstalt (AVA, aerodynamics laboratory), a position he held until 1956.

May 1945 Dr Albert Betz hands over wing research to Theodore Karman of the United States

Adolf Busemann at Langley

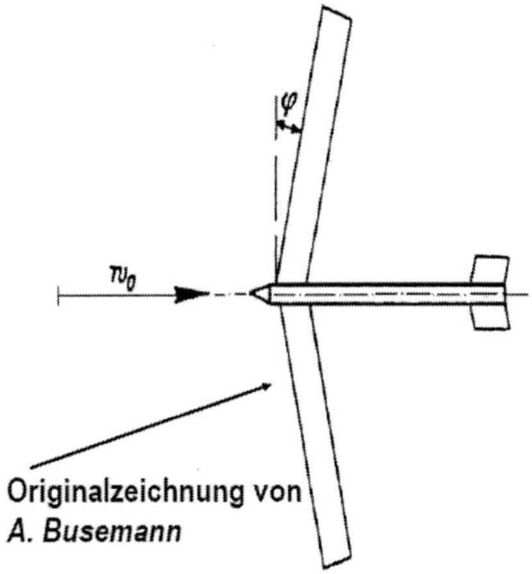

Busemann's swept wing at the Volta Conference

Also in pre-war Germany, Adolf Busemann discovered the benefits of the swept wing for aircraft at high speeds, presenting his paper on the topic at the Volta Conference in Rome in 1935. The conference was called to discuss high speed flight with reference to the aircraft of the Schneider Trophy. Busemann's paper was concerned with supersonic flow only. At the time of his proposal, flight much beyond 425 miles per hour had not yet been achieved and the speed was considered an academic curiosity. Nevertheless, Busemann continued working with the concept and by the end of the year had demonstrated similar benefits in the transonic region as well. As director of the Braunschweig labs, he started an experimental wind tunnel test series of the concept and by 1942 had amassed a considerable amount of useful technical swept-wing data.

As Germany was collapsing in 1944-45, the Messerschmitt Me-P.1101 (P. for project) was developed to flight test Buseman's designs. Messerschmitt started on the preliminary design study of a high performance jet fighter, having a high sweep-back wing this was about July 1944. The basic operational requirement agreed upon with the Reich Air Ministry which were: 1 1/2 hours endurance at approximately 10,000 ra. (32,800 ft).Rated r.p.m. 170 km/hr (106 mph) stalling speed at landing weight. l/3 fuel and armament. The Heinkel-Hirth S-109-011A engine of 2860 lbs, static thrust was selected. The fuel required for the required endurance was 1400 litres (370 U.S. gallons).

Messerschmitt submitted a proposal to these requirements in September 1944. The Messerschmitt model designation was P.1101. Authorization to proceed with the design was obtained almost immediately, (Junkers and Heinkel were also given experimental contracts for airplanes to meet the same requirement). The Messerschmitt design had three 30 mm. guns with a space for 2 additional. Its weight empty was 2600 kg (5750 lbs) with a gross weight of 4000 kg. (8850 lbs). The wing area chosen was 15.85 sq.m. (170 sq.ft) giving a wing leading of 52 lbs/sq.ft. on the 8850 gross weight. (CL Max required giving 106 mph V3 1.72). The wing used was the high sweep-back arrow wing type, having full span slots, plain flaps and conventional, inset-hinge ailerons. The wing sweep

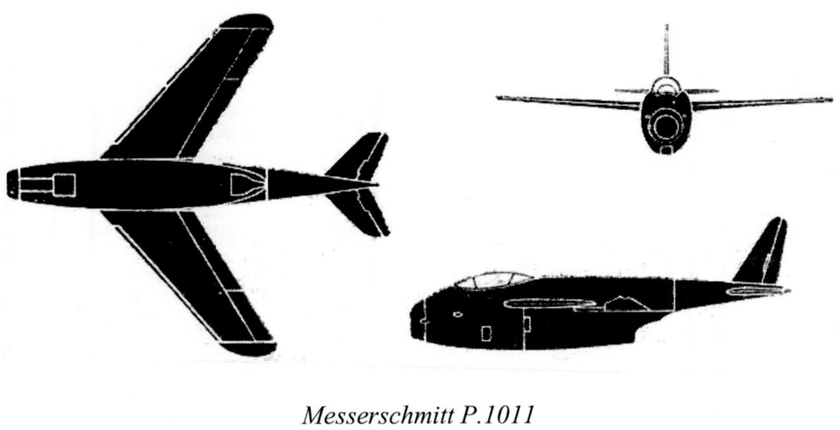

Messerschmitt P.1011

One 2860 Heinkel Hirth 109-011ATurbojet unit Weight: 5750 lbs
Loaded Weight:8960 lbs Span: 27 ft 0.75 in Wing Area: 170.60 sq. ft.
Maximum Speed at 23000 ft. – 610 mph Rate of Climb:4370 ft/min.at sea level
Service ceiling: 46000 ft. Landing Speed: 107 mph

Captured Me P.1011

Captured Messerschmitt P.1011 in American hands

Messerschmitt P.1011 with Heinkel-Hirth109-011 A turbojet engine

was 45 degrees. The root thickness was 8%, (measured parallel to plane of symmetry) and the tip thickness 12%. The tip was made relatively thick because:

(a) This thickness could be tolerated without compressibility difficulty in view of the three dimensional flow at the tip;

(b) Greatest attainable torsional rigidity was desired to maintain aileron control at high speeds;

(c) The thicker wing per se and the larger chord slat that could be fitted to it would both help to prevent tip stall.

An incidental advantage was that both the slat and the flap could be made of constant cross section throughout their span. The resulting slat chord was 13% of the wing chord at the root and 24% at the tip. The Me-P.1101 aeroplane was then designed with the engine and intake in the fuselage nose, with three guns, ammunition and chutes wrapped around the duct. The nose wheel of the tricycle landing gear retracted aft, with the plane of the wheel rotating 90° for stowage upon retraction by means of a skewed axis joint at the upper undercarriage fitting.

The cockpit was located above the duct and forward end of the engine, making a rather deep fuselage. An ejection seat was provided for the pilot. The fuel was located in the fuselage above the engine, aft of the pilot. The jet discharge was located in a half tunnel step near the root trailing edge. The aeroplane was mid-wing, with the wing structure passing under the fuel tank and above the engine. The empennage was conventional except that it had rather low aspect ratio, high taper and large sweep-back of the landing edges of the fin and stabilizers. The main landing gear was pivoted at the fuselage, just under the wing, and retracted aft. As the design work progressed into October 1944, it became apparent that this design would not "jell". The principal difficulties were:

(a) The gun installation around the nose intake duct was very crowded and had poor ammunition boxes, chutes and feed. Armament was now four 30mm Mk 108 cannon two mounted on each side of the fuselage. Each gun could fire 100 rounds;

(b) The low thrust axis caused large changes of trim with changes in thrust;

(c) The motion of the undercarriage and wheel upon retracting into the fuselage presented a serious closing-door problem;

(d) The grouping of wing, power plant and landing gear loads was poor, requiring an excessive number of fuselage strong-points, and;

(e) The calculated performance, 985 km/hr., (6l0mph) was less than desired. For these reasons it was decided to abandon the P.1101 as a possible production prototype, but since considerable work had been completed, it was to be finished up as a flight test aeroplane to prove out the swept arrow wing. Willi Messerschmitt had obtained permission to complete the airframe as a research aircraft. It was then to be built at Oberammergau now with the Junkers Jumo 004B gas turbine, with the first flight projected during July 1945. When it was three quarters completed the P.1101 was captured by United States forces and evacuated to the USA.

While he was completing his training at Royal Air Force station Cranwell, Frank Whittle, completed his fourth term thesis. He had chosen as his subject, “Future Developments of Aircraft Design.” This work became his starting point on gas turbine research. He had come to the conclusion that high speed, high altitude flight could not be met by a combination of propeller and piston-engine. Whittle was thinking in terms of rockets and gas turbines fitted with propellers attached to aircraft flying at 500 mph. Towards the end of 1929 while serving at the Central Flying School, Wittering, Whittle continued to research aircraft propulsion methods. He thought of a low pressure fan being driven by a piston engine. He concluded that his arrangement was not an advance on the piston engine but he decided to fit a turbine instead of the piston engine. This simple type of engine produced an exhaust jet instead of powering a propeller. His conception was using gas turbines for jet propulsion and it is this association of these two principals which distinguishes him from others.

He discussed his idea with W.E.P Johnson, one of his instructors and through a range of personal arrangements was instructed to report to the Air Ministry in London. There it was established he had made a miscalculation in his conclusions and that the Ministry was not in a position to take on his ideas. Returning to Wittering he discovered

Above the first Whittle gas turbines and to the left the first Whittle W.1

another mistake which on correction enhanced his calculation. Encouraged by Johnson, who was once a patent agent, Whittle took out his first patent and this was followed by another patent, these were patents GB347206A and GB347766A. No fewer than six of his patent drawings were published in nine German technical journals prior to 1939. Four patents were also purchased by German companies with one going to Heinkel and the other Gottingen University.

GB244206A was his initial patent, applied for 16 January 1930 (No 1521/30) granted 16 April 1931. In this patent Whittle specifically mentions the turbine is for aircraft use. By 1937 his patents were specifically more aeronautical, *"...for example in a turbine or through the propelling jet of an aircraft propelled by fluid reaction ....."* This was from British patent 471368 granted 3 September 1937. After exploring manufacturing of his aircraft gas turbine with British Thomson-Houston, who was not in a financial position to undertake manufacture, Whittle received a service posting. By March 1936 Whittle had formed Power Jets to manufacture gas turbines. This company had been formed under the direction of the Air Ministry. British Thomson-Houston became a shareholder together with the Glasgow Company of J&G Weir. Weir gave Whittle access to research on engine metals. Also at the time, working at Weir's in Glasgow, was the German rotary wing pioneer Otto Reder. Weirs were working on a thrust augmenter for Power Jets, at the time Reder was at Thornliebank. The helicopter sub-contractor for Weir helicopters was the firm of H. Morris & Co. Ltd cabinetmakers and wood engineers, who believed Reder was a German technical agent or spy.

Even with financial cash flow difficulties, Power Jets had a prototype gas turbine running by 12 April 1937 and continued testing to 23 August 1939. Power Jets then received a contract for a flight engine on 12 July I939 and a short time afterwards, 30 August 1939, a contract was placed with the Gloster Aircraft Company for the manufacture of an experimental aircraft to specification E28/39, designed by George Carter. In the small jet, the fuselage design was necessitated by the engine being in the fuselage behind the cockpit, giving the aircraft a bulky appearance. In point of fact the aircraft was about the same size as a Tiger Moth. The lines of the circular-section fuselage were very fine and the smooth surface was practically unbroken by panels. The wing was straight-tapered in plan and despite its thin section, the undercarriage was housed in it with only slight bulges in the under surface. Considering the large side area forward of the C.G. the fin and rudder were surprisingly small. They may have been a little too small, for by 1945 the aeroplane revealed small fins added near the tip of the horizontal tail surfaces. All three units of the undercarriage were of the Dowty levered-suspension type and were remarkable for their shortness. The surface finish of the E28 was very good indeed and all joints in the skin and rivet dimples were invisible in the smoothness.

With the advent of war in September 1939, finance was later received from the Ministry of Aircraft Production who wrote a specification round the aircraft for a six gun jet fighter. Very much a

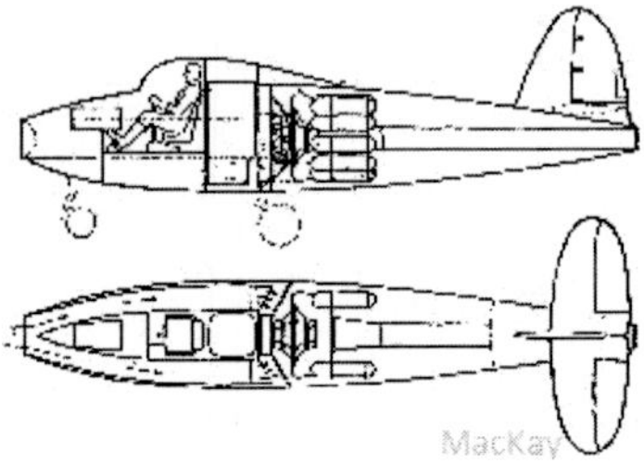

The Gloster E28/39Britain's first jet

1928 making models at Cranwell
This one for Sir Phillip Sassoon

Frank Whittle – 1946

Frank Whittle shakes hands with P.E.G "Jerry" Sayer at the first flight of the Gloster E28/39 on 15 May 1941

J.P. Herriot, Frank Whittle and Stanley Hooker of Rolls-Royce with the design of the Rolls-Royce B-41 Nene

pilot's aeroplane the aircraft was flown by P.E.G. "Gerry" Sayer at Cranwell on 15 May 1941. The aircraft flew with the W.1 engine which was cleared for 10 hours flight test. Previous to that in April the E28/39 commenced taxiing trials with the Whittle W.1.X. From a handling standpoint, under test, the E.28/39, "Gloster Whittle," would have made a good fighter but it would have been badly underpowered and was short on range; though on some occasions, the test pilots demonstrated aerobatics. Performance wise it achieved its maximum level speed of 466 mph at 10,000ft, the highest height and Mach number Captain Eric Brown achieved was at 35000ft when M 0.82 was achieved in a 40° dive to 20,000ft. The landing speed of the E28/39 was 80 mph. The E28/39 proved the concept of the jet fighter and led to Britain's first operational jet fighter, the Gloster Meteor.

In the United States a tail-first pusher, called the Curtiss XP-55 "Ascender", was one of several novel designs that stemmed from a 1940 United States Army Air Corps request to generate new, high performance, unorthodox fighters which would be superior to the best European designs. The design included a low aspect-ratio, all-moving canard pitch control, a moderately swept wing of thirty degrees and rudders mounted near the wing tips. The fore-plane location was not selected primarily for good stall behaviour but for pitch control, improved visibility and more efficient gun installations. Wing sweep was incorporated, not for transonic flow benefits (drag reduction), but to provide an aft location for the vertical fins for directional stability and control. Four .50 calibre guns were mounted in the nose and the all-up weight of the aircraft was only 7300 pounds. Three were built, but stability and engine cooling problems led to cancellation by the Army in late 1943.

The Curtiss XP-55 Ascender

Before the United States of America entered the Second World War they had sent a group of "Special Observers" to the United Kingdom with Major General "Hap" Arnold of the USAAF. At that time, Col. (later Brig. Gen,) A. J. Lyon was General Arnold's representative in England for all technical matters. General Electric had sent D. Roy Shoults, a senior staff member of the gas-turbine division, to Great Britain to assist Colonel Lyon in the early stages of his association with the British Ministry of Aircraft Production (MAP) in connection with the servicing and use of turbo-supercharger equipment.

The group had been formed at Washington and held its first meeting at the British War Office, London, on 19 June 1941. The Observers were there to inspect Britain's war effort and technology and how Britain waged war. The team inspected such things as the workings of Fighter Command, the use of RDF (Radar), British signal intelligence gathering and code breaking and the work on aircraft gas turbines etc. On 21 July 1941, R. Cox, and Roy Shoults of General Electric visited the Ladywood Works and the Gloster factory. By 12 August 1941 the Americans were requesting assistance from the British on the Whittle Jet Engine. The Americans recognised that there would be production difficulties with the centrifugal impeller. They also believed that the General Electric Company was in a good position to work on the Whittle gas turbines for the United States. They estimated that fifty gas turbines could be produced per week. The Observers knew that Rover was producing thirty, hand-made jet engines, per week at the time. The Americans were also aware that the British were on the verge of producing a twin engined, jet fighter with four cannon, a speed of 385 mph at sea level, with an altitude performance of forty thousand feet with a maximum speed of 425 mph.

It was the existence of the Whittle Jet and the Gloster E28/39 that gave the United States the impetus to produce a jet fighter. Then in June 1941 the Americans requested a Whittle engine, all the test data on the engine, an E28/39 and Whittle himself to come to America as a consultant. They wanted their request to be dealt with by the British immediately with engine and designer going to Wright Field. By the 4

The Power Jets team in the United States, October 1941, W/O J. A King, D.N. Walker chief test engineer and G. B. Bozzoni, head test fitter.

September 1941 the Americans had decided to produce the Whittle engine themselves for a twin engined fighter. They also kept pressing the British for the Whittle engine, the E28/39 prototype, Frank Whittle himself and all key engineering personnel wishing them to be sent to the United States. On 10 September 1941, they further pressed the British for the release of the material, Whittle and two engineers.

The next day, 11 September 1941, agreement had been reached between the United States of America and the British concerning American demands for the Whittle gas turbine. A Whittle W1X test engine would be despatched to the United States from Prestwick. All production drawings from Rover would be made available. The Gloster E28/39 was not available due to its test programme but the drawings for the Gloster twin jet fighter would also be made available. The Minister of Aircraft Production agreed that once the prototype Gloster fighter had flown it would be made available to the Americans at Wright Field. General Chaney was in charge of the observers' team but only for twelve days. Chaney was ordered to return to the United Sates and he left Prestwick for home on 20 June 1942 at 1910 hrs, on Boeing Stratoliner, N-19908.

On 29 September 1941 the W1X was shipped by road to Prestwick, from there it was flown to the United States by Liberator.

Boeing Stratoliner, N-19908 and crew which flew General Chaney home from Prestwick 20 June 1942

The aircraft landed at Boston and the engine was taken by truck to the General Electric works at Lynn, Massachusetts. Accompanying the engine in the truck was Colonel Don Keirn of the USAAF, D. N. Walker, G.B. Bozzoni and J.A. King of Power Jets. The W.2B drawings and other information were sent by sea. This engine, the W.2B was to be built by General Electric where it was known as the "exhaust turbo-blower Type I." Gas turbines produced in the United States with the "I" prefix are thus based on Whittle gas turbines. General Electric had been chosen to produce the type due to their experience with engine superchargers. Frank Whittle finally arrived at New York on 4 June 1942, having crossed the Atlantic by clipper flying boat. Frank Whittle's visit to the United States was from June-September 1942, there he assisted and advised General Electric, the USAAF and the Bell Aircraft company. General Electric Co. worked so fast that they had their version of the W2B (the 1-14) on the test bench by April 1942, and the Bell Aircraft Co. was rapidly building the XP-59A(Bell Model 27)— a twin engined fighter to be powered by two I-14's. When he visited the US Navy Department, Whittle saw the research and development which was taking place. He was able to advise the futility of their project which resulted in it being dropped. What struck the Americans was the negative view of the Ministry of Aircraft Production to Power Jets.

Whittle returned to the United Kingdom 14 August 1942 and on 2 October 1942 the Bell XP – 59A Airacomet took to the air at Muroc Field, California (now Edwards Air Force Base). Later the Royal Air Force received one P-59 for evaluation this was the third prototype

Bell XP-59 in the air

XP-59 on the ground

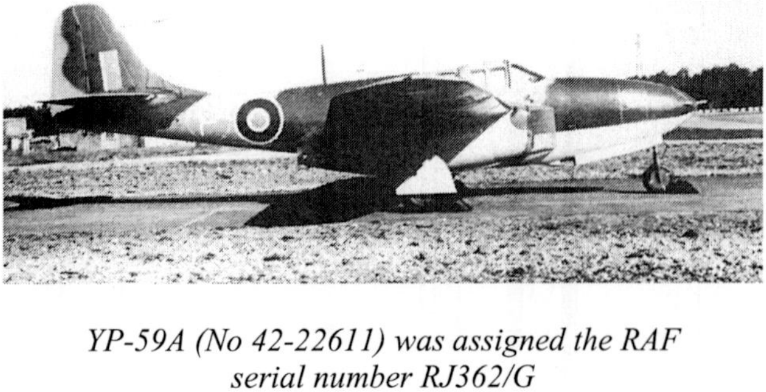

YP-59A (No 42-22611) was assigned the RAF serial number RJ362/G

YP-59A (No 42-22611). It was assigned the RAF serial number RJ362/G. The YP-59a was exchanged for the first production Gloster Meteor Mk1. Upon arrival in England, it was assembled by Gloster at Moreton Vallance where it was flown for the first time by a Bell test pilot on 28 September 1943. It was then transferred to the Royal Aircraft Establishment at Farnborough on 5 November 1943 where it was flown by Wing Commander H.J. Wilson. It was on the top-secret Jet Flight list (along with the Gloster E.28/39, the De Havilland Vampire, and the Gloster Meteor) but the Airacomet was flown very little because of unserviceability and the lack of spares. The RAF test pilots found the aircraft to be badly underpowered with an unacceptably-long take-off run. It made only a few flights up to April 1944 but after ten hours running, the engines were removed, stripped and inspected by Power Jets Ltd. With the engines re-installed, a further seven flights took place and the aircraft was then returned to the USA early in 1945. Like all other early jet-powered fighters the Airacomet suffered from very poor engine acceleration. Later General Electric decided to build and put into production their I-16 which was based on the Power Jets W2/500. Then Pratt and Whitney entered the gas turbine field after the war using the Rolls-Royce Nene as a basis for their J-42 and J-48. General Electric started their Jet engine work based on the Whittle designs and developed the I-A, J-31 and J-33.

In Germany, the research resulted in the use of axial-flow compressors in the Jumo 004 and the B.M.W. 003 turbojet engines. The Junkers Company were the first firm to take an active interest in a practical turbine design for aircraft under the direction of Dr Mader. Their first compressor was designed and made for them by Professor Encke at Gottingen. The original engine being developed at Junkers under Herbert Wagner's direction was not progressing well and in the autumn of 1939 a 39-year old graduate of the University of Graz, Dr. Anselm Franz, began work on the engine which became the Junkers Jumo 004, the engine which would power the Me-262. The first Jumo 004 axial flow jet engine was built at the Junkers Magdeburg factory in 1936. An experimental Junkers engine, the 004A was first run on 11 October, 1940 and by January 194l, had developed almost 1,000

Junkers Jumo 004

B.M.W. 003

pounds of thrust. Some redesign was called for and by December, 1941, more than 2200 pounds of thrust were being demonstrated on the engine test stand. The engine was flight tested beneath a Messerschmitt Bf 110 on 15 March 1942. Between 25000 and 30000 hours of development bench running had been completed on this type of engine by 1945 with over 5000 being produced.

The B.M.W. Company became seriously interested in jet engines in 1937 and produced their 003 axial flow design in 1939. This work was under the general control of Mr. Bruckmann, the Chief Engineer of the Group, Dr. Oestrich being chief designer. The B.M.W. design was regarded as more practical and a sounder design than the Jumo 004. The compressor was also based originally on Gottingen work but was subsequently modified by Dr. Oestrich, using NACA blade profiles. About 5000 hours of development running has been done on the bench, and about 600 engines had been produced by the end of the war. The B.M.W. 003 was planned for an output similar to the Jumo, about 5000 engines per month.

In Germany, was the firm of Heinkel-Hirth who were building a turbo-jet to a design ascribed to von Ohain. He was working with Max Hahn and produced the HeS2A which was first run on a test bench during September 1937 and fuelled by gaseous hydrogen. Initially all these von Ohain turbines were designed to run on hydrogen. This engine ran some months after the Whittle Unit. There is a patent, taken out in 1939 by Heinkel, identical to the design ascribed to von Ohain but the patent is with Max Hahn.

{Author's Note: - Von Ohain has no traceable, public, aircraft gas turbine patents in this period, though he has a joint one with Heinkel

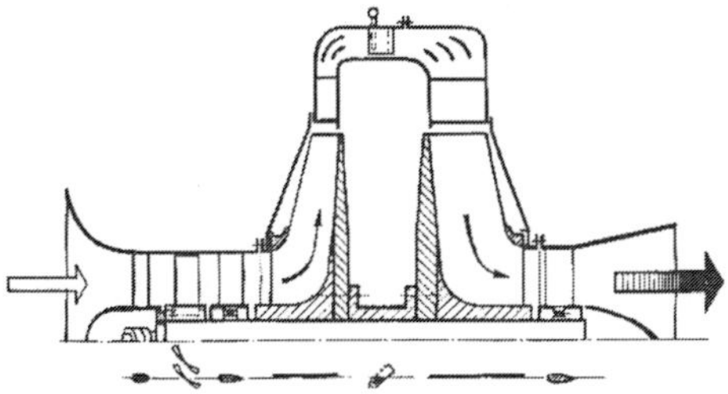

HeS 2 March 1937

HeS3A Spring 1938

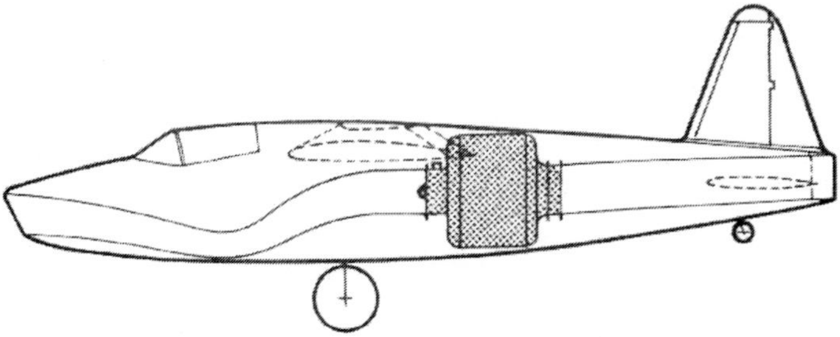

Heinkel He-178 gas turbine installation

The completed Heinkel He-178

The Heinkel He-178 in flight

in 1939, Max Hahn has one dated 27 May 1939 (US2256198) joint with Ernst Heinkel. Frank Whittle was the inventor of and the first to run, the aircraft gas turbine which was proved by his first patent.}

The HeS2A was followed by the HeS2B and then began the flight testing of the HeS3A in the spring of 1939 built under the wing of a He118 V2 dive bomber. By 24 August 1939 Heinkel had developed the HeS3B which flew in the Heinkel He178 research aircraft. The aircraft had wooden wings, a duralumin fuselage with a nose air intake, in the tail a jet exhaust was installed and the pilot's cockpit was installed close to the air intake. The tests were carried out under the direction of Dr. Ing. Schiff who was the technical director of Heinkel-Hirth. On 24 August 1939, the He 178 piloted by Erich Warsitz made a historic 6 minute flight from the airfield in Rostock-Marienehe at about 4 am. This was the first aircraft in the world to fly utilizing a turbojet engine and it flew in a straight line before landing. The second flight was three days later flown in a circuit round the airfield. The He 178 was also the first jet aircraft to experience a bird ingestion problem during this flight, causing no harm. During this flight Warsitz cut the engine and made a dead-stick landing. Again this was a six minute flight with the undercarriage jammed down. After the flight the engine was declared worthless.

Convinced that the gas turbine was the way forward for aircraft power plants, Heinkel developed the twin engined Heinkel He280 fighter. Shortly after the demonstration of the He 178 to the Reich Air Ministry on 1 November 1939, Heinkel started development of a twin engine fighter which was designated the He 280 to be built at Rostock. The aircraft could not use engines of the HeS 38 type because of the large engine diameter and low performance. At this time, however, the axial flow engine (designated the HeS 30) that was being developed by Mueller who had arrived at the Heinkel Rostock plant, was experiencing serious development problems. Recognizing that the axial flow engine would not be ready in time, a back-up solution designated the HeS 8 which would employ a radial rotor similar to the HeS 38 combined with an axial vane diffuser and a straight through flow combustor. Only 14 months were available for this development, as the He 280 airframe was developed much faster

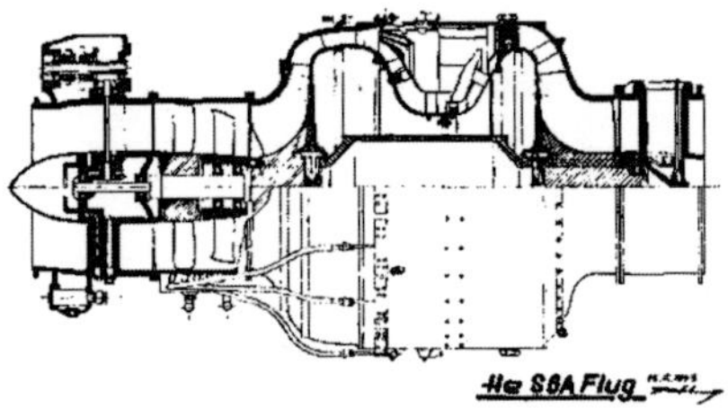

Heinkel He s8

He 280 on the ground

He 280 takes to the air note lack of engine cowlings

He 280 in the air

He 280 awaits scrapping

than its engines. The HeS 8 engine managed to meet the minimum requirements and was ready in time for the first flight of the He 280 which took place in late March 1941, though the aircraft had poor low speed characteristics. It was said to have a maximum speed of 500 mph and a designed speed of 577 mph at 20000 feet. The HeS 8 engine progressed and was in the stage where it was being developed for manufacture and the Heinkel Hirth engineers contributed towards this task. In July 1942, the HeS 8A was running well, but by this time the Me-262 and its Junkers Jumo 004 engines had been chosen to be the first production jet for the Luftwaffe. Ultimately, the HeS 8 program, the HeS 30 program and the He 280 fighter aircraft were officially cancelled in early 1943 as dead-end technology.

At the same time Messerschmitt were working on a twin engined fighter for the German air Ministry on June 1939 termed Project 1065. This aircraft was purely an experimental design though Messerschmitt had included an operation role of interceptor fighter. Project 1065 was an all-metal low-wing cantilever monoplane with a fully retractable tailwheel undercarriage and two BMW P3302 turbojets in the wing roots or two axial flow power plants developed by Junkers. The calculated maximum speed of the 1065 was 900 km/h (559 mph). A full scale mock-up was inspected January 1940 and on 1 March 1940 Messerschmitt received a contract to build three airframes for flight testing and one for static testing. The official designation for the design was Project 1065 which was also allocated the Messerschmitt type number Me-262.

By now the Me-262 was in an advanced state of construction. Its wings were sweptback about eighteen degrees but this had been done for stability and control reasons. Under the direction of Willi Messerschmitt work was begun on a Me-262 with thirty-five degree sweep (Swept Wing II). This airplane was ready for testing in January 1945 when another Me-262 stalled in the landing pattern and crashed on top of it. Another Me-262 with forty-five degree sweepback was under construction at the end of the war. By this time the entire German aircraft industry had picked up the idea and there were many experimental airplanes with swept wings at Junkers, Arado, Focke-Wulf, etc.

Me-262V1 prototype fitted with a Junkers Jumo piston engine

ME-262 with a tail wheel

Due to a shortage of power plants the Me-262 V1 flew as a piston engined aircraft. Fitted with a Junkers Jumo G210 piston engine, the Me-262 V1 made its maiden flight 4 April 1941. The first pair of BMW 109-003aA turbo jets did not arrive till mid November 1941, but the airframe still had the Jumo piston engine. Flown by Fritz Wendel the Me-262 made its first turbine flight only to have the power plants cut out, only the piston engine prevented a serious crash. On 17/18 July 1942, flown by Fritz Wendel and powered by Jumo turbines, the Me-262 V3 made its first flight on purely turbine power. The flight went completely unobserved by the German Air Ministry due to official apathy towards Messerschmitt. It was nearly a year later that the Ministry acknowledged the existence of the Me-262 on 19 May 1943. But on 17 August 1943 an air raid destroyed the chance of getting the aircraft into mass production for the Reich. Production of the Me-262 was then placed in the hands of the Speer ministry. None of the officials had any aircraft manufacturing experience thus the Me-262 fell behind in production, it was calculated that they had lost 18 months production by 1945. By the end of February 1945 results were being seen but production was now placed in the hands of SS Obergrupenfuhrer Kammler. From March 1945 production was dispersed from place to place and despite the disruption 1443 Me-262s were produced to April 1945. Aircraft manufacture ceased when Allied troops took over the factories and the Me-262 was grounded for a time.

Luftwaffe pilots had, since June 1944, been training in the first production version, the Me-262A-1a. Erprobungskommando 262 was the training unit at Lechfield with the task of both to transition fighter pilots to the revolutionary new aircraft and to develop suitable tactics for the Me-262A-1a's use. The unit was formed in December 1943 and began operations as early as April, 1944, with the acquisition of 15 pre-production types. The greatest problem for the unit was maintenance of the engines and developing sound tactical doctrine for the fighter's use. Actual training seemed to vary from pilot to pilot, late in the war when everything was collapsing; pilots sometimes received little more than a cockpit checkout before being launched into combat.

Me-262 in flight

The superb view from the cockpit

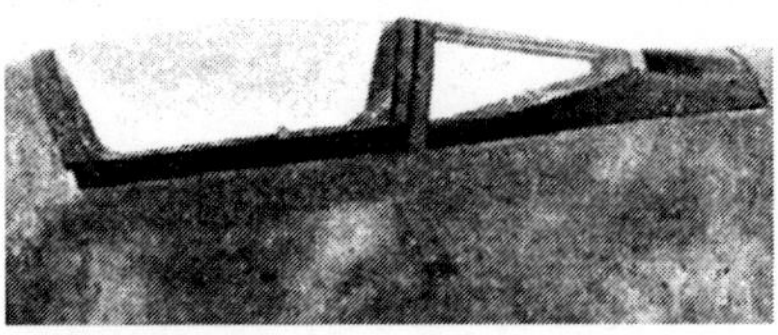

The standard cockpit and high speed cockpit

The Messerschmitt Me 262A-2a fighter bombers entered operational service in August 1944 when Kampfgeschwader 5l, the "Edelweiss", converted from twin engine Messerschmitt Me 410's to the new jet, the unit was commanded by Major Schenk. (The first Allied jet squadron to see operational service was 616 Squadron formed on 21 July 1944 with Gloster Meteors. They became fully operational on 27 July 1944). Then Jagdgeschwader 7 (Nowotny) equipped with the ME-262 and under the command of Oberst Johannes Steinhoff, was formed in December 1944; it stayed in operation until the end of the war. By 1945 the war was coming to its conclusion, other units, principally former bomber squadrons, were converted to the Messerschmitt Me 262. Despite all their efforts, the shortages of equipment and the air superiority of the Allied air forces prevented them from achieving effective operational status. As a means of desperation the Nazis formed JG44 an elite unit formed with the best of the Luftwaffe pilots.

JV 44 trained with JV 7, then moved to Munchen-Riem on 31 March 1945, for a last ditch effort. This time the Luftwaffe had more Me-262s than pilots. At Munchen-Riem the ME-262 was equipped with rockets. JV 44 fought on until it was overrun on 3 May 1945. The unit, with its elite personnel, had scored 50 victories during its short existence. Though the Me-262 did not have it all its own way all the time, it was vulnerable to attack on take-off and landing. During this phase of its flight envelope it was protected by FW-190s with bright red painted leading wing edges – this was to stop friendly fire in the flight circuit. The main drawback with the Me-262 was found to be the time between overhauls (TBO) of the Jumo 004 engines. Initially it was fifty hours then came down to twenty five hours and at the collapse of Nazi Germany twelve and a half hours.

On 2 April 1945, Republic P-47 Thunderbolts of the 367 fighter squadron were flying over Noerdlinger, Germany at 7000 feet. Four P-47 Thunderbolts were preparing a strafing run over Ottingen airfield. The group was attacked out of the sun by four Me-262s. Cutting off the Number two, Lieutenant J. Usiatynski gave the Me-262 a burst at 70 degrees deflection at 700 yards. He turned with the enemy aircraft observing strikes, both diving at 60 degrees; he gave

Line-up in front of F9/40 DG205/G which was fitted with W2B/23s and first flew on June 12, 1943. Left to right: John Crosby-Warren, test-pilot; Michael Gaunt, chief test-pilot; Frank McKenna, general manager; Frank Whittle, W G Carter, designer

The first production Gloster Meteor EE210/G sent to the United States for test April 1944

1945 Meteor being serviced at an RAF station. The Gloster Meteor was the first jet fighter to enter squadron service in the world.

the Me-262 another burst at 600 yards with 30 degrees deflection. He observed further hits on the aircraft's tail section; the aircraft then hit the ground and exploded.

With peace in 1945, German, Austria and other countries were littered with the flotsam of war. The Allies were anxious to procure examples of German airframes for test. Ten Me-262 aircraft were selected and flown to Cherbourg for onward transportation to the United States aboard the carrier vessel HMS *Reaper.* The aircraft were offloaded at Newark, then assembled and flown to Freeman Field, Indiana, with one stop en-route at Pittsburgh; at Freeman Field the planes were given "FE" numbers for test purposes, "FE" for Foreign Equipment.

One Me 262 was sent to the test centre at Wright Field and was flown on quite a few comparison tests against the P-80. It was found that the wind noise around the Me-262s cockpit, though not objectionable, contributed greatly to the noise factor. Maintenance for the Me-262 could be compared to the P-80, if the engines had been maintained by a trained maintenance crew. Despite a weight difference of 2000lbs, the Me-262 was superior to the Lockheed P-80 in acceleration, speed and approximately the same in climb performance. "*..The handling characteristics of the Me-262 airplanes tested were very poor. However, it is believed that, with the exception of the directional hunting or yawing, they would have been considerably improved if the aileron and elevator servo tab had been connected. TheMe-262 apparently has a higher critical Mach number from a drag standpoint than any current AAF fighters.*" (AIR MATERIEL COMMAND WRIGHT-PATTERSON AFB OH 1 February 1947).

The Me-262 was a sound design, both structurally and aerodynamically but the jet turbine gave much trouble because of the poor quality steel used in its manufacture but it killed more pilots than the Allies. Built with considerable sweep-back on the leading-edge, the all-metal, single-spar wing was made in one piece and featured a thin section which behaved well at high Mach numbers; full-span automatic slots were fitted and also slotted flaps. Built in four sections, the fuselage was of triangular section, blending to circular

Abandoned Me-262 beside an autobahn – engine inspected

Captured Luftwaffe aircraft aboard HMS Reaper

Me-262, Wk. Nr. 111711 under test 20 Aug 1945 it crashed when both engines caught fire.

nose, the nose section being a steel plate structure, while the remainder of the fuselage was all-metal monococque. The pilot's cockpit was designed for pressurization, one of the few aircraft of the time were so designed. The jettisonable cockpit canopy was of tear-drop form, the hood hinging to starboard for access. Suspended beneath the wing, so that there was no interruption in the main spar, were the two Junkers Jumo 004B 8-stage, axial-flow turbines, some of the motor auxiliaries being mounted on top of the unit at the forward end, thus producing a slight bulge above the leading-edge. Three fuel tanks in the fuselage provided a total capacity of 600 gallons of aircraft fuel. Hydraulically operated, the main wheels of the retractable tricycle undercarriage folded inwards into the wing, while the nose strut folded back into a fuselage well; all three wheels possessing hydraulic brakes. Armament installations on the Messerschmitt Me-262 were quite varied.

The standard arrangement for armament in day fighters was four 30 mm. Mk. 108 cannon mounted in the steel fuselage nose cap but as a bomber with two 500-lb. bombs slung under the fuselage, the number of cannon was reduced to two.

With the German collapse in the West in the spring of 1945, the Allies sent into German industry inspection teams. These teams were termed Alsos, T Force and also B.I.O.S./F.I.A.T./C.I.O.S. The key factories which were inspected were involved in the aircraft industry including gas turbine manufacture. The Allied inspection teams acknowledged that the work completed by the Germans on airframes and jet engines would greatly assist research into supersonic flight, some of their designs were quite fantastic but when looked at in terms of research and development were quite feasible.

North American Aviation had successfully produced the P-51 Mustang, B-25 Mitchell bomber, T-6 Texan and the P-82 Twin Mustang by 1945. With the mass of details existing on gas turbines North American Aviation produced two fighter designs for the Air Force and the United States Navy. These designs were the Fury (Navy) and the P-86 (Air Force). The P-86 grew out of North American's several straight-wing configurations of the XFJ-1 Fury (the projected Navy jet fighter) and engineering (including wind-tunnel data) on swept-wings obtained in Germany after V-E Day and the design details of Messerschmitt including those of the Me-262. From these projects the USAF selected one similar to the XFJ-1, for which three-prototypes were ordered. The contract for the fighter being placed with North American, on 18 May 1945, with the designation XP-86, one machine to be used for static tests. The first mock-up was approved in June 1945 and was of a conventional straight-wing type. This machine was to have had a top speed of 582 mph. and a service ceiling of 45000 ft.

Earlier in 1944 U.S. research and design people had no basis for understanding the significance of wing sweep at high speeds. However, just a few months later, in January 1945-R.T. Jones, of the NACA Langley Aeronautical Laboratory, completed a theoretical study showing that the compressibility drag rise could be delayed and reduced by use of a swept wing. In a little more than 2 months, the United States began to receive information acquired by the Allied inspection forces in Europe indicating that the supersonic advantage of sweep that had been discovered in Germany by Adolf Busemann.

In the spring of 1945, a picked team of technical personnel, including North American representatives, was sent to Europe. One group interviewed Busemann and Dr. Betz. Dr Albert Betz then handed over all the German aerodynamic research material to Dr Theodore Karmann of the USAAF Scientific Advisory Board. The North American team brought back captured Luftwaffe data on the swept wing which saved North American about three years of research. Based largely on the high-speed advantages of the swept wing as revealed by the German data, North American proposed changing from the straight wing design of the XP-86 to a swept wing design. Maj. Gen. L. C. Craigie—then Chief of the Engineering Division at Wright Field quickly gave his verbal approval.

At North American's request, a captured Messerschmitt Me-262, sweptwing was sent to the company for study of its slat configuration. Leading edge slats were required on the sweptback wing to solve the problems of low speed operation in an aircraft designed for unprecedented high speeds. The slats extending and retracted automatically in response to aerodynamics forces on the wing, these

Me-262 in Allied hands with a set of wings on the hangar floor

slats provide low stalling speeds and satisfactory stalling characteristics. In the XF-86, the fully-swept design version of the Me-262 as envisaged by Willi Messerschmitt was adopted almost unchanged following Busemann's ideas as originally put forward at the Rome conference in 1935.

The Army Air Forces (AAF) then accepted a variant of the straight-wing XFJ-1 design in May 1945, ordered two prototypes and applied the designation XP-86 to the aircraft. This aircraft also had a slimmer airframe in relation to the XFJ-1 Fury. North American engineers found that adopting the Messerschmitt 262 swept-wing with a design of 35 degrees, would give the XP-86 about 70 mph (60.7 knots) greater speed. The aircraft was then ordered to General Operational Requirements (GOR) of May 1945. Both the XFJ-1 and the XP-86 were designed around the General Electric J35 engine.

The GOR called for a day fighter of medium range that could work as an escort fighter and attack bomber. Speed was one of the primary military characteristics of which the AAF was most insistent. The straight-wing XP-86 under letter contract, with an estimated top speed of 582 mph, fell short of the minimum 600 mph required. A wind tunnel test in June 1945 showed that the airframe of the XP-86 was limited and could not be developed. Then came the design change on 1 November 1945, the AAF endorsed North American's proposal to scrap the straight wing design in favour of the 35 degree swept-wing, even though this would probably mean a year's delay in delivery. It was felt that of all the German wing data that was available showed

June 1945 mock-up of the straight wing XP-86, only the left side was finished and inspected on May 1945 (NAA)

Model of the original NA-140 with straight wing and tip tanks

that the wing leading edge slat was most promising, if the slats were made automatic and could overcome low speed stability problems of the swept wing. An Me-262 wing was sent to Los Angeles to study the leading edge slats. Thus on 1 November 1945 a proposal to redesign the XP-86 to have swept wings was submitted to the Air Force and accepted. More wind tunnel tests followed and the wing leading edge slats were designed to be fully automatic, opening and closing with a change of aerodynamic forces on the wing.

The definitive contract of 20 June 1946 replaced the contract of May 1945 was superseded by a definitive research and development (R&D) contract that raised to three the number of prototypes ordered. The production go-ahead for the XP-86 came 20 December 1946.

Although the prototypes were still under construction, a production order was released. Unit cost of the first 33 P-86s authorized for procurement was set at $438,999.00-more than twice the aircraft's eventual price.

To test the concept of the 35 degree swept wing, Bell modified two Bell P-63 Kingcobras to have swept wings; these became the Bell L-39. The airframes were modified amongst other tests, in order to study the low-speed performance of the Douglas 0-558-2 Skyrocket and the Bell X-2. First flight of the Bell L-39-1 was on 23 April 1946. A lighter three-bladed P-39 propeller was substituted for the four-bladed P-63 propeller and a ventral fin similar to the P-63C's was added. The second Bell L-39-2 flew on 29 May 1946; the fuselage was configured with a plug making the fuselage longer and an even larger ventral fin. The two prototypes made it clear that slatted, swept wings would provide stall-speed performance for fighters. Flight test and evaluation using the first Bell L-39 was completed by Bell on 26 August 1946, after which it was ferried to NACA Langley, Virginia, for a wind tunnel and flight correlation test program. The second Bell L-39 was rebuilt in mid-1946 to support Bell's X-2 program. The wing was modified to represent a fully swept wing with a circular-arc aerofoil and the leading edge was extended forward to the side of body. After completing their swept wing test programme in December 1949, both Bell L-39 aircraft were reportedly transferred to NACA Lewis where they were scrapped.

Swept wing Bell L-39

Following the wing tests Bell L-39 prototypes Bell built the model 60, X-5 which was the first aircraft capable of changing the sweep of its wings in flight. The Bell X-5 was inspired by the untested Messerschmitt P.1101 fighter. The P1101 prototype was recovered by United States troops in the summer of 1945 from the experimental facility at Oberammergau, Germany and was brought back to the United States. Although damaged in transit, the prototype was delivered to the Bell factory at Buffalo, New York where company engineering staff studied the design closely and led by Chief Designer Robert J. Woods, submitted a proposal for a similar design in contrast with the German design, which could only have its wing sweepback angle adjusted on the ground. In profile, the X-5 differed little from the P-1101, the wing area, fuselage length, and gross weight differed little between the two aeroplanes. Although the P-1101 was not a variable-sweep aircraft project and never flew, it was perfectly clear that the post-war transfer of German data on swept wings and the availability of the P-1101 prototype in the United States contributed significantly to the development of the world's first variable-sweep aircraft. For the X-5 Bell engineers devised a system of electric motors to adjust the sweep in flight to three sweep positions: 20°, 40° and 60°. On 26 July, 1949, two Bell X-5 prototypes were ordered under a $2.4 million contract (No.AC-3298), the first of which was to be delivered within a year. The tests were carried out by Bell at Edwards Air Force Base, the flight characteristics were tested out by the NACA High-Speed Flight Research Station. In addition to the flight trials at Edwards Air Force Base, tests were carried out with models of the Bell X-5 with a 35 degree sweep in the Langley wind tunnel. The results of these trials were made at low speeds in the Langley 300 mph 7- by 10-foot tunnel of a 35 degree swept-wing model of high aspect ratio and a 1/4-scale model of the Bell X-5 airplane, NACA reported".... *having 35 degree swept wings indicate that deflector and spoiler-deflector types of controls can be designed to provide considerable gust alleviation (reduction in lift-curve slope) for a swept-wing airplane while still maintaining stability and control.*" In addition to the XP-86, wing data was incorporated into

North American FJ-1 Fury on a carrier and with kneeling nose wheel

Bell X-5 showing swept wings

Bell X-5 makes its maiden flight 20 June 1950.

Prototype XP-86, 45-59597

In the air prototype XP-86, 45-59597

Nose view of prototype XP-86, 45-59597note leading edge slats

the Boeing B-47 six jet engine bomber and the Douglas D-558 Skyrocket. First flight of the prototype XP-86, 45-59597, came 1 October 1947. The aircraft had been taken by truck to Edwards Air Force Base at Muroc on 10 September 1947. There it was flown by George Welch, North American test pilot. The XP-86 was powered by a Chevrolet-built General Electric J35-C-3 turbo-jet, delivering 3,750 lb. static thrust, this was later re-equipped with the more powerful J47-GE-3 engine. A re-engined prototype (YP-86A) first exceeded the speed of sound, Mach 1, on 25/26 April 1948. The flight testing period was 1947-1949. Category II flight tests were started in December 1947; Category III, in January 1949, one month before the first F-86As entered operational service.

The pilot's field of view and ground control was described as excellent. After a ground run of 3020 feet the aircraft took off at 125 mph. From sea level to 20000 feet the aircraft acceleration was 4000 feet a minute. Service ceiling was described as 41300 feet with a warning buffet of 6 knots above the stall and immediate recovery when speed was regained.

Additional procurement for the Sabre came 28 December 1947 when North American received a second production order for 188 P-86s, but these aircraft, as ordered at the time, never materialized. They actually came off the production lines as early F-86As; they also received a 5,200 lb. static thrust General Electric J-47-GE-3 engine. Subsequent F-86A productions were successively fitted with the J47-GE-7, -9, and -13. The first flight of a production aircraft took place 20 May 1948. The Air Force accepted two other initial productions of its first swept-wing fighter on 28 May 1948 and changed their P-86A designation to F-86A and the following month June 1948 an order for another 333 F-86As was awarded. With the type entering operational service February 1949. During this period on 18 September 1947 the air arm of the United States armed forces became the United States Air Force organized within the Department of the Air Force. Designations changed, the "P" for pursuit was dropped 1 June 1948, only to be replaced by "F" for fighter in the USAF.

The 94th Fighter Squadron of the 1st Fighter Group received the first F-86As at March Field, California. The Group was completely

North American F-86A-1 (S/N 48-158) of the "Hat in the ring" squadron

Lockheed F-80s over Korea

An F-80 pilot removes his flight gear as the ground crew checks the aircraft after a mission

equipped by the end of May. Overseas Deployments commenced 1 December 1950. The 4th Fighter Group of the 4th Fighter Interceptor Wing (urgently deployed to Japan in November 1950) was the first F-86 unit to reach the Korean war theatre.

The first jet combat encounter took place between a Lockheed F-80 and a MiG -15 on 8 November 1950. At 20000 feet Lieutenant R. Brown, engaged a MiG-15 but was warned not to cross the Yalu River. The MiG went into a climbing left turn with Brown following firing short bursts with the MiG diving towards the Yalu River. At 1000 yards Brown fired another burst causing an engine fire suddenly the MiG-15 blew up. Though this was an American success it proved the capability and the superiority of the MiG-15 over the Lockheed F-80 Shooting Star.

On 6 April 1946, Soviet aircraft designers were summoned to the Kremlin for a meeting with Joseph Stalin. The designers were told to produce a day interceptor with a speed up to Mach 0.9 and have an altitude of 36089ft. It was to have a heavy armament and to be easily maintained in the field and to have swept wings using captured German data. The weakness of the fighter design was the lack of a suitable turbojet. The German gas turbines were considered obsolete and the only available Soviet turbojet, the TR1A lacked the thrust and was years away from development. The only engines that Soviet Intelligence said were up to specification for the new fighter were the Rolls-Royce Nene and the Derwent. It was the Nene that caused the most interest.

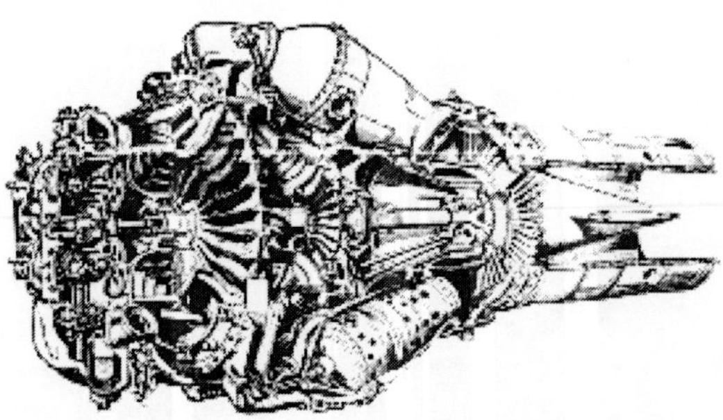

The Rolls-Royce B-41 Nene

The British Rolls-Royce Nene 1, developed 50001b thrust, though it had a large centrifugal impeller it was simple and robust and had an electrical starter. The engine was ideal for the new fighter. Due to political considerations between East and West, Stalin had his doubts about obtaining the engine; he is reported as saying, "What a fool one must be to sell one's secrets." Little did he realise there were two fools in the British Labour Government at that time, firstly Sir Stafford Cripps, President of the Board of Trade and Harold Wilson his successor. Cripps gave his approval.

On 28 March 1947, the British Prime Minister Clement Attlee ruled that once an item had been removed from the Secret List its sale to the Soviet Union could not be prevented. The first ten Derwents and ten Nenes were delivered between January and July 1947. The Soviets ordered a further 20 Derwents and 15 Nenes early in 1947 for delivery by November and this was approved in May. Another 24 units (four Derwents and 20 Nenes) were requested by the Soviets in July. This was subsequently increased to 15 and 25 respectively but the original 24 ordered in July proved to be the last engines delivered. Rolls-Royce wished to continue supplying at the current rate of four Derwents and three Nenes per month after the orders for 55 were completed at the end of November. Orders for spares were also placed in early August.

Factory No 45 built the first Soviet copy of the Rolls-Royce Nene, called RD-45, in August 1948. The MiG design bureau received a complete set of RD-45 installation drawings in February 1947. The first production engine was the RD-45F, not RD-45 and was fitted to the first production MiG-15 (101003) which made its first flight on 30 December 1948. Armament was two 23mm cannon and one 37mm cannon. Testing the MiG-15 commenced 14 June 1949 and was completed 7 January 1950 with deliveries to the Soviet squadrons starting immediately. By sheer coincidence the first Soviet regiment equipped with the MiG-15 was certified as combat ready in the same month, June 1950, in which North Korea invaded South Korea, precipitating a major war with the United Nations. By this time the MiG-15 had established a reputation for basic simplicity, toughness and combat readiness.

The first production Mig-15

Despite a shortage of F-86 aircraft (only 15 of the 19 F-86As initially deployed to Korea were combat ready,) the 4th Fighter Group began combat operations in support of the Far East Air Force on 16 December 1950. The following day, 17 December 1950, the first recorded combat between swept-wing fighters ended in favour of the F-86A. Four other Russian-built MiG-15s were claimed during the week without any F-86 losses. The retreat of United Nations (UN) ground forces in the last days of 1950 forced redeployment of the F-86As to Japan. Despite the availability of the long-range F-84Es, B-29 raids over North Korea could not be resumed until late in February 1951, when the F-86As returned to Korea.

Following their first successes, the F-86As quickly captured the air superiority gained at the onset of the Korean conflict by the inferior F-51s, F-82 Twin Mustangs and a few F-80 jets, skilfully piloted against indecisive opposition. Sino Communist MiG-15s later threatened this supremacy. F-86As of the 4th Fighter Group, although designed to escort the B-29s and fighter-bombers of the Fifth Air Force operating deep in North Korea, at first were used primarily as an air superiority force. They were pitted against large numbers of MiG-15s that could take refuge on the Manchurian side of the Yalu River where they enjoyed the immunity of UN aircraft. Of the Group's 4,885 sorties between 16 December 1950 and 28 June 1951, only 336 resulted in combat. Yet, the Group destroyed 40 MiG -15s, probably destroyed 6, and damaged 71. In contrast, it lost 7 F-86As - one due to an operational accident.

A brace of Sabres take-off and head for the Yalu River

F-86 Sabre heads for combat in Korea

Sabre awaiting an engine change

F-86 leaves its Korean revetment heading for combat

F-86 Sabre "Miss B" 50-602 receives gunsight maintenance while the pilot leans on the wing

Royal Air Force pilots in Korea serving with the 51st Fighter Interceptor Wing Front row left to right Flt.Lts. T.J. McElham, J. H. Granville White, J.A. Ryan, Flg.Off J.N. Murphy and Flt/Lt J.E.Y King. Back Row Flg. Off J.A. Mansell Flt.Lts. J.J.J Lovell, R. French, J.R. Dickson and J. R. Maitland

The F-86A's initial performances balanced those of its Russian counterpart. In light of later model improvements, the Air Force eventually judged the two aircraft roughly equal. Meanwhile, the F-86A success over the MiG-15 rested chiefly in the ability and aggressiveness of its pilots. Paradoxically, the F-86's lopsided victory score in 6 months of operation also pinpointed a serious combat deficiency. Inadequate armament (the M-3.50-caliber machinegun in particular) explained the high number of MiGs "damaged and probably destroyed" against those positively "destroyed" (77 to 44). Despite all efforts, this armament problem persisted in the F-86E that followed the F-86A into production and combat.

The F-86A's gross weight was also criticized - 16,000 lbs against the MIG's 12,000lbs. Some of this excess derived from such "gadgets" as emergency fuel pumps, self-sealing fuel tanks (that did not hold against the MiG-15's 23 and 37-mm cannons) and an unreliable, electronic gunsight that was hard to maintain. Fuel pump and fuel tank improvements in subsequent F-86 models and another gunsight introduced in the last F-86A off the production line took care of difficulties in an otherwise sound aircraft.

In the last 24 F-86As produced, the Mk 18 gunsight was supplanted by the A-1CM sight, which was coupled with an AN/APC-30 radar installed in the upper lip of the aircraft's nose intake. Earlier F-86As were retrofitted with the A-1CM sight, which was linked either to an AN/APG-5C radar or, more commonly, to the AN/APG-30.

As a progressive development of the F-86A, the F-86E featured a new tail with both tailplane and elevators controllable (all flying) and linked for coordinated movement. All controls were power-operated. The F-86E retained the F-86A's M-3 guns and the J47-GE-13 engine of the latest F-86As. First flight of the production Aircraft took place 23 September 1950. The United States Air Force accepted its first two F-86Es in February 1951 just a few months after the aircraft's first flight. The F-86E entered operational service May 1951 the first aircraft were assigned to ADC's 33d Fighter Interceptor Wing and overseas deployments July 1951.

The Soviet Union was desperate to acquire an F-86 airframe. In North Korea, the 64th Fighter Aviation Corps was primarily interested in the F-86 Sabre for its engineering value. Soviet intelligence officers assigned to the unit went to great efforts to acquire and ship to the Soviet Union F-86s which had been downed but remained relatively intact. At least three F-86s were shipped to the Zhukovski Central Aerohydrodynamics Institute and the Sukhoi Design Bureau in Moscow.

The Air Force furnished FEAF whatever F-86s it could spare from air defence. Almost as soon as operational, F-86Es joined the F-86As in the Korean War. Initial provisioning of logistics for the F-86 was based on peacetime consumption rates. Hence, the 51st Wing's unprogrammed conversion to F-86Es severely strained logistical support. By January 1952, 45 percent of the war-committed F-86A and E fighters were out of commission for want of parts or maintenance. Supplies of external fuel tanks, without which the range-limited F-86s were badly handicapped, also were nearly exhausted. "Peter Rabbit," a crash project for buying a 1-year supply of all urgently needed items, solved most of these problems but it took several months. The F-86As, first deployed to the Far East, were flown by highly qualified, regular and reservist, career pilots. Most of these men were being rotated as 100-mission veterans by mid-1951, when the F-86Es arrived and supplying qualified replacement pilots for service in Korea became a challenge. During the winter of 1951-1952 the 4th FI Wing (still flying a mixture of F-86A and E) and the F-86E-equipped 51st received pilots whose previous experience had been attained in multi-engine transports and bombers. This problem persisted until March 1952, when large numbers of jet fighter pilots began to arrive from replacement training centres in the United States. The USAF in Korea was largely outnumbered by an enemy favoured by the odds of combat but 3 F-86Es of the 51st F1 Wing destroyed 25 MiGs during January 1952. Most of the kills were achieved by patrols that entered the combat area at 45,000 feet and made astern attacks on the elusive enemy aircraft, sighted at lower altitudes.

Due to reduced flying time caused by logistical deficiencies, the 4th and 51st Wings could only claim the destruction of 17 MiGs during February, but impressive victories were recorded soon afterward. Although some MiG pilots continued to avoid action, enemy tactics changed and MiG formations were met at lower altitudes in March and April. In these months, at the cost of only 6 F-86s, 83 MiGs were destroyed.

The operational suitability tests ended in July 1952, after the F-86E had already acquired some 12 months of combat experience. In essence, the F-.86E was a relatively general purpose aircraft, facing the specialized MiG-15 fighter under combat conditions which favoured the Soviet type. Experience called for improvement of the aircraft's overall performance. This was particularly urgent because of the enemy's increasing capability. Yet, none of the several courses of action available to the Air Force appeared too promising. The F-86E could be retrofitted with the more powerful J-47-GE-27 engine; for this possibility had been taken into consideration before production, but this engine was in short supply. As recommended by North American, the thrust of the F-86E's J-47-GE-13 engine could be boosted. This would alleviate the aircraft's most serious shortcoming by increasing its rate of climb. However, neither General Electric nor the Air Force favoured this second solution. The former, because it would severely reduce the engine life; the latter, because it would pose a difficult, "if not impossible," supply and maintenance problem.

After combat testing proved its effectiveness, a kind of expedient was adopted that later became a standard feature of subsequent F-86 models. Referred to as the "6-3 wing," this modification, credited with speed increases of several knots and gave the F-86E wing a slightly increased sweepback. This was achieved by extending the wing inboard and outboard edges by 6 and 3 inches, respectively, and by eliminating the slats of the wing's original leading edges. The "6-3 wing" modification kits were inexpensive, $4,000 each, but only 50 had been sent to Korea by the end of 1952, and they were not plentiful until mid-1953. The United States Air Force took delivery of its last six F-86Es in October.

Because of the Korean War demands on American production, 60 of the Air Force's 396 F-86Es were built by Canadair Aircraft Company. Like other F-86Es, they were powered by the J47-GE-13 engine. They were shipped to Korea on an aircraft carrier and landed on lighters. Eighty F-86Es were accepted in 1951, 218 in 1952, and 98 in 1953. Fifty-five of the 60 USAF F-86Es bought from Canadair were received in FY 1952, the remaining five in FY 1953. Of the 396, 225 were ordered as F-86Fs but completed as F-86Es, owing to a shortage of the F's powerful J47-GE-27 engine.

Flyaway cost per production Aircraft was $219457.00 for the airframe, $145326 for the engine (installed), $39990 electronics, $6358 cost of ordnance, $4138; armament, $23645. Like the F-86As, the F-86Es began leaving the Air Force operational inventory soon after the end of the Korean War. The Air National Guard operated140 F-86Es by mid-1956 and still flew a few of them in 1960. Also, several foreign countries received badly needed F-86Es through the Military Assistance Program-using them until the end of 1958.

Canadair's origins date to the formation of Canadian Vickers Limited. In June 1911, at the invitation of the government of Canada, the ship builder Vickers Sons & Maxim established Canadian Vickers (CV). In 1912 it began construction of a shipyard in Montreal to produce vessels for the Royal Canadian Navy. Vickers built nearly 300 ships of various types and a few submarines for the navies of Canada and the United States. The submarines were under contracts from the Electric Boat Co. of Groton, Connecticut. With the encouragement of its parent company Vickers, Canadian Vickers set up an aircraft design staff in 1924 and began to work on a forestry patrol aircraft. The first design was the three seat Vickers Vedette. Between 1924 and 1930, Canadian Vickers built 60 Vedettes, mostly with Wright Whirlwind or Armstrong Siddeley Lynx engines. Of these, 42 were delivered the Royal Canadian Air Force (RCAF), twelve were for Canadian provincial governments and commercial operators; six amphibious Vedettes went to Chile.

In 1936 they received an order for 40 Supermarine Stranraer flying boats. The last one was delivered in 1941, that year they received an order for Consolidated PBY-5a Catalina flying boats, named Canso in the RCAF. In 1943 Canadian Vickers received a contract for 230 OA-10As, a version of the PBY-5, for the U.S. Army Air Force. The wartime agreement between the United States and the

United Kingdom was that Britain would concentrate on building fighters and bombers. Out of this came the agreement for Canadian Vickers to build a version of the C-54/DC-4.This version was to be powered by Rolls-Royce Merlins and not the Wright R-2800 radials of the C-54/DC-4, the Merlin was chosen because it was felt to be superior at altitudes over 20000 feet.

In 1944 Canadian Vickers had a huge order book to produce ships for the Allies. With such a heavy workload the company asked the Canadian Government to be relieved of the aircraft manufacturing side of its business. The government agreed to this plan and allowed Canadian Vickers to withdraw from aircraft manufacturing. As a result on 3 October 1944 Canadair war formed for the production of aircraft. The order for PBY's was continued by Canadair with the final completion of the last 57 taking place on 17 May 1945. Canadair also took part in conversion of the C-47 (Dakota) for the RCAF and RAF. Canadair also had the ability to supply aircraft spares for the C-47 type. In April 1946 the Electric Boat Company purchased 10% of the stock of Canadair. Then in January 1947 the Electric Boat Company purchased the entire stock of Canadair.

The first Canadair aircraft the C-54M, the XC-54GM, now named North Star, flew 15 July 1946. This prototype was built mainly from Douglas parts with Rolls-Royce Merlins fitted. The initial order was for 44, twenty for Trans Canada Airlines (TCA) and twenty four for the RCAF. The twenty for TCA were pressurised while the order for the RCAF was unpressurised. Then in July 1948 British Overseas Airways Corporation (BOAC) decided to buy twenty two pressurised North Stars plus spares. The first was delivered in March 1949 another seven by July 1949 with the balance being delivered within seventeen months, eight months ahead of schedule. BOAC then changed the name from North Star to Argonaut. It was the Argonaut that made BOAC profitable; the company felt it was the reliability of the Merlin and the time between overhauls that produced cost-saving dependability. The aircraft also clipped 18 hours off the timetable used by the York, Lancastrian, Hermes, etc. One of the Argonauts, "*Atalanta*", left London for East Africa and Australia on 31 January 1952, with Princess Elizabeth and the Duke of Edinburgh on board.

Prototype Canadair North Star

Canadair North Star engine nacelle and Rolls-Royce Merlin installation which made the aircraft such a noisy success

Treetops in Kenya where Princess Elizabeth received word of the death of her father King George VI

Canadair Argonaut Atalanta lands with Queen Elizabeth II at London Airport

Queen Elizabeth II descends Atalanta's stairs to be met by (r to l)Winston Churchill, Clement Attlee, Anthony Eden and Lord Woolton

Atalanta returns from Lagos to London after the Royal visit to Nigeria in 1956

Six days later, it returned from Kenya, with Queen Elizabeth and Prince Philip to London following the death of her father, King George VI. Then in April 1952 the Electric Boat Company changed its name to the General Dynamics Corporation still retaining its interest in Canadair.

The first operational jet fighter for the USAAF was the Lockheed P-80 Shooting Star. The aircraft had been sent to Europe in 1948 on the USS *Sicily* and the *Barney Kirschbaum* to Glasgow or flown across the Atlantic to Stornoway, then to the United Kingdom from there to Germany, to bolster Europe's air defences. The sixteen from Stornoway were flown to Odiham and flew to Germany on 25 July 1948. USS *Sicily* returned to the United States on 16 August 1948. Later as the F-80 Shooting Star it saw service in the Korean War. In mid-1947, Lockheed took a P-80, lengthened it by 3ft. 2.5in., added a second cockpit, this became the Lockheed TF-80C trainer. Its maiden flight was on 22 March 1948 and in May 1949 the USAF renamed it the Lockheed T-33A. On 13 September 1951, the Canadian Government announced that Canadair would build a version of the T-33, the Silver Star, for the RCAF. It would be powered by the 5100-lb. thrust Rolls-Royce Nene 10, not by the AllisonJ33 as used in USAF T-33s. The Nene was a natural engine choice for the Canadair T-33 Silver Star. The Rolls-Royce RB.41 Nene engine's first run had been in October 1944. It was initially installed in a Lockheed YP-80A Shooting Star, 44-83027 and the engine was first flown 18 July 1945 with Rolls-Royce test pilot Wing Commander John Harvey Heyworth, A.F.C. The Nene-powered YP-80, 44-83027 had made approximately 30 test flights when it was damaged beyond repair at RAF Syerston, 6 December 1945. With test pilot Andy McDowall flying the YP-80A, a fractured fuel pipe caused the engine to flame out from fuel starvation. McDowall tried to glide to a landing but another airplane was on the runway. He touched down on the grass but the landing gears were pushed up through the Shooting Star's wings. The aircraft remains were returned to the USAAF in England at Burtonwood.

The first 16 Lockheed F-80 Shooting Stars to arrive in Europe at RAF Odiham, Major Donovan F. Smith in the cockpit

USS Sicily is towed by tugs near Dumbarton Rock heading for King George V Dock Glasgow

USS Sicily unloading Shootings Stars at King George V Dock where the aircraft were towed to Renfrew Airport

US Navy unloading an F-80 Shooting Star

F-80 being towed to Renfrew Airport with an interested audience

Engine run up for the first Shooting Star flight at Renfrew

Group Commander Colonel Henry R. Spicer is met by his dog "Chief" after the first test flight of a Shooting Star

Lockheed YP-80 with Rolls Royce and in flight Church Broughton

Lockheed YP-80A Shooting Star, 44-83027/G used by Rolls-Royce to test the B-41 Nene

Canadair CT-133 Silver Star in production

Silver Stars on delivery to Turkey and Greece at Bluie West

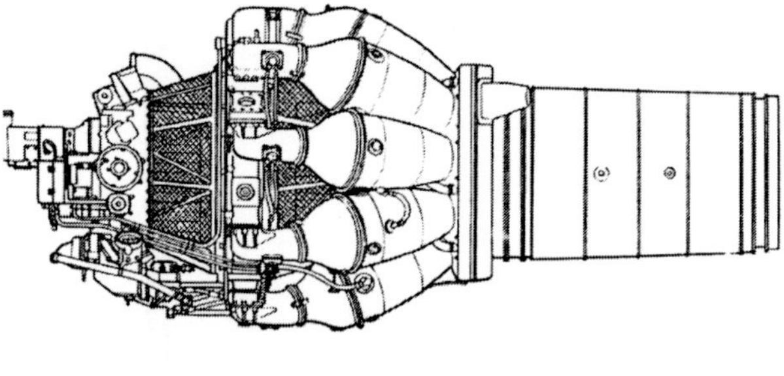

Rolls-Royce of Canada Nene 10: Silver Star Trainer turbojet. Double-sided, centrifugal compressor, nine combustion chambers and single-stage turbine. Diameter, 49.5in; length, 104in; dry weight, 1,610 1b; mass flow, 90 lb/sec; pressure ratio, 4.5:1; maximum thrust, 5,100 1b at 12,500 r.p.m. with s.f.c. of 1.00 lb/hr/lb. *Though produced by Rolls-Royce Canada one Nene was delivered from Hispano Suiza for Silver Star production.*

A contract for 576 Silver Star aircraft was signed on 1 April 1952. Canadair would design the engine installation, manufacture all but an initial quantity of 200 wings, build the forward and centre fuselage sections, and do final assembly. Beech Aircraft of Wichita, Kansas, would supply the initial wings and Canadian subcontractors would supply rear fuselages, tail units and intake ducts.

The Canadian government then decided to manufacture the F-86 under license in 1949 and in August of that year placed an order for 100 of them with Canadair Limited as the CL-13, Sabre. Initially the order was for ten aircraft, it was then planned to manufacture the F-86A but only one example designated Sabre Mk.1 was completed. Canadair became involved in its first major tooling programme. As North American was producing F-86s, it was not in a position to release any of the tooling on which Sabre parts were made and any components assembled for manufacture. Canadair therefore had to manufacture its own tooling for the Canadian Sabre programme. The first North American F-86A, pattern aircraft arrived at Canadair November 1949 and the initial Sabre production rate hit 20 planes a month and peaked at 50. This required a moving assembly line, more like those found in the car industry rather than in aircraft manufacture. Canadair introduced the made-in-Canada policy. In the beginning, Sabre components were almost 90 per cent U.S. made; by 1956 Canadian-government-supplied parts (with the exception of the engine) and components built to Canadair specifications, were 95 per cent Canadian-made and raw material was 83 per cent Canadian.

The first Canadair Sabre and the sole Sabre Mark 1 produced by Canadair (RCAF No. 19101) was an F-86A assembled from U.S. components assembled at Cartierville. It was completed on 28 July 1950. As the main Cartierville runway was being lengthened at the time, 19101 was towed to Dorval Airport where it took off on its first flight on 8 August 1950. That year two Sabres had been loaned to the Royal Air Force, Central Fighter Establishment at West Raynham for trials. The RCAF specification was for the latest "E" version of the F-86 but North American had not completed the F-86E design phase when Canadair started production. To avoid having to stop production and restart when the final F-86E design details became available, the

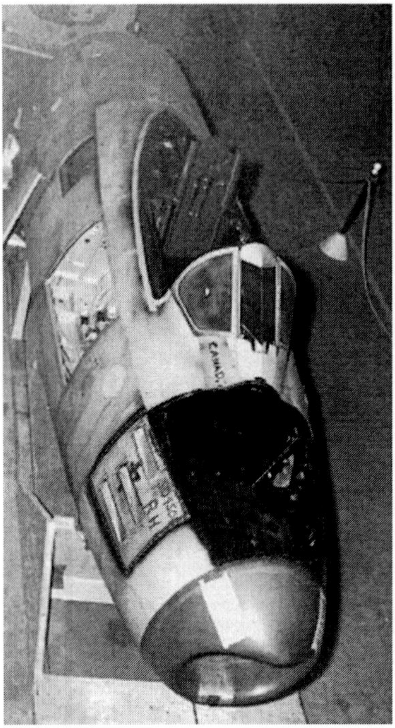

On the left the pattern Sabre received from North American Aviation, sans gun sight and battery ahead of the cockpit

Above the first production Canadair Sabre 20 March 1951

Canadair Sabres in production

Sabres awaiting assembly

Nearing final completion

first 20 or so Sabres produced at Canadair were all F-86As. As soon as they came off the line, they entered a modification program to convert them to F-86Es.

The E-model differed from the A version in having many of the improvements of the all-weather F-86D, the major change being the introduction of the "all-flying" tail surfaces. The Sabre E had power-assisted flight controls in contrast to earlier aircraft, in which the pilot's "stick" was connected directly to the ailerons and elevator. The F-86E Sabre stick movements operated hydraulic actuators which in turn moved the control surfaces. Whereas on the F-86A back and-forth stick movement controlled only the elevator, on the F-86E when the pilot moved the stick forward, both tailplane and elevator moved as a unit. When the pilot pulled the stick back, the tailplane and elevator moved first as a unit and then the elevator alone. The ultimate effect was an improvement in the Sabres overall manoeuvrability. The first production Canadair F-86E, now the Canadair Sabre Mk2, flew for the first time on 31 January 1951. A mere two weeks after the first F-86E Sabre built by North American at Los Angeles!

The power plant for the Canadair Sabre Mk2 was the 5,200-lb. thrust General Electric J47-GE-13 engine. A total of 350 Sabre 2s was produced in 1952 and 1953 for the RCAF. In the first half of 1952, 60 early Sabre 2s were supplied to the USAF in Korea. They were modified with U.S. equipment and allocated USAF numbers 52-2833 to 52-2892. They were flown to Fresno California between April and July 1952 where they were fitted with US equipment. Many returned from Korea to serve with the Air National Guard squadrons.

From the beginning of the Sabre programme the RCAF had intended to use a Canadian engine other than the GE J47 in the F-86. The Canadian designed Avro Orenda engine (Orenda the Indian god of power) was the favoured powerplant. But the Orenda required alteration to 30 per cent of the Sabre airframe structure in the engine bay. These tasks took Canadair much longer to complete than had been anticipated.

T.P.M. (Mike) Cooper-Slipper, D.F.C Test Pilot Orenda Engines

Canadair Sabre engine test

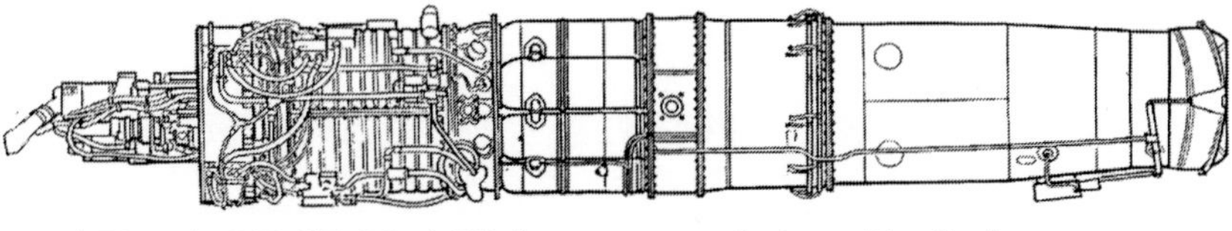

General Electric J47-GE-33. A.W. interceptor turbojet, with afterburner. twelve-stage compressor, eight combustion chambers, single-stage turbine and afterburner with two-position clamshell nozzle. Diameter, 36.75in; length, 228in; dry weight, 3,200 lb; mass flow, 102 lb/sec; pressure ratio, 5.5:1; maximum thrust, 5,500 lb at 7,950 r.p.m. with s.f.c. of 1.01 (with reheat, 7,650 lb with s.f.c. of 2.0).

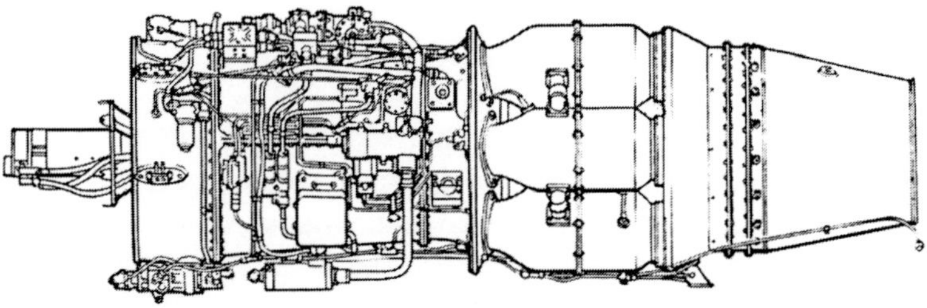

Orenda Engines Orenda 14. Single-shaft turbojet. ten-stage compressor, six combustion chambers and two-stage turbine. Overall diameter, 43in; length, 123in; dry weight, about 2,470 lb; mass flow, about 130 lb/sec; pressure ratio, about 6:1; maximum thrust, 7,200-7,500 lb at 7,800 r.p.m. with s.f.c. of 0.9.

In December, 1951, Canadair was asked by the RCAF to study the possibility of installing the Canadian-designed Orenda turbojet in the Sabre airframe. By the middle of 1952, Canadair had installed a prototype of the 6,000-lb thrust, Orenda 3 engine in the 200th production Canadair Sabre. This was the first and only Canadair Sabre Mk 3, number 19200. The Avro Orenda 3 was an axial-flow turbojet engine with a 10-stage compressor, six combustion chambers and a single-stage turbine. It produced 6000 pounds of thrust, a 15% improvement over the General Electric J47-GE-13 installed in the standard Mk2 Sabre. The Orenda was 121.3 inches long, 42 inches in diameter and weighed 2,650 pounds.

Jacqueline Cochran was an internationally recognized pilot with many aviation awards from over two decades of flying who had got her flying licence in 1932. In June 1941 she was the first woman to fly a Lockheed Hudson bomber from Montreal across the Atlantic to Prestwick. Later she recruited twenty five American women pilots to fly in the aircraft delivery service of the Air Transport Auxiliary. In twenty years of flying Jacqueline Cochrane to 1952 she had amassed 10000 hours flying. She had flown the F-51 Mustang and at the time owned a Lockheed Lodestar named, "Wings of Beauty." Then in 1952, she decided to challenge the women's speed records held by Jacqueline Auriol of France. First she tried to borrow an F-86 from the USAF but the chief of the U.S. Air Staff, General Hoyt Vandenberg, refused. She had been forbidden to fly jets solo by USAF regulations; she held the rank of full Lieutenant Colonel in the USAF Reserve. At a dinner party held in New York in November 1952, she was introduced to Air-Vice Marshal W.A. Curtis, chief of the RCAF. She appealed to Curtis to let her use an RCAF Sabre for the record attempt. Curtis realised she was serious and took her request to the defence minister, Brooke Claxton, who authorized Canadair to let Cochran use the Sabre 3. She then became a consultant to Canadair Ltd. in addition to being a director of North West Airlines.

Canadair sent a 16-man support team, led by Lewis Chow, to Edwards Air Force Base, California for the attempt. Cochrane made her first flight 12 May 1953 and on 18 May 1953, Cochran set a new

Jacqueline Cochran with the British Air Transport Auxiliary

Jacqueline Cochran standing on the wing of her Canadair Sabre with (L) Yeager and (R) Longhurst of Canadair

Jacqueline Cochran's Canadair Sabre Mk 3, 19200

100 km speed record of 652.5 mph. Later on 3 June, she set a new 15 km closed circuit record of 670 mph. On May 18, 1953, at Rogers Dry Lake, California, Cochran flew the Sabre Mk 3 at an average speed of 652.337 mph. On 23 May 1953, carrying drop tanks for extra fuel, she flew a 300 mile circular course at 590.273 mph and on 3 June she set a 9 mile closed circuit record of 670 mph. The Sabre was fully aerobatic carrying external wing drop tanks. Between the record attempts, she took the Sabre Mk 3 up three times to 48000 ft. and each time put it in a vertical dive and exceeded 790 mph, once again becoming the first woman in the world to break the sound barrier. 19200 was then flown back to Montreal, the Orenda was removed and a General Electric J-47 installed. By 13 April 1954 the new 6:3 wing had been installed and the aircraft flown again as a Sabre Mark Four.

A number of modifications were introduced by Canadair after the 353rd Mk.2: the aircraft's designation changed to Mk.4, of which 438 examples were built. The principal change in the Mk. 4 was the installation of the A-4 gunsight; the Mk. 2 had the A-1c gunsight. There were also changes to the cockpit and the cabin air conditioning, pressurisation controls and canopy jettison mechanism. The new flat windscreen, introduced with the F86-10 was adopted for the Canadian Sabres. Armament remained the same as six Colt Brownings. This was the only difference between the Mark 2 and the Mark 4. 19453 was the 353 Sabre produced and the first Mark 4. Most Mk. 2s and Mk. 4s were fitted with "6-3" extended leading edge wings and otherwise modernized. They were then designated F-86E (M) the M denoting modified - and delivered under the MDAP programme to other nations. Delivery began in 1954, when Greece received 104 and Turkey 105 of these fighters; though some sources give Turkey 107, 82 Mk2/4 ex RCAF Sabres and 25 Mk 4 from the RAF. They also received free of charge 277 spare engines and a year's supply of spares and equipment. The Greek Air Force flew its Sabres with 337, 341 and 343 *Mire*, of No 111 Combat Wing. Transference also applied to many of the RAF's Sabres, which were overhauled by civilian contractors, notably at Ringway and Stanstead but also at Speke, Prestwick and Yeovilton and then transferred to other European air forces. Italy received 180, and Yugoslavia received 121

First production Canadair Sabre reportedly used about 90% American components in its construction. First flight 31 January 1951, flown by Canadair pilot W. Longhurst. Delivered direct to No. 410 (F) Squadron at RCAF Station St. Hubert, PQ, coded "AM N". Category B damage at RCAF Station Trenton, Ontario on 16 May 1952. Also with No. 431 Squadron at RCAF Station Bagotville, PQ in 1954, carried the name "Iroquois". Overhauled by Canadair, MDAP contract, at Cartierville before passing to Greek Air Force. Ferried to UK by No. 1 Overseas Ferry Unit via Bluie West, with RCAF serial and Greek roundels. Destroyed in a crash-landing on 22 August 1955.

or 122 aircraft to equip two squadrons. The aircraft were supplied in as new condition. Yugoslavia and the other Western Powers, signed the Mutual Defence Assistance Pact (MDAP) on 14 November 1951, this meant that the nations could be supplied with modern combat aircraft and equipment. Canada and the United States agreed, as part of Mutual Defence Assistance Program, to supply the RAF with around 430 Sabres, Canada donated the airframes, the United States the engines. Sabre 4 production was delayed because General Electric could not supply more than 30 engines a month, 20 for North American and 10 for Canadair. At one stage the delivery ratio was reversed. The RAF Sabre Mk. 4 served in Britain and Germany until replaced in mid-1956 by the Hawker Hunter and then they were transferred to the Italian Air Force. A further 120 ex-RAF Sabre Mk.4s were also transferred to the Yugoslav Air Force. Former Royal Canadian Air Force Mk.2 and the Mk.4 aircraft, after being retrofitted with extended-wing leading edges were allocated to the Royal Hellenic and Turkish air forces. In the spring of 1955 the first Hawker

Hawker Hunter Mk 4 WV325, the Hunter effectively replaced the Sabre in RAF service. This example was later sold to Jordan.

Hunters reached RAF Germany and started to replace the Sabres. By the end of June 1956 all the RAF's Sabres had been withdrawn and replaced by the Hunter, the last one to leave being XB670 of No. 3 Squadron.

In 1953, the first fruits of the exhaustive testing of the sole Sabre Mk 3 had borne fruit. Tests with the Orenda-powered Sabre had been highly successful and Orenda Engines had evolved a special version of the Canadian turbojet for Sabre installation- the Orenda 10 of 6355 lb. static thrust. The 791st machine (23001) off the Cartierville assembly line was the first aircraft to receive this new engine and dubbed CL-I 3A Sabre Mk. 5, was completed on 21 July I953 and flew for the first time nine days later, on 30 July. The Orenda engine was slightly larger in diameter than its American predecessor, necessitating the enlarging of the frame openings over the engine bay, the provision of different pick-up points and some minor local structural changes.

Canadair Sabre Mk.5

The Sabre Mk. 5 employed the "6-3 leading edge," in which the chord of the wing was increased six inches at the root and three inches at the tip, and the slats removed and replaced by small fences at roughly seventy per cent span. This wing had been introduced on late production Mk. 4s, and although it raised stalling speed and produced a yaw-and-roll effect before the stall, which necessitated a faster landing approach, it resulted in benefits at the upper end of the Sabre's speed range, 1.5 g at Mach 0.92 at 30,000 feet being gained before buffeting appeared. The Sabre Mk. 5 could attain an altitude of 40000 feet in half the time taken by the Sabre Mk. 2, despite a 500-lb. increase in loaded weight, time to this altitude being attained in nine minutes.

On 20 April 1954, the thousandth Canadair Sabre was produced slightly less than four years after the roll-out of the first Sabrejet.

C.D. Howe initials the 1000th Canadair Sabre 20 April 1954

The final Canadair Sabre was the Mark 6, powered by a 7440-lb thrust Orenda 14. On 2 November 1954, the very much improved Sabre Mk. 6, or CL-138, began to leave the assembly line with aircraft number I 161 (23371).The first example (No.23371) had flown on 19 October 1954 and deliveries to the RCAF in Europe started shortly thereafter. The early Sabre 6s retained the unslatted hard wing of the Sabre 5 but this was soon changed and all subsequent "6s" had slatted wing leading edges.

The Sabre Mk. 6 differed from its predecessor in having the 7275 lb. s.t. two stage Orenda 14 turbojet which radically improved the fighter's climb rate and altitude performance. Normal loaded weight was reduced from the 16900 lb. of the Sabre Mk. 5 to 16094-16426 lb. (varying according to modifications on individual aircraft) and an altitude of 40,000 feet could be reached in two-thirds of the time taken by the Mk. 5-six minutes! In 1955 the RCAF's No I Air Division in Europe began to receive the improved fighter, which, although primarily a high-altitude interceptor, could be used for ground attack with bombs and rockets. The CL-13B Sabre Mk. 6 was undoubtedly among the finest day fighters extant at that time. Despite its greatly improved climb and altitude performance, the Sabre Mk. 6 was still subsonic in level flight although Mach unity could be exceeded in a 45 degree dive. To further improve performance one Sabre Mk.6 was experimentally fitted with an afterburner and tested by the National Aeronautical Establishment. A proposed production version with an afterburner was designated CL-13C and the CL-13D was a project in which climb and acceleration were to have been boosted by an Armstrong Siddeley Snarler rocket motor. The CL-13E was a standard Sabre Mk. 5, in which the fuselage was re-faired to take some advantage of the "coke bottle" area rule theory, while the CL-13F was a proposed two-seat all-weather version of the Mk. 6.

On 23 March 1955 a hangar fire destroyed an Orenda Sabre, two CF100s, an Orenda test bed Lancaster and much aircraft test and research material. This resulted in a six month setback for testing, research and development. The fire was traced to a short circuit in a switch box and a storm blowing 80 mph winds. This resulted in a loss to Canadair of £1785000.

West German Air Force Canadair Sabre 6 JB-106

Sabre 6 production totalled 655 of which 390 went to the RCAF. In July 1955 the South African Air Force ordered 34 Sabre 6s; in April 1956, the Colombian Air Force bought six and in December 1956 the West German Air Force ordered 225. Israel had ordered 24 in 1955 but when the Suez War broke out in November 1956 the aircraft were sitting on the dock at Montreal but the Canadian government wanted no direct involvement in the Suez crisis and cancelled the contract.

Italian Canadair Sabre Mk 4 in United Nations service over the Congo, as 19784 flown by the Philippine Air Force formerly RAF XB896

UN Canadair Sabres being prepared for flight, left is 19655 formerly RAF Sabre XB801 of No. 229 Operational Conversion Unit at Chivenor, UK, coded "Z".

In the former Belgian Congo the break-away state of Katanga continued to defy both the central government in Leopoldville and the U.N. Security Council which had urged its re-integration into the Congo state. This stalemate continued as the leadership of the United States and the U.N. General Secretary changed. Congo was also beset by other insurgencies in the eastern half of the country, which involved aircraft and resulted in U.N. causalities. In one case, 14 Italian airmen flying in a C-119 into Stanleyville were brutally killed.

The situation became more serious when Moise Tshombe, the leader of Katanga, bought an air force and white mercenaries to help fight off the U.N. and the central government forces from Leopoldville. The air force consisted of a wide variety of airframes: Fouga Magister armed trainers from France, Vampire fighters from Portugal, and an assortment of light transport aircraft from South Africa, plus aircraft left behind by the Belgians. Mercenaries included ex-French Foreign Legion paratroopers from the 1st Regiment Etrange Parachutiste (1. R.E.P) which had been disbanded in disgrace in Algeria after a mutiny. Also known as the Katangan Gendarmerie, these formations would continue to play a major role in conflicts in the Congo and later Zaire.

In 1963, Italy sent five Sabre 4s it had received from MDAP to support UN peacekeeping efforts in the Congo. While there they were flown by members of a Philippine Air Force, the original Italian pilots losing their lives earlier in the conflict. During its brief stay of four months in the Congo, the Sabres flew air reconnaissance and support of Israeli troops who moved into hostile areas. The unit, together with the Iranian and Swedish contingents attached to the UN Command in the Congo, undertook persuasion flights over an area roughly twice the size of Luzon in the Philippines. After hostilities the aircraft were just left in situ and by 1964 scrapped at N'Djili. Several Sabre 4s that had been transferred from the RAF to Yugoslavia were later resold as surplus to the Honduran Air Force in the late 1970s. South Africa's Sabres remained in service until 1979.

On the night of 12/13 August 1961, the East Germans suddenly construction of the Berlin Wall and thus signified the start of the "Berlin Crisis." As a result, numerous USAF units were called upon to strengthen European forces and in addition, a number of Air National Guard (ANG) squadrons were called to active duty. Significantly, three ANG F-86H Sabre squadrons were called up and sent to Europe. The 101st and 131st Tactical Fighter Squadrons (TFS), Massachusetts ANG and 138th TFS New York ANG were activated on 1st October 1961 under Project "Stair Step," deploying their F86Hs to Phalsbourg AB in France under Tactical Air Command

North American F-86H en route to Germany via Prestwick

(TAC). The three squadrons were further assigned to 102nd Tactical Fighter Wing, under the command of Major General Charles Sweeney, who had been on the Hiroshima B-29 raid in WWII. The three squadrons flew from Loring AFB, Maine through Goose Bay in Canada, to Sondrestrom in Greenland and then on to Keflavik in Iceland. Following the earlier Becher's Broke and Leap Frog Sabre supply flights. Staging from Iceland to Prestwick, in Scotland, the wing's aircraft, officially arriving in France on 11 November. Into 1962, the Stair Step augmentation of USAFE remained and despite protests from the West, the Berlin Wall stood firm. To maintain proficiency, the three squadrons rotated through Wheelus AB in Libya for gunnery practice and also flew regular simulated tactical missions throughout Europe with the Group returning to the United States in August 1962.

By January 1966, Germany had replaced its Sabres with the Lockheed F-104G Starfighter and sold 90 Sabre 6s to Iran who quickly transferred them to Pakistan. In that year, the private firm, Merex Co., which had specialized in exporting Bundeswehr surplus weapons, purchased the ninety F-86 Sabres and twenty-eight Seahawks plus spares from Vebeg, a state-owned company responsible for the sale of such surplus stock. The Seahawks went to the Indian Navy. Neither Canada nor Germany approved of this

Ex German Air Force Canadair Sabre 6 formerly, JB-110, and JB-363, used by 17 Squadron Pakistan Air Force scrapped 1978

transfer. When they queried Iran for an explanation, Iran claimed the Sabres had gone to Pakistan for maintenance and would be returning to Iran. Earlier 102, North American F-86F Sabres were in service with Pakistan during the 1965 war armed with sidewinder missiles. The Sidewinder missile, which is still in production and designed as a passive, infrared-homing, air-to-air guided missile was developed at the Naval Ordnance Test Station (NOTS), China Lake, California. It is a simple, reliable, inexpensive and easily maintained missile for use primarily in tail-chase attack from single-place fighter aircraft. The missile has a range of less than three miles and equipped the West German Canadair Sabre Mk6 as an upgrade.

Then six years later, on Sunday 3 December 1971, hostilities once again broke out between the two nations. At the time the Canadair Sabre 6 was the leading Pakistan Air Force day fighter, during that brief but furious war with India. In the Sadek area, (near Ferozepur) in the Punjab, the ground attack Sabres attacked army vehicles inflicting no damage. At Agartala airfield in Tripura the Pakistani Sabres made several attempts to bombard Agartala but were driven away by heavy anti-aircraft fire. On the 3 and 4 December, 1971 the Indian Air Force started its retaliatory action against Pakistan. The Indian Air Force was able to destroy 8 Pakistani Sabre jets: 4 near Dacca and 3 near Jessore and 1 in another area in Bangladesh. Fourteen other Pakistan

Air Force planes were destroyed in Bangladesh; 10 Sabre jets, three light aircraft and one transport aircraft.

By this time the Canadair Sabre 6 could be equipped with Sidewinder missiles but there is little evidence that the missiles were actually used. It is the official view of Pakistan that the tenacity of its air force and the way it established air superiority in the face of India's superior numbers, including its state-of-the-art MiG-21s, led to India's sudden acceptance of a cease fire. Without air superiority, India felt that victory would not have been possible. Pakistan lost two Sabres in combat in the West, five Sabres were lost in air combat in the east and eleven Canadair Sabre Mk 6s were destroyed by the Pakistanis themselves in East Bengal, though all these figures are open to question. On 4 December, PAF Sabres bombed and strafed Pathankot, again dropping six 1000 lbs. bombs on the periphery of the airport. Some of them hit tin sheds and local villages. At 5.40 p.m. a formation of six Sabres came into the airport low at 500 ft below radar, dived to 150 ft. and dropped twelve, 1000 lb. bombs. The damage to the airport was so slight that it was repaired in thirty minutes. At Sirsa Airport they dropped six bombs. By 6 December there were only two Sabres left at Dacca and they remained in the hangars. The Sabre reportedly appeared to take little part in the overall air operations at that time.

The total number of Canadair Sabres built, including all marks, was 1815. On 22 January 1970 a Sabre Mk5, 23102, flew from Montreal – Cartierville to Trenton marking the last flight of a Sabre in Canadian Service.

Canadair CL-13 Sabre Mk5, 23102
of the Sabre Transition Unit, New Brunswick 1968

4.
Leapfrog

After the Second World War the Soviet Union made it clear that it was still pursuing a policy of world domination under its leader Joseph Stalin. As early as March 1946, former wartime British Prime Minister Winston Churchill warned in a speech that an "Iron Curtain" was descending across Europe, with freedom being denied in those eastern European countries that the Soviet Union dominated. In 1948 the Soviet Union blocked access to Berlin and the city had to be resupplied by air. As a response some European nations particularly France and the United Kingdom formed the Western Union. This evolved into the North Atlantic Treaty Organisation with the United States as the leading power. The formation of NATO balanced the threat that the Soviet Union and her satellites presented from behind the Iron Curtain. Canada was now a key player in NATO and committed 40% of her gross national product to defence.

No1 Air Division was formed as Canada's air contribution to NATO; it was to consist of four wings of day fighters. These wings were to be located on the European continent but because of war time damage to the established airfields, new airfields had to be built. Canada would deploy two wings to France (Marville and Grostenquin) and two wings to Germany (Zweibrucken and Baden-Soellingen). Initially there were two squadrons deployed to North Luffenham for the air defence of the United Kingdom. These squadrons were controlled by Fighter Command. The RCAF began the entire operation with the establishment of a headquarters in Paris France, which was subsequently relocated to Metz in April 1953.

With the formation of NATO and the start of the Cold War, Europe was seen as a battleground between East and West. Canada committed herself to providing 12 squadrons of fighter aircraft as well as ground forces in an effort to deter attacks and defend Western Europe. The aircraft would be flown to Europe using the North Atlantic ferry route that had been developed during the Second World War by Royal air Force Ferry Command. Leaving from Goose Bay or Gander in Newfoundland, aircraft would fly to Greenland, Iceland

and on to Scotland and England then to Europe. Initially in the first stage the aircraft would be delivered to Europe by aircraft carrier

Glasgow was no stranger to aircraft carriers at King George V Dock. The first vessel we know of was the aircraft carrier HMS *Argus* delivering fighters to the Mediterranean between 1940 and 1942. This was followed by the USS *Wasp* delivering Spitfires to Malta in Operation Calendar and Operation Bowery in April May 1942. Then in 1948 the Americans once again returned with a transport USAT *Barney Kirschbaum* on 4 August and the carrier vessel USS *Sicily* carrying P-80 Shooting Stars. These fighters were flown to Germany to re-inforce the Allied presence in response to the Soviet Union blocking access to Berlin. After leaving the Clyde the *Barney Kirschbaum* headed for Europe to collect the American war dead who were to be repatriated.

By 1945 the Royal Canadian Navy had amassed a great deal of experience in working with aircraft carriers, their first aircraft carriers being *Nabob* and *Puncher*. On 14 January 1945 the Royal Canadian Navy was offered two carriers by the British, these were the carriers *Warrior* and *Magnificent.* As soon as the policy in respect to *Warrior* and *Magnificent* had finally been settled in April 1945 and with the Canadian suggestion for the air component as a guide, the Admiralty started to form RN air squadrons for the ships with a mixed complement of RCN and RN personnel. HMCS *Warrior* was a Colossus Class aircraft carrier, built by Harland & Wolf, Ltd, in Belfast, Northern Ireland and commissioned into the Royal Canadian Navy under the command of Captain F. L. Houghton, CBE, RCN, at Belfast on 24 January1946, at 1530hrs. After serving with the Royal Canadian Navy, *Warrior* was returned to the Royal Navy on 28 March 1948. *Warrior* then served with the British Fleet and in 1956 was completely modernized, including the adoption of the angled flight deck, the fitting of a steam catapult, improved radar and new communication systems. In 1957 she sailed as flagship of a Special Service Squadron and took a leading part in Britain's first full scale hydrogen bomb tests in the Pacific. On 4 November, 1958, the Republic of Argentina took possession of her as its first aircraft carrier and *Warrior* was renamed *Independencia.*

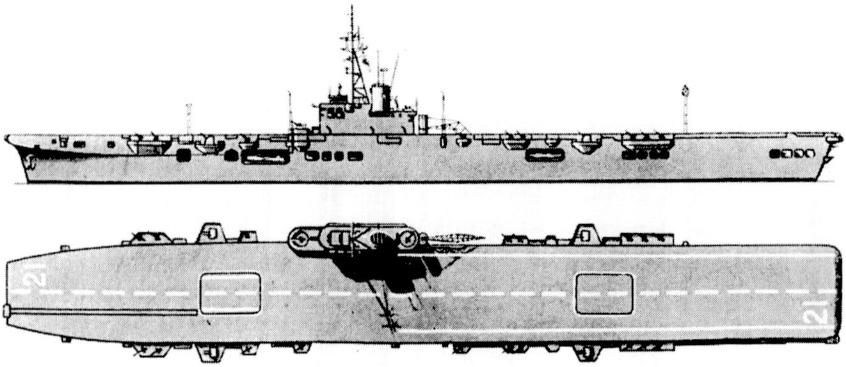

HMCS *Magnificent*

The next Canadian Navy aircraft carrier was HMCS *Magnificent* built by Harland and Wolf, Ltd, Belfast, Northern Ireland. She too was a Colossus Class aircraft carrier but differed from *Warrior* in being three feet longer, being modified for cold weather operations and having different messing facilities for the crew. Her initial operational aircraft were the Hawker Sea Fury and the Fairey Firefly. Up to the autumn of 1950 she worked with other Commonwealth Navies in the Atlantic and in British waters. In December 1950, HMCS *Magnificent* went into dry-dock at Saint John, NB where amongst other improvements was the replacement of her three bladed starboard propeller with a four bladed one to reduce vibration.

HMCS Magnificent at King George V Dock Glasgow with her cargo of Sabres, note Sea Furies to the left on the dock

On 29 October Commodore K.F. Adams Broad Pennant was struck and, under Captain K.L. Dyer's command, the ship embarked the officers and men of 410 Squadron Royal Canadian Air Force. 410 Squadron was under the command of Squadron Leader Larry Hall and the first RCAF squadron to equip with Sabres. On 10 April 1951, 410 had one Sabre at its temporary Dorval base and by the end of May had its full complement of fighters. HMCS *Magnificent* stopped at Norfolk, Virginia to embark 35 Canadair Sabre jet fighters for passage to King George V Dock, Glasgow, Scotland. 24 were carried on deck with 11 being carried below deck in the aircraft hangar. The deck Sabres had been preserved with cocooning while the 11 below

Loading Sabres Norfolk Virginia

Sabres on the deck of HMCS Magnificent

On the Firth of Clyde at the Tail o' the bank and docking at King George V Dock Glasgow

Unloading at King George V Dock

Loading the Sabres onto the carrier's lift

Canadair Sabre being towed from King George V Dock to Renfrew Airport

in the hangar had no preservation. The carrier developed a list more than it ever had in its history due to the extreme weight of the Sabres on the top deck of aircraft carrier. At the peak of a storm at one time the ship's Captain was ready to start dumping aircraft one at a time over the side when the storm finally eased. Encountering more severe weather en route, the ship hove to on two occasions to re-secure the Sabres and in due course off-loaded them at King George V Dock on the Clyde on 13 November 1951. The Sabres were then towed by road from King George V Glasgow, to Renfrew airfield where the cocooning was removed and the aircraft were serviced for one test flight in preparation for the flight to North Luffenham. The Sabres were delivered from Renfrew to North Luffenham from 26 November to 4 December 1951. The Sabre's place was taken on *Magnificent* by some new Hawker Sea Furies, which had been purchased from the UK. These aircraft from Abbotsinch were waiting for *Magnificent* as she docked.

410 Squadron was the first RCAF squadron to equip with Sabres. The Squadron received its first Sabre on 10 April 1951 at its temporary Dorval base. Then another two Sabres were received on 19 May and three more on the twenty fifth of May. Fully equipped by November 1951, 410 became the first squadron in No. 1 RCAF Air Division, to be prepared to sail aboard HMCS *Magnificent* for the UK, where it would be based at North Luffenham as part of Fighter

Command. It was planned to sail the wing from Halifax Nova Scotia but problems with the Sabre and the Canadian Navy meant that the wing sailed from Norfolk, Virginia. Also aboard *Magnificent* were the Sabres of 441 Squadron, aircrew and ground crew personnel for 441 Squadron crossed the Atlantic on the "*Empress of France*" in February 1952 and disembarked at Liverpool. Their aircraft were stored in the hangars at North Luffenham till the aircrew and ground crew arrived.

Technical personnel of 410 Squadron had been established at Renfrew Airport by 26 September 1951 awaiting the deliveries of the Canadair Sabre from King George V Dock. The Canadians had been accommodated at RAF Bishopbriggs, just outside north Glasgow. On the 14 November 1951, 410 Squadron was disembarked at Renfrew under the command of Flying Officer Prince to re-activate the aircraft before flying them from Scotland. The squadron had two test pilots posted to Renfrew F/O's Found and Joy. By 21 November three aircraft were ready to be flown from Renfrew to North Luffenham and arrived there that day. More aircraft followed, with more arriving on the 22 November. The pilots were flown to Renfrew from North Luffenham by an Avro Anson from No 12 Group. If the weather was inclement the pilots went to Glasgow by train. By 26 November six more Sabres had arrived at North Luffenham and by the 29 November a total of twenty three Sabres had arrived. A further eight aircraft arrived on 30 November 1951.

When those Sabres arrived on 30 November the first major accident occurred at Renfrew Airport when 19 year old Aircraftman W Richards Com.Tech. (A) was sucked out of his boots into the air intake of a Sabre. The Airman suffered possible fracture of the skull over the left eye, and possible fracture of the right knee and undetermined internal injuries. He was taken to the Southern General Hospital, Govan Road, Glasgow, Scotland where he was placed on the seriously injured list. When he was X rayed it was found he had torn ligaments in his right leg and two black eyes. He was underneath the nose of the aircraft when the fitter ran up the engine to full power. Suddenly he slipped and fell and was sucked into the intake. The mechanic in the cockpit, R.B. Gelinas, felt the bump and shut down the engine immediately, Richards was pulled out the fuselage unconscious by Gelinas. For his quick thinking, Leading Aircraftman R.B. Gelinas received the British Empire Medal.

Seven more Canadair Sabres were flown from Renfrew to North Luffenham on 4 December. Bad weather hampered the deliveries but the final date for deliveries was expected to be the 7 December 1951. That day local flying was started by the squadron. Earlier three more Sabres were received at North Luffenham on 5 December with four unserviceable aircraft at Renfrew; these Sabres were flown out to the Canadian base on 9 December 1951. The technical personnel arrived on the ninth, from Renfrew and Bishopbriggs and by 14 December 1951 all Royal Canadian Air Force personnel had left Renfrew and Glasgow. They reported to the squadron that the co-operation of the Ministry of Transport at Renfrew was excellent. No civilian contractors were utilised at Renfrew for the move of the Sabres to the south, all work was completed by service personnel.

As a further commitment to western defence, in addition to the two squadrons of Sabres aboard *Magnificent*, Canada commenced a series of resupply exercises to Europe termed, "Operation Leapfrog." The Sabres were to fly from Labrador, Canada to Greenland, Iceland, Scotland and then England. 439 Squadron was the first Sabre squadron to fly on Operation Leapfrog 1. They departed Uplands at 09:30 hours on 30 May 1952 on "Leapfrog 1" and arrived at North Luffenham on the 14th of June 1952.

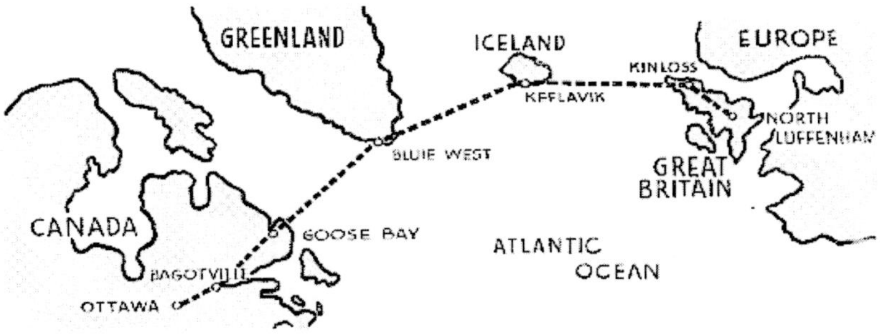

The North Atlantic Ferry Route

Leapfrog II saw all three squadrons of 2 Wing fly across the Atlantic, by the same route as Leapfrog 1, to arrive at their new home at Grostenquin, France in October 1952. Grostenquin was made ready for occupation by the French it was far from being ready by Canadian standards.

416 Squadron, based at Uplands was also getting ready for departure in Leapfrog II which commenced on 28 September 1952. At that time the squadron converted from North American Mustangs and starting to accept delivery of the new Mk 2 Sabres from Canadair, Montreal. At the beginning there were only a few Sabres so the squadron trained on Harvard Mk IV and the T-33 with underslung tip tanks and Allison Engines. The Harvard two seat trainers were also used by the Royal Air Force for advanced training in the University Air Squadrons, though by 1955 the numbers were small. In 1954 the Harvards were still being overhauled by Helliwells Limited who had factories at Treforest, Aberdare and Walsall where their airfield was situated.

Prince Phillip in a Harvard cockpit

Helliwells last Harvard KF448

A few days before the wing's departure from Canada, the Canadian government held a farewell parade and ceremony for the three Squadrons heading for Europe at Uplands. 430 Squadron flew in from North Bay, 421 Squadron from St. Hubert, and all the squadron aircraft were lined up around the corner perimeter of the ramp adjacent to the old hangars. Many senior RCAF and government leaders led the inspection while another squadron did the flypast.

As there were more pilots than airplanes on each squadron, some had to ride on the North Star for some of the route. All the squadrons left from their own bases and either stopped in at Bagottville for fuel, or flew direct to Goose Bay. The North Star also from Uplands to Narsarsuaaq (Bluie West 1) in Greenland and then flew two trips on the same day through Keflavik into Prestwick. The Wing was stuck in Narsarssuack for a week due to the weather. 416 and 430 Squadrons got away on the 31 September 1952 before the fog rolled in while 421 Squadron remained in Bluie. The Squadrons started arriving at Prestwick between 2 and 9 October 1952 and included three for the Royal Air Force.

Initially Air Sea Rescue was provided by SB-17s of the USAF painted with yellow stripes. They were flown midway between weather ships and the land. They were nicknamed, "Duck Butts" because from the rear they looked like the rear elevation of a duck.

Grumman SA-16 Albatross

U.S.C.G Boeing PB-1G

Boeing SB-17 at Bluie West

SA-16 at Nuuk Greenland covering Atlantic air-sea rescue operations

Sabres prepare for take - off

Sabres at Bluie West, three Mark 6s with early wing and four Sabre Mk2s, two for Turkey two for Greece

They also provided weather information. The nickname was later carried on to the Grumman Albatross rescue plane.

The Sabres flew in sections of four and had just enough fuel to make the destination with 5 or 10 minutes of fuel to spare. The initial route was direct to Goose Bay. The Americans in Goose Bay, Bluie West and Keflavik provided search and rescue coverage with Grumman SA-16s Albatross, Duckbutt seaplanes The SA-16s orbited en route and also transmitted a weak Radio Beacon signal for the Sabres in transit. The aircrew were issued with one-piece rubber suits for the overwater flights. The suits were very tight at the ankle, wrists and throat, hot and uncomfortable.

The Wing flew to Narsarssuack (Bluie West 1), in Greenland on 30 September with a flight time of 1 hour and 45 minutes. 416 and 430 Squadrons flew to Keflavik a day or two later but 421 Squadron was delayed at Bluie West 1 due to bad weather. Midway, roughly, between Goose Bay and Bluie, and Bluie and Keflavik, a weather ship was on station which could be used as rescue ship. 421 Squadron eventually left Bluie West 1 on 8 October for Keflavik Iceland with a flight time of 1 hour and 30 minutes. The squadron left Keflavik for Prestwick on the 9th October with a flight time of 1 hour and 50 minutes and then caught up with the other two squadrons.

416 Squadron were delayed in Prestwick, waiting for 421. The plan was that all squadrons would arrive in Grostenquin at the same time and celebrate their arrival on the continent together. On 11 October 11, the Wing flew to Grostenquin with 421 Squadron landing last - again with five minutes between sections. The weather was good but one aircraft from 430 Squadron landed at North Luffenham due to engine problems but the Wing arrived safely in Grostenquin. When they arrived the accommodation was not ready and barely adequate for the needs of the Wing. There were no hangars or aircraft sheds for aircraft maintenance. Some ground crew had been flown in by North Star while others arrived by ship. At this time servicing was at a squadron level but later changed to Planned Central Servicing a few months later. Flying commenced in the middle of November 1952 but only to deploy Sabres to North Luffenham for aircraft modification, the aircraft returning to Grostenquin on the 4 December.

439 Squadron at Bluie West

RCAF Sabre at Keflavik

439 Squadron at Keflavik

In August 1953 the wing moved from its French base to Zweibrucken, while the runways were repaired.

Number 3 Wing, consisting of 413, 427 and 434 squadrons, were allocated to Leapfrog 3. The operation started from St Hubert on the 7 March 1953 and the Squadrons arrived at Zweibrucken on 7 April 1953.RAF Kinloss was the first British airfield the wing landed at on 4 April 1953. Operational flying commenced on 15 April and on 26 April the base was handed over to the Royal Canadian Air Force by the French.

Operation Leap-Frog Four was the fourth and last "Leap-Frog" operation and was planned to relocate 414 (F) Squadron, Bagotville, 422 (F) Squadron, Uplands and 444 (F) Squadron, St. Hubert, to Baden-Soellingen, Germany, as No. 4 Fighter Wing of the Royal Canadian Air Force First Division.

Like the three similar Leap-Frog operations which preceded it, Leap Frog Four Sabres followed the same route to Europe. Leap-Frog Four went in two phases, first went the squadron personnel carried to Europe in the North Stars of 426 Squadron and second the Sabre fighters flying the route. The North Stars landed ahead of the Sabres and prepared maintenance for the fighters. In addition another permanent technical, maintenance base was set up at 30 Air Material Base, Langar in England. Langar could provide support for thirty Sabres at a time and included a Technical Supply Unit and medical supplies and transport equipment. The Movements Unit was also responsible for the movement of all goods to and from the Air Materiel Base, whether by land, sea or air. Between Langar and the continental bases a regular transport service was maintained with the Bristol Freighter. The Freighter regularly, brought the equipment necessary for the maintenance of the Sabres and to rotate round European Canadian bases. They also flew Sabres in the Bristol's fuselage to contractors in the United Kingdom. The RCAF operated six Bristol Freighters from 25 April 1952 until the fleet was retired on 16 May 1967 and the remaining aircraft being a single Mk. 31 and two Mk. 31Ms. The Canadians were to be integrated with the French Air Division and also with part of United States tactical aviation under the orders of U.S. General Lee.

RCAF Canadair North Star which flew the ground crews to Europe.

Bristol 170 Freighter

Douglas Dakota

Beech C-45

The actual control of the "Leap-Frog" route was the responsibility of the USAF, Military Air Transport Service (MATS) which had operational control over long distance flights and co-ordinated all American, British, and Canadian jet moves across the North Atlantic. The RAF had established liaison staffs at the various bases between Canada and Scotland and they give a great deal of support to the RCAF.

Two weeks before the operation commenced the squadron commanders, flight leaders, and engineering officers, visited St. Hubert for briefings on the operational and technical aspects of the exercise. By Monday 24 August departure preparations were completed, and Nos. 414 and 444 Squadrons flew to Uplands to join with No. 422 in a departure ceremony at which the Chief of Air Staff was present. On 26 August days later, the administrative staff flew to Goose Bay, to await the arrival of the three squadrons at the marshalling-point.

On 27 August Goose Bay had prepared for the arrival of the three Sabre squadrons. Due to the weather, strong head winds, the St. Hubert and Uplands squadrons refuelled at Bagottville en route. At 10:28 am, exactly on schedule, the first section of No. 414 Squadron into the Goose Bay circuit. Then, at five-minute intervals, the remaining four sections of the Bagottville squadron joined the circuit, so that by eleven o'clock all nineteen Sabres had landed and were ready for refuelling. To many pilots, the most arduous part of their first "Leap-Frog 4" leg had been burning off their excess JP4 fuel after landing so that all fuel tanks could be crammed to capacity with heavier, longer-range JP1.

Due to poor visibility at St. Hubert No. 444 Squadron's departure had been delayed, No. 422, was the next to arrive. An hour later, the last of these 21 aircraft were on the ground and the first section of No. 444 Squadron appeared over the aerodrome. By 4:30 pm, the 63 Sabres which made up the Wing were safely on the ground, and preparations for the first over-water leg were rapidly going forward. Bagotville's ground support party had left for Narsarssuack at 7:30 a.m., the ground crews from the other two squadrons carried out the daily inspection on the 63 Sabre aircraft. By nine-thirty all were serviceable and ready for take-off but because of extremely strong head-winds between Goose Bay and Greenland, it was decided that there could be no departure that day.

Due to rain damage six of the Sabres had to be towed into the hangar for repair work and No. 422 Squadron's airmen worked far into the night to fix the aircraft. By daybreak all six Sabres were serviceable. To save precious fuel, the Bagotville squadron was towed to the starting point on the runway. By twelve o'clock, weather and winds were good, the weather ships and rescue aircraft were assuming positions on track, and flight control permitted take-off.

Sabres at Bluie West

Between 1:00 and 3:00 pm, sixty Sabres and a North Star took off from Bagottville for Bluie West. Due to last-minute minor troubles, three Sabres were unable to take off as scheduled. Quick action by the ground crew repaired the snags but the three Sabres were unable to take off, as Narsarssuack was closed to aircraft at dusk. By early evening all aircraft had arrived in Greenland. At Bluie the only accident of the whole operation occurred when one Sabre found the strange American runway too short, and was damaged extensively after running off the end of the concrete runway. Due to poor weather Control decided to move the group to Keflavik and to re-form the wing there. The Sabres then flew from Bluie West to Keflavik. The crashed Sabre was examined for recovery and arrangements made for the three Sabres from Goose Bay. Five men were left behind at Bluie to service the three Sabres on arrival with the three Sabres arriving on Tuesday 1 September.

At Keflavik the Sabre aircraft were parked on an unused runway on the side of the field opposite the Icelandic and USAF Headquarters. Fortunately the Americans did everything they could to make the Canadians stay easier, not the least of their services being the loan of four jeeps and their maintenance crews. On the seventh day at Keflavik the three Sabres joined the group and all was ready for departure but reports of continuing bad weather over the United Kingdom meant another day's delay

414 Squadron at Lossiemouth

The next day the group was ready. The Sabres moved into their starting position Meteorology reported that the cloud ceiling had lifted to 2000 feet over Lossiemouth and was still improving. Two hours later the last of the Sabres took off and most of No. 414's aircraft landed at Royal Naval Air Station, Lossiemouth, Scotland. There was only one problem when the sabres left for Scotland. One pilot had oxygen problems with his Sabre and the flight had to descend to a lower altitude as they made their way to Scotland. When this flight landed at Lossiemouth they only had a reserve of four minutes fuel remaining.

The Sabres had survived their last lap but four radio frequency changes had to be completed in every aircraft so that the radios could be used over continental Europe. It was a massive task and the squadrons were helped by a working party from North Luffenham. At two-thirty, 422 Squadron's Sabres were ready. In addition to the fact that the Canadian ground crews had to work with starting equipment which they were unfamiliar and in short supply, they found that many of the Sabres had suddenly decided to become temperamental and refused to start up. The airmen would not allow any difficulties to defeat them and five minutes before the last possible take-off time, the last six Sabres got airborne. On Friday, 4 September 1953 at 5.40pm the last Sabres finally arrived at Canada's new Fighter Wing base at Baden-Soellingen. 62 Sabres arrived at 4(F) Wing in Germany from Scotland. The aircraft landed in sections of three and four, at five-minute intervals with the first aircraft, a Sabre of 414 Squadron, touching down at 16:28 hours. "Leap-Frog Four" was the most

Sabres at North Luffenham

successful and fastest of the ferry operations and had actually been completed in 8 days, 4 hours, and 40 minutes.

Three weeks later, on the 28 September, 1953, came the official opening ceremony where the Wing was welcomed by General Norstad, Air Deputy Supreme Allied Commander, Europe. There was a display of 96 NATO aircraft, 36 Sabres and 60 other types from NATO countries. Norstad declared that the wing had been established three months ahead of schedule.

The initial Sabre contractor responsible for Sabre overhaul in Europe was by "Bristol"-The Bristol Aeroplane Company Ltd. Negotiations between the Company and Canadair Ltd regarding overhaul arrangements had begun before the first RCAF Sabres

Canadair Sabre under extended overhaul at the Bristol Aeroplane Company

arrived in the United Kingdom in November 1951. The fist approach had been made in August 1951 by Mr. Tim Sims, who had piloted Bristol Freighter G-AGVC on its 41000 miles demonstration tour through North and South America in 1948. To acquire the necessary technical background a team of "Bristol" engineers and technicians were sent to the Canadair plant at Montreal towards the end of 1951 where they were joined by the Company's Assistant Chief Test Pilot. From the first moment of contact between personnel of the two organisations, it was clear that there was an admirable spirit of co-operation on both sides - a cordial relationship which was maintained and greatly facilitated progress of the overhaul scheme. At North Luffenham, the volume of repair work was comparatively light, but it was clear that as further squadrons arrived and the wing approached its complete establishment, the demands on the Bristol service organisation would be considerably increased.

Work was divided into two categories - repairs which could he handled on site and extensive overhauls which would be handled at the Filton headquarters of the Company. With the first preparatory step, a Sabre aircraft was sent to Filton for examination by servicing personnel, shortly after the first Sabre squadron's arrival at North Luffenham. A little later, two Bristol Company test pilots were sent to North Luffenham to take a jet conversion course. The first aircraft to be serviced was accepted on 10 March 1952 by the team of Bristol technicians at the North Luffenham base and within fifteen days was once again airworthy. The work on site and at Filton increased

North American F-86 Sabres of the USAF in storage at Short, Northern Ireland

steadily, ranging from minor to extensive repairs. The major overhaul period for Sabre aircraft in Europe in 1951-52 period had not yet finalised. The supply of spares from the materiel base at Langar was prompt and comprehensive and a large stock ranging from small parts to major components had been established near Bristol, under the supervision of a RCAF Supplies Officer. In addition, a Canadair representative was stationed permanently at Filton. The Company was also responsible for the overhaul of the Sabres' J47 engines from the spring of 1953. The last overhauled Sabre was delivered by Bristol 19 July 1955.

With the ending of the initial Sabre maintenance contract with the Bristol Aeroplane Company, the contract was taken over by Messrs Airwork. In addition to Sabre aircraft maintenance Airwork painted the Sabre airframes though some were painted at squadron level. In July 1956 the Airwork contract expired and Scottish Aviation at Renfrew took on the work. The transfer of this contract started in April 1955 when Scottish Aviation and the Canadian Government commenced negotiations and the work provided employment of 300 engineers. (This work included the CF-100). This also meant that BEA’s maintenance hangar was closed down to be used by Scottish Aviation. Spares from Bristol were taken by lorry to Renfrew and included 14 Sabre fuselages plus 212 lorry loads of spares. Politics now took a hand. Short Brothers in Northern Ireland had been responsible for refurbishing the North American F-86 Sabre for the

United States Air Force in Europe. Short also prepared the aircraft for return to the United States by sea and cocooned the airframes. Naturally they felt they should be considered, due to their Sabre experience, for a Canadian contract for the Sabre. The unions objected to Scottish Aviation receiving the contract and lobbied Parliament but to no avail.

The RCAF move from North Luffenham in 1955, to the new NATO station at Marville was named, "Operation Rumba Queen" an operation that was planned to take two to three weeks flown by four RCAF Fairchild Packet/Boxcar transport aircraft. The four Packets flew from North Luffenham to Marville and back without refuelling with a load of 15000 lbs. The Packets were drawn from 435 Sqn (Edmonton) and 436 Sqn (Dorval). Marville was equipped with an 8200ft runway and facilities for fighters of the F-86 type. No 439 Squadron moved direct to Marville by 15 March 1955 where it was joined by 410 and 441 squadrons in time for the wing to become fully operational there on 1 April 1955. The move was relatively easy because the Sabres were left behind to be overhauled initially by Airwork, for the Greek and Turkish Air Forces. At their bases in France and Germany the Canadian Squadrons had already been re-equipped with Canadair-built Orenda-engined Sabre 5. The Sabre 5s were then to be replaced by Sabre 6. By January 1955 about 300 Sabre 5 had been flown over from Canada.

Fairchild Packet of the RCAF moving stores during Rumba Queen

Prince Phillip in a Sabre cockpit North Luffenham 1953

Sabre fuselage and engine Metz France

Sabre under maintenance

United States Air Force Sabres being refurbished by Scottish Aviation at Prestwick July 1956

North American F-86F-25-NH Sabre 52-5409 at Prestwick 1956. Formerly USAF 48th FBW then USAF 86th FBW. USAF 461st FDS (36th FDW) To Spanish AF as Ed A C.5-224 in Dec 1957. Struck off charge Oct 5, 1961 then transferred to Philippine AF

In 1956 a technical assistance agreement was made with Construcciones Aeronautics Sociedad Anonima (CASA) of Madrid, Spain, resulted in the repair and overhaul of F-86F Sabres turned over to the Spanish government by the U. S. Air Force. Later that year Scottish Aviation became involved in supplying refurbished North American F-86 Sabres to Spain.

Then came another factor in the servicing contract. The British Army wanted the Canadian de Havilland Beaver as a light transport. Scottish Aviation had supplied its own entry to the Army specification, the Scottish Aviation Pegasus. The British cabinet got involved and ultimately recommended the order for 36 Beaver aircraft for the Army. The Cabinet also felt that the Canadians would be unhappy that Scottish Aviation had won against the Beaver and would cut the repair work at Renfrew which would cost jobs. They saw that the Sabre work at Renfrew guaranteed a cash flow for Scottish Aviation and blocked the design, 900 people worked there. The wrong decision could also jeopardise aviation orders from the United Kingdom to Canada.

With the arrival of the Canadair Sabres in Europe a gap arose in NATO air defence, that of an all-weather fighter. Canada responded

Sabre Mark 5 23360

Sabre Mk 5, 23283 at the OTU, Chatham under tow

Canadair Sabre Mark 5, 23362

Canadair Sabre Mark 5s from Chatham

October 1955, F/O Bob Caskies' Sabre's nose wheel was stuck in the transverse retracting position without retracting. He landed safely at Grostenquin without mishap

Sabre 19173 in the hangar at Metz

Sabre Mark 5s at Grostenquin including 23196

MDAP Canadair Sabres in Turkish service about 1957

Canadair Sabre XB763 being loaded into a Bristol Freighter and a Sabre being off-loaded at Langar 1954

Greek Air Force Sabre Mark 2, 19108 at Filton in 1955

Greek Air Force Sabres on delivery receive a blessing

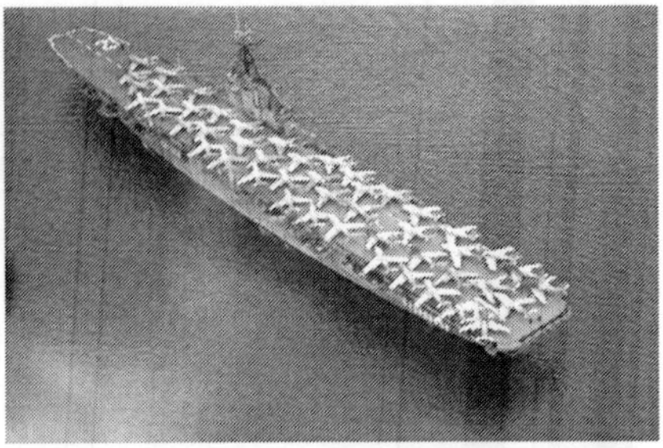

HMCS Magnificent returns to Canada with a cargo of 59 Canadair Sabre Mk5s flown from Kinloss, prepared at Renfrew, loaded at Govan

Sabre Mark 5 unloaded from HMCS Magnificent in Canada during Operation Magnificent

Canadair Sabre Mk 6 in production for the West German Air Force

Canadair Sabre Mark 6 on delivery flight

Canadair Sabre Mark 6, 23455

23757 Sabre Mk.6 of 1 Overseas Ferry Unit

RCAF Canadair Sabre Mark 6 23510 of 434 Squadron at Abbotsinch,20 June 1959

Sabre Mk6 of the West German Air Force

RCAF Mk. 5, 23092at Prestwick, waiting preservation

Mk. 6, JB-238 equipped with Sidewinder missiles

Mk.6, BB-295 in 1962 at Dijon

WGAF MK.5, BB-153 ex RCAF 23124 at Renfrew

by volunteering four CF-100 squadrons for service to NATO. Between October 1956 and August 1957, one Sabre squadron per Wing was stood-down and replaced by a CF-100 squadron from Canada. The twin engined, two-seat Avro CF-100 Canuck, was originally designated as the XC-100, by A.V. Roe Canada Ltd. The company was officially approached towards the end of 1945 to design an all-weather fighter for operations in Canada. The CF-100 was the 1946 brainchild of Edgar Atkin who was then Chief Engineer of Avro Canada and John Frost, a designer from de Havilland in the United Kingdom. Initial armament requirements was for four 20mm Aden cannons but that was replaced by eight .50 Browning machine gun fuselage belly pack. The nose radar was originally planned to be the British Mk.9A-1 but this was changed to the American AN-APS-19A system. Avro was busy post- war servicing Sea Furies, B-25 Mitchells and Lancaster. In addition Avro was designing the Avro C.102 all-jet air liner during the same time as they were building the CF-100 Canuck; due to these factors it was not until mid-1948 that tooling was ready for the project. At the end of 1949 the first CF-100 prototype was completed. The prototypes were officially designated as Mk.1s but they were never destined for military service.

The first prototype 18101 (FB-D) flew for the first time on the 19th of January 1950. As the Orenda engines were not yet ready, a pair of Rolls-Royce Avons was substituted to power the first two prototype CF-100s. No major problems were noted in the first flight and the recommendations were for better nose wheel steering and better brake pedals. On its third flight it was found that the wing root fairings were twisted and bent this had occurred after gentle manoeuvres. Avro did not want to take risks and it took some time to cure the cause. Later, after aerobatics at a Toronto air display, it was found that the skin of the wing and centre section had split. This was discovered to be caused by the main spar being weakened when the engines were relocated in the forward fuselage, after the airframe was modified to have straight wings. (At one point the design had swept wings). In late 1951 the structural problems returned. The Avro engineers worked at strengthening the joint where the wing met the nacelle but found making it stronger only caused it to fail in a shorter

Prototype Avro CF-100

Prototype Avro CF-100 with F86E used by Orenda to test engine fitting

423 Squadron RCAF Avro CF-100

Maintenance on the gun bay of Avro CF-100, 18368

445 Squadron CF-100s take off

423 Squadron CF-100s

number of cycles. Ultimately the engineers found a permanent solution. Rather than a single rigid joint, a pin joint was used. This was combined with strengthening the aircraft's centre section where the wing joined to the fuselage. This prevented the stresses from the wing to cause the nacelle skin to distort and split this caused an 8 month delay in production. Even with its faults, which were ultimately cured, the CF-100 displayed an outstanding flight envelope and performance when in service.

The Second prototype 18102 (FB-K) was finished in July 1950 and introduced the wingtip fuel tanks. This aircraft was delivered to the Central Experimental and Proving Establishment in Radcliffe, Ontario in October of 1950 but 18102 crashed around 10:30 am on 5 April 1951. The cause of the crash was attributed to the crew losing consciousness at a high altitude, possibly from oxygen failure. The two prototype aircraft were not equipped with ejection seats nor did they have flight controls in the rear cockpit.

Five Mk.2 CF-100s were produced (18103-18107) all fitted with the Orenda 2 jet engines. These aircraft were still not production models but introduced the natural metal scheme instead of the high polished black of the Mk.1s. CF-100, 18103 was used for the development of the underbelly Browning gun-pack while the remaining Mk2s were built with dual controls and designated as Mk.2Ts. The Royal Canadian Air Force began CF-100 operations in 1952 at R.C.A.F. Station North Bay and the Canuck saw further modifications including better radar, fire-control system and upgraded engines. The CF-100 was officially retired in October 1981.

As the CF–100 proved itself as an all-weather night fighter, the decision was made to replace four squadrons of Sabres with four squadrons of Canucks. This would provide NATO with a more capable interception capability, as there was no all–weather or night fighter capability in Europe. The Canucks were flown to Europe under Operation Nimble Bat, and 426 Squadron provided a North Star aircraft to carry support personnel for each stop–over. The timings for each of the four Nimble Bat operations were:

Nimble Bat I, 445 Sqn, Oct–Nov 1956
Nimble Bat II, 423 Sqn, Feb 1957
Nimble Bat III, 440 Sqn, May 1957
Nimble Bat IV, 419 Sqn, Aug 1957

At the same time Canadair Silver Stars for use by the Air Division and as Mutual Aid gifts to NATO members were also being ferried across the Atlantic, under the name Operation RANDOM. The first operation began on 11 February 1954, ferrying brand new Sabre Vs, while the last mission, Random 30 commenced on 24 June 1957, with 24 Sabre VIs and six Silver Stars. On RANDOM 14, No1 Overseas Ferry Unit flew over some twenty jets. Some were Sabre Mk6s, Silver Stars and older Sabres. The latter were being flown to Manchester for overhaul and forwarding to other NATO nations such as Turkey and Greece. The Silver Stars were for Turkey and Greece.

In just over three years of ferrying, No. 1 Overseas Ferry Unit (OFU), supported by 426 Squadron RCAF safely delivered more than 800 aircraft to Europe. No.1OFU also brought aircraft back to Canada with the introduction of the Mk6 Sabre, the now surplus Mk5s were given to West Germany or brought back to Canada for the reserve squadrons. HMCS Magnificent left the Glasgow with 48 Sabres on February 1957. 1 OFU completed two ferrying operations from east to west across the North Atlantic – Operations RANDOM WEST I and II, on 17–19 Oct 56 (20 Sabre5s) and 17–20 Nov 56 (16 Sabre 5s). (These operations were also referred to as REVERSE RANDOM).

When Belgium received 53 Avro CF–100 Canucks through MDAP, the RCAF delivered them in Operation Jump Moat. The first batch of Avro CF-100s for the Belgian Air Force in Jump Moat 1 was delivered by the RCAF, December 1957. The machines, 14 out of the total order of 53, were flown from the RCAF Station Uplands, Ottawa, by crews from 428 and 410 Squadrons. They went via Goose Bay, Keflavik, and Marville France, to Beauvechainin Belgium. There were five missions under this op name, with the numbers 3 and 4 also bringing CF–100s to the Air Division and number 5 being solely Air Division aircraft.

JUMP MOAT I, December 1957
JUMP MOAT II, March 1958
JUMP MOAT III, May 1958
JUMP MOAT IV, June 1958
JUMP MOAT V, October 1958

Throughout the 1950s the RCAF, provided other aircraft to NATO allies under the MDAP. In 1959, 19 Beech C–18 Expeditors were provided to France and another 6 to Portugal, flying to these countries under Operation BEECHFLIGHT. This operation started on 20 May and ended 4 June when the six Portuguese aircraft landed in that country. Each aircraft had a pilot and navigator while a North Star from 426 Squadron carried the 12–man support section.

Operation Western Weft and Western Weal were conducted in 1962, delivering aircraft to France and Greece respectively. On this occasion 40 Silver Stars and 10 Expeditors were given to France and 10 Silver Stars to Greece. This operation was conducted in five separate missions between 17 April and 3 August 1962.

Later the RCAF also ferried aircraft across the Atlantic inside transport aircraft to re-equip No. 1 Air Division. These operations involved putting the CF–104 inside one of the newly acquired Lockheed C–130 Hercules and flying it over in that manner. These operations, known as RHO DELTA, lasted from 1962 to 1965, ending when the last of the 185 CF–104s had been delivered. (Rho Delta is ancient Greek for 100 –Rho–and 4 – Delta).

In the autumn of 1959, the Canadian government announced that starting in the autumn of 1962 the Sabre squadrons of the Air Division would be re-equipped with CF-104 Starfighters and the CF-100 squadrons would be disbanded. 439 Squadron finally stood down on October 1963 and by the end of the year the Air Division was fully operational with the CF-104 Starfighter. The majority of the Sabres

Sabres from the North

Canadair Sabre Mark 6, 23667awaiting scrapping Prestwick, February 1963

Scrapped Canadair Sabre at Lasham (L) and Prestwick (R)

CF-100s 18449 and 18460 await final demolition with the soon to be scrapped Scottish Aviation static test Twin Pioneer

18350 and 18330 await scrapping at Prestwick 1963

and CF-100s were flown to Scottish Aviation at Prestwick where the airframes were reduced to produce and ultimately scrapped. 441 Squadron flew their Sabres to Prestwick 17-27 October 1963.One flight to Prestwick was named, Operation “Sal Siesta” and flown 3 November 1963.

The Starfighter brought a new role to the Air Division. Instead of the Day/All Weather interceptor role, the Canadian Squadrons would now be involved with nuclear strike and reconnaissance. However, during 1964 the cold winds of change were blowing and the French government announced that all nuclear weapons located on French soil would fall under French control. Therefore, in late 1963 after being recently re-equipped with the CF-104, 2 Wing sent their two squadrons to the two wings in Germany and closed their doors at Grostenquin in 1964. The other wing in France (1 Wing Marville) was converted to a strictly reconnaissance role and the communications flight (109 KU) for the Air Division moved to Marville from Grostenquin.

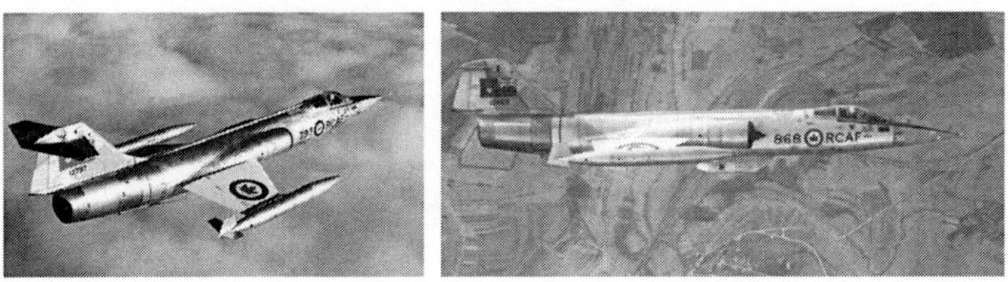

CF-104 and Vinten Camera equipped CF-104

The CF-104 aircraft was equipped with a new camera pod that Lockheed Aircraft USA, Computing Devices of Canada and W Vinten Limited of England had designed and delivered. On the centreline fuselage pod was constructed of cladded aluminium alloy it was 8 feet long; 15 inches wide; and two feet deep. The photographic equipment built into the pod comprised four Vinten F-95 70mm cameras; two in the side oblique configuration, one facing port and one starboard; one vertical camera and one forward facing camera. Normally, all cameras were fitted with lenses of 3 inch focal length. Pilot-selected shutter speeds available were 4 and 8 frames per second (fps) that represented exposures of 1/1000 and 1/2000 respectively. With an iris control located in the lens barrel, settings of “Bright”, “Hazy” and “Dull” were automatically selected by signal data from a Light Level Monitoring (LLM) system built into the pod. Data recorders built into each of the pod cameras recorded on exposed film the position of the aircraft in East/West and North/South distances from its base as supplied by the aircraft’s PHI-5 navigation system.

In March 1966, the French government announced the withdrawal of their military forces from NATO and that all the NATO forces stationed in France must leave (or fall under French command). New quarters were found for 1 Wing and 1 Air Division HQ at Base Arienne 139 Lahr, West Germany. The move of the operational equipment was accomplished by March 1967.

Sabre and Starfighter

5.

Becher's Brook

The formal surrender of Germany took place at Lüneburg Heath on 5 May 1945. In the closing few weeks of the Second World War the RAF squadrons of the Second Tactical Air Force swept into Germany alongside Field Marshal Montgomery's 21st Army Group. Second TAF had been specially equipped, trained and employed in close support of the ground battle. Germany was now occupied by the Allies and the 2nd Tactical Air Force was given a new role. As a result, on 15 July 1945 a new organisation, British Air Forces of Occupation (BAFO), came into being with its Headquarters located at Bad Eilsen. On its formation BAFO was comprised of 4 Groups, 20 Wings and 68 Squadrons which were spread across 20 operational airfields in Germany and the Low Countries.

Britain's post-war, flagging economy, made further cuts in the size of BAFO inevitable. Gone were the former Group and Wing HQs. The number of squadrons was reduced to 10 based at just three airfields and all under the direct operational control of the Air Headquarters at Bad Eilsen. Due to the political climate at the times the squadrons were moved to 30 miles from the border with the Soviet controlled German Democratic Republic.

At the end of 1947 the force consisted of 121 aircraft made up of Spitfires, Tempest IIs and Mosquitos. It was over Berlin, buried deep inside the Russian Zone of Occupation, that international relations were strained to breaking point. On 24 June 1948 the Soviet authorities closed all roads and rail links to Berlin. Pushed by the British Foreign Secretary, Ernest Bevin, the Western Allies set about the re-supply of the city by air. The integrity of the three air corridors to Berlin was enshrined in the Quadripartite Agreement of November 1945 and Operation Plainfare swung into action. This was the re-supply of Berlin from the air. Over the next 12 months aircraft of the RAF, including Dakotas, Yorks, Sunderlands and later the Hastings, together with a variety of aircraft chartered from civil companies and aircraft of the USAF, kept the city supplied with both food and fuel.

The task necessitated substantial airfield works and BAFO was required to move out of Wunstorf and Celle to allow their use by C-54s of the USAF. The blockade was lifted on 12 May 1949 but the RAF element of the airlift continued until October to allow a stock of supplies to be accumulated in Berlin in the event of re-imposition of the blockade.

During this period the RAF in Germany received its first jet aircraft in the shape of the de Havilland Vampire. By the outbreak of the Korean War, June 1950, five squadrons were equipped with the Vampire. The Vampire and the Meteor were at the forefront of the BAFO expansion and they were followed by the de Havilland Venom which arrived from mid-1952. 1 September 1951 BAFO reverted to the name Second Tactical Air Force or 2TAF. Then came the first of the new airfields, the first to open was Wildenrath, which did so in January 1952. This was followed by the opening of Geilenkirchen in March 1953, Brüggen in July 1953 and finally Laarbruch by the end of 1954. Construction of a new Headquarters at Rheindahlen began in April 1953 and the building was occupied in October 1954 allowing relocation of HQ 2TAF and HQ BAOR in a new Joint Headquarters.

In parallel with the airfield construction programme 2TAF's re-equipment programme was continued, with delivery of the first Canadair built Sabres from March 1953. The Sabres were to replace the Vampire then serving in Germany. The Allied experience of the Korean War saw the next step - change in capability and in numbers in RAF Germany. The Soviet Union had brought into service, in quantity, the MiG-15, in Korea it had proved in combat just how effective it could be, especially at altitude. The Vampire was no match for the MiG-15 which had also begun to be deployed to Soviet Forces in Eastern Europe. Neither was the Gloster Meteor a match, though some did hold their own in the Korean conflict. The Swift and Hunter were experiencing production and design delays before coming into service and were years away. With the arrival of the Sabre 2TAF gained a much needed swept-wing fighter capability some two years before the home-grown Hunter became available in quantity.

De Havilland Vampire Mk-9 of 8 Squadron

De Havilland Vampire FB-9 of 112 Squadron

De Havilland Venom FB-4, WR413

Vickers Supermarine Swift F3 and FR5

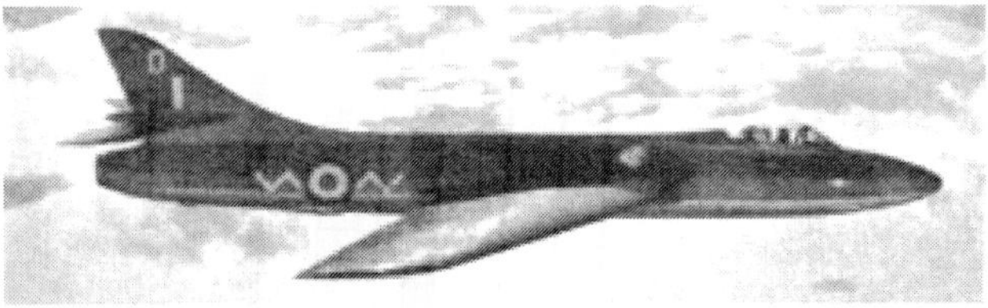

Hawker Hunter F.4

Royal Australian Air Force Gloster Meteor Mk8 deployed in Korea

De Havilland Vampire T.11 trainer

Gloster Meteor T7 trainer

North American F-86 Sabre of the type that was under test at West Raynham

One North American Sabre, F86-A5, FU-279 powered by a J47-GE 13 had gone through an engineering appraisal by the Air Ministry in 1951. That same year two North America Sabres F86As including FU-279 and FU-296 were also tested for handling. The two aircraft were tested at the Central Fighter Establishment at RAF West Raynham. FU-296 was lost in a crash in 1952 while FU-279 was returned to the USAF at Burtonwood in November 1954. The conclusion at the end of the Sabre test phase was that the North American F-86 was far superior to any British jet fighter then in production.

An Operational Conversion Unit was set up at the brand-new base at Wildenrath and eight Sabre squadrons were quickly formed. The swept-wing Vickers Supermarine Swift was also used in Germany but in the dedicated fighter-reconnaissance role and from 1954 the Canberra bomber was also to see service in Germany.

"Becher's Brook" was the name given to the supply of Canadair Sabres by transatlantic ferrying operations to the United Kingdom and West Germany. The Sabre aircraft were to be supplied to the United Kingdom through MDAP. As with all MDAP supplied aircraft, they remained the property of the United States Government and could not be disposed of without the approval of the United States, this meant that before they could be disposed of they had to be returned to MDAP control. Becher's Brook is the famous water jump which has ended the hopes of so many horses and riders in the Grand National race. Its Cold War counterpart in "Operation Becher's Brook" was even more of a jump - 3100 hazardous miles, mostly over the icy formidable Atlantic Ocean, between Labrador and Northern Britain. The course followed the transatlantic air ferrying route which thousands of bombers and fighters were flown across the Atlantic during the Second World War. Instead of cocooning and dismantling the aircraft, which was deemed time consuming, costly and unnecessary, the matter was finally settled when Air Chief Marshal Sir Ralph Cochrane, then Vice Chief of the Air Staff, made the decision to fly the aircraft across the North Atlantic from Canada.

The R.C.A.F had already planned route across the Atlantic in "Operation Leapfrog" so three R.A.F. observers were detailed to travel with the first Canadian Units in the summer of 1952 to see how the experiment worked. When "Leapfrog II" followed, three more R.A.F. pilots took part in the mass flight, this time flying in Sabres intended for R.A.F. conversion training in Britain and giving the pilots route experience. One of the three pilots was Squadron Leader T. Stevenson, A.F.C., a 36-year old R.A.F. veteran who had flown Fairey Battle day-bombers in France in 1940. His report on "Leapfrog II" persuaded the Air Ministry that "Operation Becher's Brook" was a practicable proposition and Stevenson was put in command of the pilots of the R.A.F. Overseas Ferry Unit who were chosen to fly the Sabres. In this case Royal Canadian Air Force agreed to assume operational control of the flights; the U.S.A.F. offered to provide communications and other facilities such as search and rescue. The R.C.A.F. also trained the RAF pilots in little over a month and on 8 December 1952 the first R.A.F. Sabre ferry convoy, "Becher's Brook I," left Bagotville, Quebec, for Goose Bay, Labrador.

The aircraft were to fly from Quebec via Goose Bay (Labrador), Bluie West (Greenland), Keflavik (Iceland) to Prestwick, or northern Scotland, a distance of nearly 3,000 miles, then on to R.A.F. Kemble Maintenance Unit. The ferrying was undertaken by No. 147 Squadron Transport Command (originally designated No. 1 Long Range Ferry Unit). The first squadron to fly Sabres was No. 3 based at Geilenkirchen, Germany. No. 3 Squadron received its first three Sabres on 12 May 1953. Seven of the original aircraft were with the squadron until July 1956, the oldest (XB 590) having completed more than 800 flying hours before retiring.

A Mosquito, Swift, Hunter, Javelin and Meteor T.7s await ferrying by No. 1 Long Range Ferry Unit later 147 Squadron of Transport Command

Canadair Silver Star 21548 over Niagara Falls

North American/Canadian Car and Foundry Harvard IV

To ensure success of the operation a new organisation was needed which was able to control aircraft and men spread across the route, even when communications were blacked out by magnetic storms. It was not sufficient to convert and teach the pilots how to fly the Sabres; they had to be trained to withstand the mental fatigue of frustrating delays caused by weather and other factors. They also had to be taught how to survive a forced landing in one of the most inhospitable regions of the world - the bleak, menacing Greenland ice cap. Out of these requirements grew out of Transport Command, No. 1 Long Range Ferry Unit, which was later renamed No. 147 Squadron, after one of the most famous wartime transport squadrons of the R.A.F. 147 squadron, ferried all types of Royal Air Force aircraft throughout the world, even to the Far East Air Force.

The squadron's strength was increased to 60 pilots, by selecting men with at least 400-500 hours of jet experience from Fighter Command and the 2nd Tactical Air Force. Quite a few of these pilots were N.C.O. aircrew. Squadron Leader Stevenson remained in command and pilots who had initially flown the route were made flight and section leaders. Handley Page Hastings transport aircraft were provided to fly the pilots and their equipment to Montreal and along the route. It was from Montreal where future ferry flights would start and from where the specially-trained ground crews were carried. The latter were divided into two parties, who were flown to the first two airfields on the aircraft's route, with each party subsequently flying ahead of the other to await the Sabres at each stage of their journey.

More attention than ever was given to training. New pilots had to complete 10 hours familiarisation and conversion flying in Harvard IV's and T-33 Silver Stars before moving on to the Sabre. They attended various ground courses, in England before going to Canada for a rigorous seven-day survival course in the Labrador forest. After that came even more detailed technical instruction on the Sabre and a further 15 hours' flying at St. Hubert, Montreal. It took one month to complete conversion training. The ground crews were given an equally thorough training to emphasis the fact that in such a unique operation, following the book and using specialist equipment would

First Sabres ready to depart from Canada

First Sabre take-off St Hubert

Above, the R.A.F. ferry team January 1953 comprising left to right, Sqn. Ldr. T. Stevenson. Fit. Lts. H. M. Deffee, H. F. Edwards. J. F. Sollom. Flg. Off. A. Shepherd. Fit. Sgts. C. J. S. Howard. J. A. D. Meechen and Sgt. F. W. Burney.

often be useless. The emphasis on this type of training meant that cheap hand made tools could be packed in a convenient corner and be ready to hand. Similarly the method of training in a particular job that was often satisfactory in a hangar may not easily be feasible in sub-zero temperatures under the midnight sun. Often airmen would have to do jobs outside their own specialised trades but the important thing was to do them cheerfully and keep the aircraft flying while the weather remained clement. Finally, it was decided to synchronise "Becher's Brook," whenever possible, with R.C.A.F. "Leapfrog" and U.S.A.F. ferry operations, so that full use could be made of all available safety and navigation arrangements.

Initially the Sabres flew in pairs to an altitude of 35000 feet heading for Goose Bay, Labrador. Along the route the pilots would tune into radio signals sent out by USAF, Grumman S.A.16 Albatross rescue amphibians. Using radio compass in bad weather the Sabre pilot was guided to the airfield and landed using his instruments. Efficiency was so great that the Sabre landed at its destination within half a minute of its estimated time.

Some hours before the start of "Becher's Brook", the aircrew received information on weather, the condition of airfields along the route, fuel, radio and navigation data. Two hours before take-off the liaison officers, 700 miles apart, at each end of the first leg, checked final details, while ground crews applied the finishing touches to the Sabres. After briefing, the pilots changed into their long woolly underwear, string vests, rubberised immersion suits and "Mae West" lifebelts, which gave them the only possible chance of surviving a ditching in the icy Atlantic Ocean. Personal kit was stowed away in ammunition bays and other cubby holes and after a last-minute check over the aircraft, the pilots strapped on their parachutes and helmets and clambered into their cockpits. 250000 gallons of fuel was poured through about 250 filler caps—any one of which might be so cold that it would remove the skin if touched with a bare hand - in under two hours and oil levels were checked as was oxygen and radio equipment. To conserve fuel the engines were only run five minutes before take-off.

Sabre taxiing at Goose Bay, Handley Page Hastings beside control tower

Four Sabres viewed from the Goose Bay control tower

Sabres in the Goose Bay hangar with the Hastings viewed through the hangar door

Flights varied from three weeks to two days depending on the weather with an average flying time of six and a half hours. On two occasions, due to the accumulation of Sabres, a double shuttle technique was used. This involved 64 aircraft with 32 pilots. Immediately on arrival at the first staging post the pilots returned in a Hastings to the first starting point. This was repeated till the 64 aircraft were delivered. On "Becher's Brooke One" due to various factors only eight Sabres were delivered. Their route was Bagottville to Goose Bay, Labrador then Bluie West One, Greenland, Keflavik, Iceland and finally Prestwick. Stornoway was available as a relief landing ground in case of poor weather or fuel shortage. On Becher's Brook Two, the first sixteen Sabres were planned to depart from Goose Bay on the 9 February 1953. By the thirteenth of February there were 36 Sabres at Goose Bay delayed by the weather. On the 19 February seventeen Sabres had arrived at Keflavik but again they were delayed by the weather. Supplementary aircrew were flown from North Luffenham to Canada by North Star others were flown from Heathrow by Trans Canada Airline. Weather caused further delay at "Bluie West" when sixteen Sabres were flown to Keflavik. On a flight to Kinloss from Keflavik a Sabre had to divert to Stornoway with jammed ailerons. The aircraft crashed at Stornoway. After the Sabre aircraft were delivered to Kinloss the aircrew were flown by Handley Page Hastings back to Keflavik. The five known Hastings were WD485, WD483, WD490, WD494 and WD491. By Becher's Broke Four there were 29 Sabres at Goose Bay waiting delivery. Of these three were unserviceable, six were ready for air tests and twenty ready for delivery. At Goose Bay on 13 April, Sabre XB621 was damaged in a heavy landing when it ran off the runway.

It was found at Goose Bay that there was water contamination in the engine oil of one Sabre and all aircraft had to be checked. The aircrew were closely monitored for fatigue and some were found unfit for ferry duties. There was also continuous training for the aircrew as they delivered the Sabres. Training was carried out on Sabres, Canadair Silver Stars and Harvard. Under the command of Squadron Leader Stevenson, 31 Sabres were flown from Goose Bay to "Bluie West" on 24 April 1953. Four days later 28 aircraft plus one Canadian

RAF Sabre landing at Bluie West

A flight of Sabres ready for take-off

Sabres awaiting their crews five minutes before take-off at Bluie West

Master Pilot A. "Murky" Murkowski in Sabre Cockpit

Fuelling up Bluie West

Clearing ice from the fuel caps at Bluie West

were ready to be flown to Kinloss but once again weather caused a delay of six days. The first batch flew off on the 30 April and arrived at Kinloss with the Canadian Sabre flying to North Luffenham and the balance of the RAF Sabres to Kemble. From there the pilots were flown to Abingdon by Vickers Valetta and from there by Hastings to Kinloss. 27 Sabres were then flown to Kemble and three to West Raynham. 147 Squadron left Abingdon for Benson on 4 May with the squadron personnel being given eleven days leave.

Becher's Brook Five ended on 1 June 1953; there were delays due to weather and lack of air sea rescue support at one point. This caused a delay of one hour before take-off. The USAF would not send out a Grumman Albatross, which was controlled by Prestwick for less than twelve aircraft. Three aircraft went unserviceable due to undercarriage and radio problems with one RCAF Sabre, 19441. A total of 37 Sabres were delivered to the Maintenance Unit at Kemble. Within this aircraft movement were four RCAF, Canadair Silver Stars and one Sabre Mk2 en route for Keilbrucken. Then on 8 June the squadron was made responsible for moving the Sabres to 2nd Tactical Air Force in Western Germany. At Benson continuous training was given on the Sabre for the aircrew. This was continued at St Hubert where the crews flew a total of five hours on Sabres before carrying out further ferry operations.

In July the squadron flew a mixed ferry convoy of Sabres and Silver Stars, there were six Silver stars and 34 Sabres. XD709 was left at St Hubert with hydraulic problems. At Goose Bay there was an additional 28 awaiting flight to Great Britain. There the squadron based two Hastings crew, 52 Ferry pilots and two Sabre working parties. XB289 was seriously damaged when its tail cone blew off after a minor explosion in the engine. An American operation termed, "High Flight", co-incided with the Royal Air Force operation which caused accommodation problems. The High Flight track led to Prestwick and at Bluie West on 14 July, 49 Sabres and six Silver Stars were ready to move. In this case they arrived at the Royal Naval Air Station Lossiemouth, Scotland, on 15 July. Then three days later the air convoy consisting of 47 Sabres and five Silver Stars flew out to Kemble and the Silver Stars to Benson. On the way down to Kemble

Sabre XD724over Greenland

Sabre F.2 XB531 of the first batch at Prestwick

Hand-over of Sabres at Abingdon 2 January 1953

147 Squadron pilots with Squadron Leader Stevenson

OLDER AND NEWER: The Venom pilot (left) is wearing standard R.A.F. clothing, less Mae West., with an early-type visor. In contrast, the Sabre pilot wears crash helmet, pressure breathing mask, "pigtail' intercom lead, back-type parachute and American overalls; he is also using the Sabre's alternative starboard access steps. The Venom illustrated does not have on ejector seat.

Sabres arrive at RAF Kemble Maintenance Unit including XB669

XB882 was lost when it had a generator fire. The pilot bailed out, was rescued and taken to hospital in Dundee suffering from facial injuries, abrasion and shock. Later in July the squadron flew four Sabres from Benson to Wildenrath.

By August there were sixteen Sabres at Goose Bay for movement to Great Britain but only six were serviceable. In addition there was scheduled a move of 37 Sabres from St Hubert. These aircraft left St Hubert on 7 August but were diverted to Bagottville. On 13 August 48 Sabres left Goose Bay for the United Kingdom but five aircraft were left at Goose Bay one unserviceable. Due to signalling problems regarding the destination of the Sabres there was a problem at Lossiemouth but the Sabres were delivered to Aldergrove, Kemble and Aston Down. Out of fifty aircraft in this operation 49 were delivered. This part of Becher's Brook was regarded as a complete success.

There were now no large mass formations of Sabres flying to Britain from Canada at this time, only small batches of two and three. No aircraft were available for transfer from Canadair to the 10 September. This left the squadron at continuation training at St Hubert. The Becher's Brook route was maintained by Hastings aircraft during this period. By 21 September twenty four Sabres were ready for transfer from St Hubert to Great Britain but due to the weather the operation was cancelled. Three days later the operation proceeded with 42 arriving at Goose Bay. On the 26th the convoy was ready to move after delays due to inaccurate weather forecasting. As the aircraft flew on their way they were followed by a Hastings carrying a technical support party for the Sabre. From Keflavik 33 aircraft completed the journey to Kinloss. By the end of September all the Sabres had been flown to Kemble with one Sabre being left at Kinloss. Again during October there was no mass flying across the Atlantic. Only three Sabres being delivered from Canada early in the month to British units whilst the balance of flying was local deliveries in Britain with Sabres being flown to Germany. At the end of October four Sabres were collected from Cartierville, XB983, XB775, XB993 and XB752. In total at the end of October there were 42 Sabres waiting at St Hubert for delivery.

The final delivery of Sabres from Canada was scheduled for 4 November 1953 with a total of 57 Sabres with one unserviceable, XB762. On 6 November 54 aircraft left for Goose Bay, 28 via Chatham and 26 via Bagotville. The aircraft arrived at Kinloss on the 9 November 1953 with aircraft being delivered to 23 M.U. Kemble and 31 M.U. Lyneham. During December eleven Sabres were delivered to Kinloss. According to 147 Squadron the Becher's Brook operation moved 368 Sabres from Canada to the United Kingdom with the first movement taking place to Prestwick on 19 December 1952. With the finish of the operation in December 1953 came a drastic reduction in flying personnel, 37 posted away by December, with aircraft movements of flying aeroplanes to the Royal Air Force on the continent and abroad continuing. Due to air sea rescue shortage at this time, a Coastal Command Hastings, TG504, "G" of 202 Squadron, was scheduled to operate from Prestwick on 18th December to cover the operation; it was planned to be used instead of a USAF Grumman Albatross but the operation was cancelled.

3 Sqn, Sabre F.4 at RAF Benson June 1956

In Great Britain two squadrons of Fighter Command received Sabres, 66 and 92 squadrons converted from Meteors to Sabres. They were based at Linton-on-Ouse. The Sabre Conversion Flight at Wildenrath, Germany and supplemented by 229 Operational Conversion Unit, at Chivenor where they trained a variety of pilots in addition to Sabre pilots, providing familiarisation for the Vampire, Meteor and Venom.

RAF SABRE 4 Squadrons

Squadron	Dates	Main RAF Base(s)
3	1953-56	Wildenrath, Geilenkirchen
4	1953-55	Jever
20	1953-56	Oldenburg
26	1953-55	Oldenburg
66	1953-56	Linton-on-Ouse
67	1953-56	Wildenrath, Brüggen
71	1953-56	Wildenrath, Brüggen
92	1954-56	Linton-on-Ouse
93	1954-56	Jever
112	1953-56	Brüggen
130	1954-56	Brüggen
234	1953-56	Oldenburg, Geilenkirchen

3 Squadron

Sabre XB538

In May 1955, 3 Squadron was still equipped with the de Havilland Vampire in Wildenrath, Germany. Then on 11 May 1955 the first two Sabres were delivered to the squadron becoming the first Royal Air Force squadron with swept wing, supersonic aircraft with the first formation of four being flown on the 19 May 1955. Nine days later the squadron provided a formation of Sabres at Dusseldorf for preparations for the Coronation flypast. That day six Vampires were flown away by pilots from Celle. The Coronation flypast took place on 2 June with six squadron Sabres and six Sabres from 67 Squadron.

The squadron was allocated a Meteor 7 to provide instrument ratings and for communication duties. Number 3 squadron flew the F-86 Sabre till June 1956 at Geilenkirchen: there the main hindrance to flying battle flights was the weather, low cloud and mist, there was also a great shortage of drop tanks which hindered operations. The Sabre was fully aerobatic with wing tanks but there was also poor aircraft serviceability. On some occasions, towards the end of Sabre service with the squadron, drop tanks were removed to improve handling qualities.

The Sabre run down started from 14 May 1956 with four Sabres being flown back to the UK. Sabre flying had almost finished by 12 June, when the squadron became non-operational with Hawker Hunter pilots attending conversion lectures. On 15 June one Sabre was left with the squadron and the only one left in the 2nd Tactical Air Force. The Hunter was in full operation by 21 June and was well received by the pilots.

4 Squadron

A Sabre of Fighter Command

Number 4 Squadron was operational with the Vampire at RAF Jever, Germany. The squadron became aware of the Sabre when one made a dead stick landing at Jever on the 1 February 1954, then came plans for Sabre conversion on the 26 February 1954. The squadron was to complete Sabre conversion at Wildenrath with conversion starting early March. Conversion training had finished by the 13 March 1954.

The runway at Jever had been resurfaced for Sabre operations and by fifth of April, twelve Sabres and one Vampire were on station and a Percival Prentice was brought in to supplement the Tiger Moth; the last Vampire leaving the squadron by the end of April. The squadron was operational with the F-86 Sabre and in March 1955 the Squadron first saw a Hawker Hunter F.1 which had landed at the airfield, this captured the squadron's imagination. That month the squadron carried out numerous interceptions on Venoms, Sabres, Canberra and B-45s.The Sabre was also being used at the time to tow banner targets. In April all the Sabres were grounded for a check on the ejector seat gun. During July the squadron started to re-equip with Hawker Hunters when five Sabres were flown away and two Hawker Hunters arrived from Oldenburg. Then four Hunters arrived later that month to rapidly convert the remaining pilots of the squadron from Sabres. By the latter half of the month the remaining pilots of the squadron had commenced conversion training. The pilots felt that the Hawker Hunter was not as complicated as the Sabre but the Sabre had one or two good points. By the end of August there were only two Sabres left on squadron charge and by 9 September 1955 there was only one Canadair F-86 Sabre remaining.

20 Squadron

Sabre XB982

20 Squadron reformed at Royal Air Force Jever on 1 July 1952 equipped with Vampire Mk9 for the ground attack role. Later that

month the squadron flew to Oldenburg with eight Vampires. At Oldenburg the great problem for the squadron in its first year of operation was the shortage of aircraft and too many pilots. In August of 1952 the squadron deployed to Duxford for two weeks for bomber interception sorties against Avro Lincolns, B-50s and fighters. During June 1953 the squadron started Sabre training when aircrew were sent for a conversion course at Wildenrath.

By November 1953 the first Sabres had arrived with a total of sixteen arriving by the fifth of the month. The great handicap for the squadron was the lack of Sabre spares. On its first delivery flight with the squadron the Commanding Officer lost control when the aircraft started pitching and he blacked out as he did a fast run over the airfield. He regained control when he recovered consciousness as the aircraft righted itself. This incident had been caused by lack of knowledge concerning the aircrafts ballast position. Even though the squadron had 16 Sabres the squadron strength was set at 22. The Sabre was liked by the pilots and the ground crews adapted very quickly to the engineering qualities of the aircraft. There were technical problems with the aircraft though when all Sabres were grounded in January 1954 to check the tail trim actuator motor. Added to this there were undercarriage retraction faults in four Sabres. This resulted in two Sabres receiving major damage when the undercarriage fell down under "G" loading.

The F-86 Sabre lasted with the squadron till November 1955. Sabres were being ferried out in July 1955 with XB892 being recorded as leaving that month with the squadron establishment being reduced to fourteen Sabres. During August pilots were given further training in preparation for receiving the Hawker Hunter. Flying was given in the Vampire T11 to familiarise pilots with instrumentation. The last Sabre day was 29 November when Hawker Hunter conversion began with nine aircraft being allotted by serial number and three accepted awaiting pilots. Cold weather showed up the defects of the Hunter, cracked windscreens, frozen fuel valves and slow undercarriage retraction. Twelve Sabres remained with four flying to Geilenkirchen and two to the United Kingdom. The last

Sabre on the squadron lost a drop tank on 25 May 1956 with no damage to property, this was XB914.

26 Squadron

Sabre XB577

Early in 1951 26 Squadron was at RAF Wunstorf when it was equipped with Vampire Mk5 and Mk9. Still at Wunstorf in July 1952 in addition to the Vampires, it was operating a Meteor T7 and a Mosquito T3. In August 1952 the squadron moved to Oldenburg practising battle formation, tactical training and air to ground exercises without the Mosquito T3. Whilst at Sylt, 30 October 1953, on an armament practise camp, the squadron received a signal that it had been allotted ten F-86 Sabres. Conversion training started at Wildenrath at the beginning of November, with the Commanding Officer and seven pilots went on the course. Later in the month another eight Sabres were allocated to the squadron.

By the 18 November the squadron was operating as a mixed unit with Sabres and Vampires. The F-86 pilots were busy this month local flying to give themselves familiarisation on the Sabre. By 1 December there were only two Vampires left which were used for continuous training. In addition to the bad weather in December, Sabre operations were hampered by unserviceability. The following year the performance of the Sabre was hampered when operating with Vampires and Venoms. The Sabre could not fly at full throttle and had to use half air break when operating with the other types. Then two new Sabres from Brüggen were flown in during March. Later the squadron practised tail chases, battle and close formation. There was also trouble with the Sabres brakes; no spares were available which caused concern. Then there was formation flying over Hamburg to practise for the Queen's birthday on 10 June.

On 20 September the squadron moved to RAF Ahlhorn during Exercise Battle Royal. In addition to practise interceptions they worked in concert with anti-aircraft guns flying between 12000 and 20000 feet. Their primary purpose during the exercise was to fly practise interceptions; they were not permitted to fly ground support operations. After the operation the squadron returned to Oldenburg. Towards the end of the year all Sabres were grounded due to a serious starter generator fault and aileron inspection. This lasted three days with the backlog being cleared by the ground-crews working long hours. Significantly they were posted in pilots who had flown the F-86 Sabre operationally in Korea. During May 1955 the squadron provided six Sabres on detachment to RAF Habbaniya in Iraq. Then the squadron returned to Germany via Cyprus on the 16 June when the first three Hawker Hunters arrived to convert the squadron from the F-86 Sabre. The last three Sabres left for 20 Squadron on 26 August 1956.

66 Squadron

Sabre of 66 Squadron

At the beginning of 1951, 66 Squadron was re-equipped with Gloster Meteor Mk 8s at Linton-on-Ouse. Primarily the squadron concentrated on interception and air to air gunnery. Flying the Meteor continued to November 1953 when the squadron commenced training for the introduction of the F-86 Sabre. In preparation for the Sabre pilots were sent to Farnborough for fitting of new flying clothing and by December the squadron had completed the conversion course at Wildenrath. Actual conversion commenced 22 January 1954 with 57 hours being flown and 22 pilots converted with the pilots being very enthusiastic. At the beginning of January the squadron was operating Sabres, Meteors and a Vampire T11, the latter being used for instrument ratings. Though by the 31 January 1954 all the Meteors had been disposed of and replaced by 21, F-86 Sabres. Sabre conversion continued into February but was held up by the weather with 22 pilots becoming operational on the type. Though the squadron recorded that the Meteor had left, the pilots still managed to clock up nearly 93 hours on the type. By the end of March the squadron was considered operational.

By June 1954 the squadron was concentrating on air armament exercises and cine-gun familiarisation in preparation for Exercise "Dividend". The squadron flew 660 hours during the exercise but its success was hampered by the loss of three Sabres. One aircraft caught fire, the pilot successfully ejecting and two flew into the hills with the loss of two pilots. Practise interceptions were carried out against USAF B-47, RAF Washington B.1 (these resembled the Soviet Tu-4) and Canberras. The main interception problem was found with the ground controller directing the aircraft to the targets. This was cured by the flight commanders working more closely with the controllers. November's flying was hampered by the loss of another Sabre when the engine seized and the cockpit suddenly filled with jet fuel fumes. The pilot ejected in the Binbrook area where the Sabre fell to earth. He was then carried twenty miles out to sea on his parachute where he was found in his dinghy by a Lockheed Neptune from Topcliffe. He was then rescued by an air-sea rescue launch from Grimsby. In December the 6:3 wing was fitted at squadron level giving the Sabre better performance and handling characteristics at altitude.

In addition to sector exercises and lectures on the F-86D the squadron practised intercepting the B-36 bomber. This was in March

1955 and the Sabres were intercepting the bombers at 42000 feet quite easily. The bombers were coming in at four in the morning which the squadron easily coped with. One aircraft was lost on 16 March when it was seen to flick and spin in. In December the squadron was warned that it would be re-equipping with the Hawker Hunter. Sabre flying continued to March 1956 when the Sabres started to be ferried out and five Hawker Hunters arrived. As a stop-gap four Gloster Meteor Mk8s were re-introduced which were enthusiastically received by the pilots who had not flown twin jets before. Twelve Hawker Hunters were in service by April. By May there were five Sabres with the squadron but they were flown out to various airfields with two going to Airwork at Stanstead.

67 Squadron

Sabre F.4 B of 67 Squadron

67 Ground attack fighter squadron was formed at RAF Gutersloh on 1 September 1950 equipped with Vampire 5s. At the end of April 1952 the squadron moved to Duxford in England for exercises and bomber affiliation with Avro Lincoln bombers. With the ending of exercises on 5 May the squadron moved to Wildenrath where the runway was being extended by 700 yards. In October 1952 the squadron was warned it was being moved to Cologne, Butzweilerhof airfield. There the squadron was to practise landings on pierced steel planking a 2000

yard runway. With the ending of the trial on 11 November, the squadron returned to Wildenrath.

At the turn of the year four Vampires were sent up to intercept 18 Meteors from 56 Squadron from Waterbeach. No interception was made because the Meteors came in at 5000 feet while the Vampires were patrolling at 30000 feet. Later in March fourteen Meteors were intercepted at 31000 feet. Around 10 March 1953 the squadron was warned it would be equipped with the North American F-86 Sabre and on the 12 March three Sabres arrived with the first six being used to convert pilots. Pilots commenced cockpit familiarisation on the newly arrived Sabres as soon as they were available with the squadron organising a small conversion unit with six Sabres that they had. Actual training took place on 24 March with three Sabres completing taxiing trials. As a mixed fighter squadron with Sabres and Vampires, they continued to practise interceptions on B-45 Tornadoes and F-84 Thunderjets during April. Five pilots were detached to the conversion flight for F-86 training and did not take part in interceptor exercises.

On 12 May 1953 two Sabres arrived from the MU at Kemble for squadron use. On the 18 May the first squadron Sabre XB674 carried out its first acceptance check and was joined by four other Sabres. The next day a total of eight Sabres were on squadron charge. By the 22 May the de Havilland Vampire Mk5 had left the squadron with the unit becoming a fully equipped Sabre unit. Then the squadron received a further five aircraft on 26 May 1953. The squadron provided six Sabres for the Coronation flypast over Dusseldorf in June. At the end of June the squadron moved to Duxford to take part in the Coronation Review at Odiham. In order to conserve airframe hours, the aircraft were checked at 50 hours, then little Sabre flying was done. Ten Sabres was the usual size of the squadron flypast flight. After the flypast on 15 July the squadron returned to Wildenrath.

The following year, 1954, the squadron was based at Sylt for an air firing programme. The Sylt detachment was marred by a Sabre suffering a nose wheel collapse on 17 February. When the squadron returned to Wildenrath on 12 March, of the ten aircraft the squadron had at Sylt, two Sabres were left behind as unserviceable. For the rest of the year the squadron practised high level interceptions, low level attack and close formation flying: though that year the Sabres were flown in the summer without wing tanks. In 1955 the Sabres had leading edge modifications made to the wings and some were discovered to have cracked mainplanes which resulted in wing changes. It was also found in aircraft with the wing leading edge modification that the compass stopped working. This was traced to the sensing unit situated near the leading edge; the trouble was overcome by altering the position of the sensor unit.

On 12 June 1955 the Squadron was deployed to RAF Nicosia on Cyprus for air firing. The squadron personnel were flown to Luqa, Malta but engine problems with the Hastings transport meant a delay of 24 hours, the squadron arriving in Cyprus on 14 June. Eleven squadron aircraft arrived two days later. After the deployment to Nicosia the squadron left for home on 4 July. The Sabres were refuelled at Turkey, Greece and Ciampino, Rome arriving at Brüggen on 6 July. The squadron continued to fly the Sabre for the rest of the year with un-serviceability being the major problem. This was due to experienced technicians leaving the squadron and not being replaced. On the 11 January 1956 the first Hawker Hunter arrived and by the 26 March the last three Canadair built North American F-86 Sabres left 67 Squadron.

71 (F) Eagle Squadron

Squadron Sabres possibly "B" Flight

71 (F) Eagle Squadron was formed by Operation "Glean" on 16 November 1950 at RAF Gutersloh, West Germany with de Havilland Vampires. During March 1951 the squadron moved to Sylt for one month on an armament practise camp. The squadron's scores were good and the best in BAFO, bettering the Tempests. The squadron returned to Gutersloh at the end of March from Sylt.

May 1952 was a month of great change with the squadron moving to Wildenrath on 8 April. Little flying was done in its first week of moving due to lack of equipment, bad weather and radio difficulties. During May the squadron rotated with Duxford for practise interceptions but three Vampires were damaged in various accidents, VZ829, WA163 and VZ106 during the month. Later in May 1952 the squadron took part in a simulated raid on London with practise interceptions from Duxford continuing.

At Vienna on 7 September 1952 the squadron performed aerobatics for the British ambassador. These were the first British jets to visit that great city but on the way to the city the squadron was intercepted by Soviet MiG 15s. At the end of October the squadron was once again at Sylt but bad weather cut the flying programme. By 1 March 1953 pilots of the squadron were attending lectures on the F-86E Sabre. By the end of the month almost half squadron technical personnel had received instruction on the Sabre. In May two detachments of six pilots were sent to the Sabre Conversion Unit and by the end of the month seven pilots had been converted. Trials were also conducted with IFF to see the effect on television. By the end of June half the ground crews had completed Sabre servicing training.

During June there were five major aircraft incidents: WG840 and WA250 were struck by lightning, WG840 had compass failure and crashed at Eindhoven, VV699 engine overheated, WE848 hit on port mainplane by cannon ricochet in air to ground firing. Between the 2 and 8 June, nine pilots were sent to the Sabre Conversion Unit. In September the squadron readied for the F-86 Sabre, nine pilots were sent to the Sabre Conversion Unit for a refresher course. The Sabres arrived by October but there was little flying due to the weather. Two Sabres had incidents: XB880 had a burst tyre and XB739 made a heavy landing. In November the squadron came up to strength with

22 Sabres when seven F-86s were flown in. There was a height restriction of 15000 feet on the Sabre which restricted training. At the end of December the squadron was still a mixed squadron with Vampires and Sabres. There were restrictions on the Sabre flying time due to supply restrictions and the weather.

By June 1954 pilots were flying Sabres without wing tanks to give them handling experience and to spin the aircraft at Mach 1. The squadron also received a Meteor T7 (WA714) to increase the squadron's instrument ratings. There were two Sabre incidents in June: XB550 had a heavy landing and XB687 had turbine failure, both were Cat 3 incidents. Flying was only achieved that month by heavily robbing aircraft parts from unserviceable airframes (Cannibalising) to keep the others flying. In July the squadron was flying against the United Kingdom at an altitude of 40000 at Mach 0.74 on Exercise Dividend. The squadron flew 51 sorties against United Kingdom with the defenders response being assessed as disappointing. Unusually in August on an APC at Schleswig the squadron had 17 Sabres and the Meteor serviceable. In November all Sabres were grounded due to trouble with the generators.

In April the Sabres went through a wing modification programme at Geilenkirchen. The programme was suddenly stopped with nine aircraft being completed and six awaiting completion. That month the drop tanks were removed which reduced flying time to 52 minutes but increased turnaround time. In May the squadron were warned that twelve Sabres were to go to Cyprus for three weeks but the problem was the provision of spares which could keep the aircraft with enough flying hours. The squadron was due to leave on 15 June but there were problems with sights, fixed rings had been fitted to the aircraft. There was also confusion in settling training features for the Sabre pilots. They were to fly to the Middle East to give the squadron more air to gunnery practise and to prove the route to the Mediterranean. In Cyprus the squadron flew two detachments to Amman (five aircraft) in Jordan and Abu Sueir. There the Sabres flew against de Havilland Venoms. When the squadron returned they landed at Bruggen not Wildenrath.

Then XB880 crashed on 17 July killing the pilot Squadron Leader L.H. Cherry, he crashed on finals. That month the squadron also practised ground attack against Belgian tanks but there were problems with split fuel tanks and ailerons. In August four Sabres flew as bombers in a Canadian exercise. It was also found that the Canadair Sabre 5 and 6 were far superior to the Sabre 4 in performance. September finished with an armament practise camp at Sylt. In November the squadron prepared for the Hawker Hunter when a pilot was sent to RAF Oldenburg on a Hunter course. In January the Sabres flew against Lincolns and Canberras of Bomber Command on Electronic Counter Measure sorties. Dogging the Sabre aircraft during this period was a continual lack of spares and unserviceability. The squadron had received its first Hunter aircraft on 23 April 1956, with full Hunter training taking place on the 26th of that month. In April the squadron was down to ten pilots and at one point eight. The Sabres intercepted the Tupolov TU-104 on four occasions and an Avro Ashton at 38000 feet. Ten Hawker Hunters had been delivered at the end of the May and by July the squadron was fully equipped. The last Sabre, XB869, was flown out on 5 June 1956 with the squadron disbanding at Bruggen on 27 April 1957.

92 Squadron

Sabre XD727

At the beginning of 1952 , 92 Squadron was fly Gloster Meteor Mk8s at RAF Linton-on-Ouse. That year the squadron carried out bomber affiliation with Avro Lincolns and B-29. Some of the squadron took part in, "MiG Alley" interceptions with positive results. Later in 1953 the squadron flew against F-86 Sabres in dogfights for fighter assimilation. During July the squadron had posted in Flight Lieutenant R. Knight who had flown Sabres in Korea. It was felt he would be a great asset to the squadron when it was fully converted to F-86 Sabres. Knight took command of "B" Flight. In August the squadron was on continual exercises and standby. The latter was gruelling for the pilots because they had to sit in the Meteor cockpit for hours. Thankfully this was changed to a one hour rotation but the squadron finished the month with battle close formation and cine-gun practice: though the Meteor Mk8s were showing their age, with rivets popping and engines overheating and poor serviceability. In October the squadron prepared for Sabre conversion when three pilots were sent to Wildenrath to familiarise themselves on the type. The following month three ex 147 Squadron ferry pilots, with Sabre experience joined the squadron and another pilot was sent to Wildenrath.

At the turn of the year there were only six Meteors serviceable but the aircrew were fitted with Sabre flying kit. On 23 February 1954 the first Sabres arrived at Linton on Ouse with all pilots being checked out on taxiing and cockpit drill. The pilots were then checked out on a Vampire T.11 which had American instruments. By the end of March the squadron had re-equipped with Sabres with the Meteors flying out. Pilots and ground crew were enthusiastic about the new aircraft with morale and serviceability being very high. For the Queen returning from her Commonwealth Tour the squadron deployed to North Luffenham to fly with the Canadians on escort. In September one Sabre was lost in a night flying accident with the loss of the pilot. Then first Sabre, modified at squadron level, with the "hard" wing flew on 30 November 1954. In April 1955, after an armament practise camp the squadron's establishment strength was reduced by two aircraft. The squadron became more selective in using Sabres for high altitude gunnery, pilots choosing the best Sabres that were available. This increased the squadron gunnery scores.

In April the squadron flew against the Hawker Hunter for the first time but due to serviceability only two Sabres were available. This was during Exercise “Skyhigh.” The squadron pointed out it only had one instrument corporal to service the A.4 gun sights and instruments whereas the USAF had one master sergeant and eight mechanics! There was a weakness with .5 Browning gun armaments on the Sabre, it was found the guns had to be continually harmonised. Added to this it was found that the fuel content gauges had a fault which was traced to the leading edge slats. Canadair introduced a modification which reduced the wing servicing time which cured the problem. The Canadair representative for electrical systems was Mr. H Eldridge. In May three Sabres went into minor servicing including a second engine change. These were XB677, XB837 and the engine changes, XD769 and there was also a shortage of drop tanks for three aircraft. Next month a civilian work party changed the wings on XD779 and four Sabres went through minor servicing, XB957, XB726, XD769 and XD736. That June in addition to the Sabre and Vampire T11 the squadron had on charge a de Havilland Chipmunk and Meteor 7 and 8.By October the squadron was finding the Sabre more delightful with its cockpit demister and heating system in the cold autumn weather. What dominated the year was the turnover in pilots, 15 pilots total with 7 flight and deputy flight commanders. The squadron was scheduled to re-equip during 1956 with Hawker Hunters but a shortage of Hunters meant a squadron mix of Sabres, Hunters and Meteors. The Sabres put up a final display for the Air Ministry in April 1956 when four Sabres put up a final demonstration. The last Sabre was flown out in June 1956.

Tupolov TU-104

93 Squadron

Sabre XB712

93 Squadron was reformed on 15 November 1950 at RAF Celle, Germany, flying De Havilland Vampire Mk 5 fighter-bombers. The squadron was at Celle till February 1952 when it was warned it was to move to RAF Jever. The move to Jever was carried out in 3 March when the squadron left its former base. Problems with the radios curtailed flying but one pilot, Sgt Walker, completing a high "G" manoeuvre was reported to have a collapsed lung. On examination Walker was found to have a punctured lung. There was continuous flying and testing redundant ammunition which resulted in a better rate of cannon stoppages for the squadron. The armament section invented a cannon cover for the gun safety flap, the section was recommended for an award. Weather was dominated by snow which curtailed flying.

During May the Battle flight practised interceptions against Lincolns and B-50 bombers. The weather unusually warm and clear and the squadron aerobatic team flew to Gutersloh for a display. Later the squadron was vectored onto a B-29 which was in their sector. Added to the squadron activities in May, five French pilots were attached to the squadron and were integrated within the squadron activities. That month they were at Sylt for live firing but the activities were curtailed. Target towing at Sylt was by Hawker Tempest and at times was hampered by the few which were available to carry out that duty. But later in June, during Exercise "June Primer" the squadron intercepted Varsities, Wellingtons, Lincolns and

B-50s. In the evening ten B-50s overflew the airfield in a farewell formation and were promptly attacked! At the end of June the squadron moved to Duxford on detachment.

At Duxford the squadron was joined by a Gloster Meteor. The squadron then intercepted Lincolns and had its first interception against Canadair Sabre. The four Vampires gave a good account of themselves then battled with Gloster Meteors in flights of five. There was a downside when in a simulated fight with F-86s, two Vampires collided with one pilot managing to escape the other pilot losing his life. The squadron then returned to Jever on 14 June with ten aircraft. After the Vampire Mk5 the squadron was upgraded to Vampire Mk.9's on 25 November, 1953, due to weather five were delivered on the 27th. Later in December the squadron moved to Sylt for an armament practise camp for the month of January; there it was a mixed squadron with Vampire 5 and 9. Back at Jever the squadron intercepted Venoms which were much too fast for them. During February the aircrew were prepared for Sabre conversion with the first Sabre arriving on 8 March 1954: the squadron still being at Jever.

The squadron Vampires were flown to RAF Alhorn on 14 March where they were taken over by 4 Squadron. That day five pilots went to Wildenrath for Sabre conversion. The next day the squadron moved to its new base at RAF Alhorn with twelve pilots leaving for the second Sabre conversion course on the 28 March. The squadron was at Alhorn waiting the resurfacing of Jever's runway. The squadron received its first Sabre XB856 on 25 March while it was at Alhorn and on the 7 April three Sabres from Bruggen arrived.at Jever. The Tiger Moth and Prentice were still being utilised with the Prentice demonstrating aerobatics on the 28 April. A further Sabre arrived on 26 May from Bruggen. On 1 June two Sabres landed in a stream and collided after a tyre had burst on the first machine. Both aircraft were assessed as Cat 4 and were returned to Airwork in the UK. These two aircraft never re-entered Royal Air Force service. The squadron was visited by Canadair's representative, Mr Holloway, who gave a demonstration talk to the squadron on the J-47 engine. Then the Sabre completed its first air to ground sorties, seven in total and on 17 June eighth Sabre arrived. Another Sabre was due from Wildenrath on 22

June but when the pilot went to collect it the Sabre was unserviceable. At the end of June all the flying was completed by the Sabre, Meteor, Prentice and Tiger Moth, there was no Vampire flying.

In July the squadron's flying was dominated by Exercise "Dividend" and flying in battle flights. In August there was an air to ground firing practise, in this case, unusually all six guns were used instead of four. In September the squadron took part in Exercise "Lucifer" which consisted of low level flying and interceptions which were felt to be of no value. There was also an armament practise camp at Sylt where radar ranging was used for the first time. By November the squadron had fifteen Sabres on charge but all Sabres were grounded up to the 5 November when four became serviceable. On 22 December all squadron Sabres were again grounded to check for wing cracks, by the end of the day two were ready to fly and four were serviceable. At the end of 1955 the average squadron strength was 15 Sabres. It was planned to convert to the Hawker Hunter in July 1956 but the plans slipped. The squadron Sabres had already flown in mock combat with Hunter but found the Sabre had better combat manoeuvrability due to the all-flying tail. Three Sabre pilots had converted to the Hawker Hunter in November thanks to the co-operation of 118 Squadron. One pilot then converted to the Hawker Hunter on 8 December 1955 though preparations for the ground crew had started early in November. In December the unit had become a combined Hunter/Sabre squadron. Five more Hunters had arrived by 17 January 1956 and on 20th four Sabres were ferried to RAF Geilenkirchen. At the end of January another six Sabres were readied for ferrying to Benson but bad weather stopped the move, the aircraft were then ferried on the 30th. One Sabre aircraft having undercarriage failure on landing at Benson: six Hunters were in service by the end of the month. In February the squadron flew just over an hour on Sabres and they were anxious to be rid of the last three due to serviceability concerns. The squadron had nine Hawker Hunters on charge by the beginning of March. There were only two Sabres on charge by 9 March, Sabres gradually left service at Jever, one left on 20 March for Geilenkirchen with the last Sabre Mk 4 leaving on 22 March 1956 flown by Flying Officer Sanderson to RAF Benson.

112 Squadron

Sabre XB956

During the Second World War, 112 Squadron flew Gloster Gladiators, Curtiss P-40s and Mustangs. Then the squadron gained its trademark which was a set of sharks teeth painted under the nose of their aircraft. The squadron disbanded on 30 December 1946 at Treviso, Italy. The squadron was re-formed at RAF Fassberg in Germany on 12 May 1951, equipped with de Havilland Vampire Mk 5s and a Meteor T.7. In September it put on a rocket demonstration for the American and German press and took part in Exercise "Bertram Mills." That month it operated as a battle flight for the first time much to the enthusiasm of the pilots. In October, during Exercise "Counter Thrust" they were visited by General Eisenhower, this was the first time they flew as a squadron. They also visited APS Sylt on an armament practise camp where the squadron scored exceptional well. At Sylt two of the squadron pilots flew the Hawker Tempest target tugs. During this training period the squadron noted there was a great shortage of fuel bowsers which reduced squadron flying hours. By the end of the year the squadron had only eight pilots on strength for flying duties.

At the turn of the year, now with nine pilots, flying was curtailed by poor weather but the squadron performed cross country flying at 20000 feet. In February the squadron practised interceptions and prepared to move to Jever but flying was again curtailed due to the death of the King. Practise interceptions were made against Avro Lincolns with 118 Squadron with no results. On 7 March they left

Fassberg for Jever. At the beginning of April the squadron practised interceptions against B-29 Superfortresses and flew with 98 Squadron. Once again the squadron flew at Sylt APS for an armament practise camp in May. The squadron returned from Sylt on 15 May and its pilot strength was increased by three. At the end of the month flying was curtailed by poor weather but they flew with the Royal Netherlands Air Force. By the 16 June only one Vampire and the Meteor 7 were serviceable. Instead of receiving brand new Vampire 9s the squadron received second hand Vampires from 26 Squadron; these Vampires were the oldest in Germany at the time.

In Exercise "June Primer" the squadron intercepted ten B-50s at 27000 feet and three B-36s. Serviceability was much improved with pilots sitting in their cockpits for long periods on standby. The battle flights practised rocket attacks at Oldenburg and flying against light anti-aircraft guns. At the end of June there were fifteen pilots and no NCO aircrew. On 11 July the squadron received its first camouflaged Vampire from Fassberg. At the end of the month the squadron was flying reconnaissance missions and flying practise missions against the army. This was Exercise "Catswhisker" and they were flying with four unarmed aircraft at the time. Unfortunately the squadron had its first accident since it was reformed when a Vampire crashed on take-off 12 June. Then on the 27th there was another fatal incident when Pilot Officer C.R. Donaldson was killed in an interception exercise. Between the 17 and 21 August three Vampires were flown to Kemble to have new ten channel radios. Then the squadron had a successful interception of a USAF B-45 Tornado, the Tornado did very little to escape to the disappointment of the pilots. On the 28th the squadron managed to intercept a Bomber Command Lincoln.

During September the squadron practised snake climbs and descent to 23000 feet. Then it was under canvas for ten days during Exercise "Holdfast." Nine squadron aircraft flew in formation over Jever and Oldenburg at the end of the month and in October the squadron flew battle flights with other squadrons including 4 and 93, bad weather hampered the month's' flying. What impressed the fourteen squadron pilots was the performance of the de Havilland Venom and the F-86 Sabre above 30000 feet. In November the squadron flew to Sylt APS for an armament practise camp but very bad weather curtailed flying. The camp lasted to the 17 December when the squadron returned to Jever but had to leave one Vampire behind due to unserviceability. At the end of December it was impossible to fly due to the weather. January was dominated by battle flights and interceptions. The squadron flew to RAF Butzweilerhof near Cologne to undertake a trial with PSP (Pierced Steel Planking) on the runway. On the 29 January eleven Vampires flew from Jever to Cologne. One aircraft was lost when the engine stopped and the pilot bailed out. The deployment at RAF Butzweilerhof was from four to six weeks. During the24 days of trials the Vampires lost 24 main wheel tyres, four nose wheel tyres and they made 584 landings. The squadron returned to Jever on 6 March.

During 1953 the squadron was once again at Sylt and returned to Jever in June but they were notified on 26 June that they were to move to Bruggen: the move took place on 6 July. On 22 July they temporarily moved to Florennes in Belgium for Exercise “Coronet.” Later the squadron was used aggressively to bomb Bristol during Exercise “Momentum.” In September, during Exercise “Monte Carlo,” the Vampires were flown without drop tanks and they finished the month flying battle flights. In December the squadron prepared for the Sabre and on 17 January 1954 “A” flight’s pilots were given familiarisation on the F-86 Sabre and soloed on the type. The second batch of pilots converted seven days later on 24 January. By the 26 January there were only six Vampires left on charge with 13 Sabres on charge with only two serviceable. By the 16 February the squadron was fully equipped with Sabres, the last two Vampires being used for familiarisation.

In April the Sabres were flown in battle flights against USAF B-47 bombers up to an altitude of 45000 feet. On 16 June a Sabre was lost at low altitude due to control failure, the pilot had to eject between 1000 and 1500 feet and survived. In September the Meteor T.7 also crashed killing both pilots. For high level flying in October drop tanks were fitted to all the aircraft and in November a member of the squadron went to USAF Bitburg to see the American gun harmonisation methods. In June 1955 the squadron flew to RAF

Geilenkirchen to take part in Exercise "Carte Blanche". During the exercise sections of four aircraft were at readiness from 0300 with two other sections of four aircraft at readiness within an hour. At the close of the exercise the squadron returned to Bruggen. While carrying out solo operations near Haarlem Holland Flying Officer Smith was killed when his Sabre crashed. In August there was poor Sabre serviceability due to lack of manpower, the squadron also received a signal stating there was a fault with Sabre fuel tanks only four aircraft were affected. In September the squadron had eighteen Sabres on charge with only ten being available at the end of the month. December saw flying curtailed due to bad weather. The bad weather continued to February 1956 with heavy snow falls limiting flying, excellent flying weather returned in March. In April the squadron flew to Luxeuil Saint-Sauveur in France to fly with F-84s of the French Air Force. During the month all fourteen Hawker Hunter 4s arrived at Bruggen. On return from France the squadron was declared non-operational and all Sabre flying ceased. It was found when flying in mixed Sabre/Hunter formations the Hunter was the more powerful aircraft. The first Sabres to leave out were flown by three ferry pilots on 1 May 1956 and the next day four more were flown to Aviation Traders at Stanstead for overhaul. The last Sabre left 5 June 1956. Flying Officer Crompton then designed the new shark's teeth for the Hawker Hunter aircraft.

130 Squadron

Formation of 130 Squadron Sabres

130 Squadron was reformed at RAF Bruggen, Germany, 5 August 1953 equipped with de Havilland Vampires to give air defence cover to the British sector. For the first month it shared No2 hangar with 112 Squadron till it moved to its own hangar at the end of the month. Their first five aircraft arrived from Fassberg on 8 August but one was found to be unserviceable. On 11th another three Vampires arrived with another two to follow, two pilots were sent to the Sabre conversion unit for the security part of the conversion course. During Exercise “Momentum” three Vampires of the squadron flew with 112 Squadron from Merryfield. Later in August they started to fly ground attack sorties and another aircraft was collected from Celle. Poor serviceability during Momentum meant that on some occasions only three Vampires were available for flying. Later on they simulated bomber streams and were intercepted by F-86 Sabres and Meteors.

In September the squadron took part in Exercise “Sunspot” flying on army support and then they prepared for Exercise “Monte Carlo” which was due to start on 10 September. Without drop tanks the squadron operated against targets in the high hills east of Bruggen. On 11 September the squadron started to fit drop tanks giving the Vampire the 130 mile additional range to the target. The exercise ended on 13 September but poor serviceability dogged the squadron during the exercise. Later in the month the squadron practised anti-shipping strikes over the Rhine. By October the squadron had twenty pilots and they tested the Belgian air defences, then the aircrew also took time to study the F-86 Sabre pilot notes. At the end of the month the squadron flew a formation of aircraft for the first time. In November, now with 24 pilots, the squadron intercepted B-29s operations were carried out in pairs of Vampires. Then the squadron flew to Sylt APS for an armament practise camp with 112 Squadron. At Sylt the squadron flew air to air and air to ground sorties with lectures given on the 0.50 Browning. Flying was marred by an air collision between a Vampire, WA129 and a Hawker Tempest: the wing of the Vampire and the vertical tail surface of the Tempest were damaged. On 19 December the squadron returned to Bruggen. With two pilots at the Sabre Conversion Unit, Wildenrath, the squadron aircrew concentrated on studying the Sabre Pilot’s Notes.

At the turn of the year the squadron had twenty eight pilots and seventeen Vampires eagerly expecting the F-86 Sabre. The Vampires were starting to return to Great Britain with three returning to the Maintenance Unit at St Athan in the first batch. At the end of January a Meteor T.7 was allocated to the squadron from Oldenburg with the first three Sabres expected on 29 January by now the squadron had twenty six pilots. The arrival of the Sabres meant that eight Vampires were kept outside the hangar, another Sabre arrived 2 February and another on the 3rd. With the Vampires being kept outside they

Hawker Tempest Target Tug SN329

quickly became unserviceable, some with blown undercarriage glands.

The squadron planned it would be re-equipped with the Sabre at the end of February, commencing with "A" Flight. On 13 February eight more Sabres arrived at Bruggen, making a total of thirteen and the ferry pilots then took away seven Vampires. Then cockpit time was given to pilots who had not flown the Sabre, assisted by pilots who had completed the Wildenrath course. Later in the month three Vampires were flown for disposal to Benson. A restriction came in, due to pilot experience, limiting flying if visibility was less than four miles and cloud ceiling was 3000 feet. By now poor weather and strong winds was limiting the flying of five Sabres and one Vampire. On 2 March the squadron was informed that the wing slatted Sabres were to be sent to Wildenrath and the unslatted Sabres were to be retained. During March Sabre XB894's nose-wheel door opened in flight and the aircraft was assessed as Cat 3 damage a day later the same thing happened to Sabre XB790: there was also a delay in delivery of non-slatted Sabres for a month. The last Vampire in the squadron WA201 was allotted to 19 MU and on 9 April two more Sabres arrived. It was felt that the squadron changing the Sabre wings from slatted to non-slatted gave the ground crews a lot of extra work and retarded training.

In a practise flypast two Sabres collided, XB595 touched XB916 when joining the formation for the Queen's flypast; the two aircraft were later replaced. In early May the weather was fine and the squadron practised battle formations for the rest of the month. On 3 June 1954, XB648 burst a tyre on take-off, swung on to the grass; the nose wheel collapsed causing Cat 4 damage. The squadron then moved to APS Sylt for an armament practise camp on 25 July. Through the summer camp there were burst tyre incidents, this was due to pilots landing on the short runway: a series of lectures was given to the aircrew to try to cure the problem. XB932 undershot, damaging the port dive brake bringing the squadron serviceability down to three aircraft. The target towing aircraft for the camp were still Hawker Tempests and some of the squadron were briefed on the T-33. The squadron then returned from Sylt on 18 August, the camp was regarded as disappointing due to the bad weather.

During September weather permitted normal flying though the station Meteor crashed killing one of the squadron pilots. In October twelve Sabres were grounded, cracks being found in the compass mounting brackets. New brackets were made on station but the Sabres needed their compasses swung after they were fitted. Then the squadron practised night flying and night cross-countries. During the night flying one Sabre was lost with the pilot when it crashed near Kassel. At the beginning of November all Sabres were grounded for a generator check, XB918 had total electrical failure which affected the whole squadron. In addition to generator failure cracks were found in the exhaust cones. Then on 19 November the aircraft were all grounded again due to cracks being found in the horizontal stabiliser artificial feel control brackets. By the end of the month replacements for XB927 and XB988 had not yet arrived and XB951 was to be returned to the UK to have its nose-wheel door and fuselage repaired. During December the squadron pilots went over to Wildenrath to inspect the two Hawker Hunters which had flown in from the UK. Weather curtailed most of the December flying along with further technical inspections with aircraft being left outside the hangar, this also caused starting problems.

1955 was characterised by more flying incidents such as loss of drop tanks in flight, shortage of drop tanks, fuel tanks cracking and restriction of flying to 15000 feet due to time expired oxygen regulators. It also took nearly a year to change the wings of the squadron Sabres to the 6-3 wing. The squadron also took part in Exercise "Carte Blanche," Exercise "Foxpaw" and Exercise "Beware." In January 1956 the squadron moved to APS Sylt for an armament practise camp, but achieved little due to the weather. In February the Sabres were once again grounded due to undercarriage problems. Then on 27 March 1956 the first Hawker Hunter was delivered but more problems were found in the Sabre wings and cracks were found in the aileron actuators. Five more Hawker Hunters had then been allocated to the squadron and they arrived on 6 April with another three on 9 April. By the end of April only two Sabres were left on charge and poor weather hampered the conversion to the Hawker Hunter. On the 3 May one Sabre was air tested and flown out leaving one Sabre but the month's high-point was flying in a Danish Catalina and landing in a fresh water lake. On 5 June the last Sabre XB959 was air tested and left around the 14 June for Benson.

Danish Air Force Catalina used for air experience

234 Squadron

Sabre XB872

[Operational Record Book between 1950 and 1956 for this Squadron are not available from the National Archives].
In 1944 the squadron was recorded as operating Meteor Mk.III jet fighters and was disbanded then on 1 August 1952, No.234 reformed at Oldenburg as a Vampire ground attack squadron in Germany. In November 1953, it received Sabres for day fighter duties. By December 1953 the squadron had received seven Sabres and by the end of the month three more Sabres had arrived. The squadron moved to RAF Geilenkirchen, with its new aircraft, on 8 January 1954. In July it simulated attacking bomber formations against the air defences of the United Kingdom. During April 1955 the squadron took part in Operation "Sky High" when the Sabres intercepted Canberras flying at high altitude. In June they were involved in Exercise "Carte Blanche" with other Allied forces across Europe. In July the squadron flew to Cyprus for an armament practice camp. This camp was followed by one to APS Sylt in September.

Weather was poor during January 1956 with fog and snow hampering operations. During Operation "Argus", 12 January 1956, the squadron practiced interceptions of Canberras from the UK, but the heights the Canberras were flying made it impossible to reach them. For interception a flight of four Sabres was used and it took 1 hour 20 minutes to reach 37000 feet. Then they were joined for lunch by eight pilots of the RCAF who flew in on their Canadair Sabre Mk 6s. By the end of January little flying could be done due to poor weather, low cloud, and snow. On the 2 January the first Supermarine Swift arrived on the station for 2 Squadron and a support mission was flown with a Meteor Mk9. During February an eight aircraft detachment was sent to Chaumont on an exchange visit with 494 Bomber Squadron where they had fine flying weather. Then the Technical wing found that the wrong lubricating oil had been used on the Sabre controls which caused freezing. The detachment at Chaumont was for seven days and included practice interceptions, dog fights and battle formations. This type of flying carried into March and included air to ground firing with the Easter stand down from 30 March to 2 April.

During April the squadron used the Percival Prentice as a "Hack" and flew three pilots to the UK for a wedding. Then on 6 April all aircraft were grounded in the afternoon to have their spars X-rayed for a fault and the wedding party returned. Three days later the squadron was controlled by 618 Signals Unit who vectored the aircraft at 10000 feet over Aachen. The fine weather that day meant that the Sabres were turned around in eight minutes. Then on 16 April they were informed by the C in C 2TAF that the squadron was to be equipped with Hawker Hunters. The next day they intercepted a Soviet, Tupolov TU-104 on its way to London Heathrow with three Sabres; one aircraft took cine film of the aircraft. A week later they flew on an air to ground sortie using tracer ammunition for the first time and set the range on fire. On the 26th they were visited by two Hawker Hunters in preparation for conversion. Conversion was to take sooner than later in place of Three Squadron in the second week of May. They were also told not to "Shoot at" TU-104s! At the end of the month they were told that they would cease operations of Sabres within two weeks. The plan was to get rid of the Sabres slowly and operate at any one time as a mixed squadron. In preparation for the Hunter they flew a Balbo of eleven Sabre aircraft in formation without drop tanks over the airfield. Then eight squadron Sabres were offered up for disposal at the end of the month.

On 1 May the squadron flew the last Sabres without drop tanks at high Mach speeds, they were recorded at flying at Mach 1.05 and 1.06. The first Hunter arrived from Bruggen on the 3 May and was taken to the Technical Wing as an instructional airframe. Pilots were then shown the Hunter's aircraft systems such as oil, hydraulic and electrical. On Monday 7 May three Hunters arrived, they were XF311, XF943 and XF936 - "…and looking very smooth." Two days later they were joined by Hunters XF932, XF944 and XF935, to be joined on 10 May by one more Hunter. On 14th some Sabres were flown away and some were taken to 3 Squadron and a day later two more Hunters arrived. On the 17th the squadron flew its first Hunter sortie with the pilot landing, "…and came back in raptures…..the aircraft is well liked morale is high." The second last Sabre was flown away on Thursday 24 May. By July the squadron was fully converted to the Hawker Hunter with practise interceptions against four F-100s (Super Sabre), a B-29 and a Canberra. The date of the final Sabre leaving is not recorded in 234 Squadron Operations Readiness Book.

Over 300 Sabres were returned to the USAF with Bristol Siddeley receiving two for test work with the Bristol Siddeley Orpheus. The balance of Sabres was overhauled for deployment to other nations but they were not all taken up. Some were scrapped at the contractors while others were bought by Staravia. The Staravia aircraft were dismantled at Lasham then Church Crookham where they were gradually broken up for spares. The remains lasted at Church Crookham till the early seventies then they were moved back to Lasham where they quietly disappeared. All surplus Royal Air Force Sabres had been struck off charge by December 1958. Up to July 1956, the Royal Air Force Sabres had flown a total of 120000 flying hours representing a distance covered of 48 million miles at a cruising speed of 400 mph.

Sabre XB748

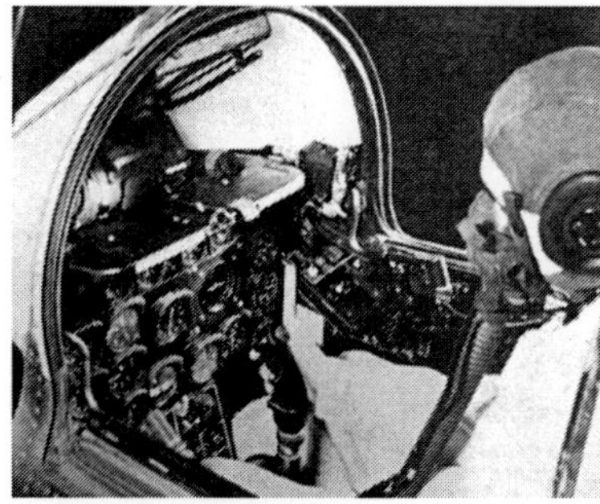

The Redifon Sabre flight simulator

Maintenance in a Sabre tail

First flight of the Orpheus 12 Sabre, 10 November 1959

19771 ex XD773and 19642 exXB768 at Staravia, Church Crookham

19687, exXB833 at Yeovilton to the Italian Air Force

Italian Air Force Sabre 4-11

Staravia, Church Crookham 11 September 1964

SERIAL NUMBERS FOR CANADAIR SABRES

Type Sabre	Serial	Comment
Mk. 1	19101	Prototype Canadair Sabre
Mk.2	19102-19199 19201-19452	60 of these were delivered to U.S.A.F. receiving U.S.A.F. Serial Nos. 52-2833 to 52-2892
Mk.3	19200	Sabre used by Jacqueline Cochran
Mk.4	19453-19890	
Mk.5	23001-23370	
Mk.6	23371-23760	
Mk.6	For the West German Air Force Canadair Constructor Numbers 1591-1815	
Mk.6	For Columbia 2021-2026	
Mk.6	For South Africa 350-383	

R.A.F. serial numbers for Mk. 2 and 4 aircraft delivered to the R.A.F.:— XB530-XB550, XB575-XB603, XB608-XB646, XB664-XB713, XB 726- XB769, XB790-XB839, XB856-XB905, XB941-XB990, XD102-XD138, XD706-XD736, XD753-XD781

6.

"Kissing Cousins"

Before and during the nineteen fifties there grew a common bond between the USAF Strategic Air Command and RAF Bomber Command. Strategic Air Command was originally established in the U.S. Army Air Forces on 21 March 1946 and transferred to the United States Air Force on 26 September 1947, initially under the command of General George C. Kenney. He was later replaced on 19 October 1948 by Lieutenant General Curtis LeMay who had under his command 60 aircraft that were nuclear capable. On July 17-18, 1948, at the invitation of British Prime Minister Clement Attlee, some sixty United States Air Force B-29 Superfortress strategic bombers landed at three British air bases on a thirty-day training deployment. For the first time the United States Air Force had stationed combat aircraft in another sovereign nation during peacetime.

Unlike the situation in Germany, where the United States had acquired its bases by right of occupation, the United States had no bases of its own in the United Kingdom. Moreover, the two nations had no formal agreement allowing this deployment. Six squadrons of strategic bombers constituted a sizeable military force to be deployed on British soil in peacetime without formal agreements between the host nation and visiting forces. The bases that were allocated to the United States Air Force were Royal Air Force (RAF) Scampton, RAF Marham, RAF Waddington, and RAF Lakenheath. Later in August a fighter group of Lockheed P-80 Shooting Stars was deployed from the Panama Canal Zone to Germany on a training basis. The aircraft were brought by carrier (USS *Sicily*) and transport ship (USAT *Barney Kirschbaum*) to King George V Dock, Glasgow with the P-80s being assembled and flown to Europe from Renfrew Airport. By 13 November 1948, the British Air Ministry advised Washington that long-term use of RAF stations by the USAF "was assumed." Thus, less than four months after the arrival on a thirty-day deployed task force, the governments of the United States and the United Kingdom had agreed that the basing of U.S. forces in the United Kingdom would continue indefinitely.

As part of the rationalisation of Royal Air Force, Bomber Command was formed in 1936. During the Second World War this air arm came into prominence with such raids as the Dambuster Raid and 1000 bomber raids on Germany. When the war finished the Command was under Air Chief Marshall Sir Arthur Harris. By 1951 the command was under the authority of Air Marshall Sir Hugh Lloyd. Both commands, Bomber and Strategic, trained together, competed together and had the same targets in a joint mission of deterrence. Twice a year the staffs of Bomber Command and Strategic Air Command would meet in England and Omaha, Nebraska to discuss targeting. Both commands firmly believed that by maintaining the nuclear deterrent the danger of nuclear destruction was kept remote. There was also a wide-ranging personnel exchange programme, whereby each of the commands on both sides of the Atlantic had USAF and RAF personnel attached. There was considerable exchange of views at the top between commands and between the Air Force departments in the Pentagon and the Air Ministry later Ministry of Defence in London. The Royal Air Force had now experience in operating and deploying such American aircraft as the Boeing Washington (B-29) and the North American Sabre. On the other hand the United States Air Force had ordered a version of the English Electric Canberra the Martin B-57 Canberra.

English Electric Canberra B.2 WD932
demonstrated to the USAF

Atomic weapons were first used by the United States in the Second World War against Japan. The genesis of this weapon can be traced to the United Kingdom sharing its atomic secrets with the United States from 1941. Post-war, Great Britain embarked on a nuclear weapons programme in 1949 and exploded its first device on 3 October 1952 at the Monte Bello Islands off Australia. Four years later in October 1956 the Royal Air Force dropped its first air dropped atomic weapon at Maralinga in Southern Australia.

To carry out the successful delivery of these weapon systems the Americans and British sought knowledge of the defences of the Soviet Union. In 1949 the Soviets had exploded its first atomic bomb. To deliver this bomb the Soviet Union embarked on a heavy bomber programme. Initially this was centred on a cloned copy of the Boeing B-29 the Tupolov Tu-4 code named "Bull". The British and the Americans had an intelligence requirement to investigate the Soviet aircraft industry bomber potential and Soviet defences. Both nations found it frustrating that no knowledge was forthcoming in both fields; nothing was coming out of Russia. To counter this lack of knowledge the United States and United Kingdom embarked on a programme of high altitude reconnaissance flights over the Soviet Union.

TU-4 a copy of the B-29 Superfortress which gave the Soviet Air Force a strategic capability and the ability to deliver a nuclear store

During May 1945, English Electric Company received a study contract valued at £1,000, confirmed on 13 June 1945. The contract was for work on a high-speed, high-altitude jet bomber to specification E3/45. By December 1945 the design had become a twin jet, high altitude bomber and the contract to proceed was signed on 15 January 1946 with a change from E3/45 to B3/45. The basic specification of the aircraft was a still air range of 1,400 nmls at a cruising speed of Mach 0.75, at 45000ft with 6,000 lbs of bombs. By the spring of 1949, the first prototype, VN799, was being assembled at Warton and it was rolled out for first engine runs at the beginning of May. Problems with the Rolls-Royce Avons meant that the Rolls-Royce RB41 Nene was substituted in their place with the second prototype VN813. Taxi trials with the first prototype were started on 7 May and the test pilot, Roland Beaumont took VN799 off the ground on the 9th for a short 'hop' to check unstick speed and low-speed control feel. A few more hops were made before, on Friday 13 May, VN799 was cleared for flight. Beaumont took off at 10.46am for a 30 minute flight.

Built to specification B5/47, the Canberra B2 was the first variant of the Canberra to enter quantity production and was the Royal Air Force's first jet bomber. It had a third crew member who sat in an ejection seat alongside the navigator or lay prone in the visual bomb-aiming station in the nose. The Canberra B2 had Avon RA3 engines of 6,500 lbs thrust. The Canberra B.2 started to enter service Royal Air Force service with 101 Squadron in January 1951 and a further squadron, 9 Squadron equipping by the end of the year. The production of the Canberra was accelerated as a result of the outbreak of the Korean War and orders for the aircraft were increased but outpaced production capacity, as the aircraft was designated as a "super priority". A further five squadrons were able to be equipped with the Canberra by the end of 1952. The first RAF pilots to fly the Canberra were all very impressed with its performance and handling and they recommended a few relatively minor modifications to the design. In February 1951, a Canberra set world record when it became the first jet aircraft to make a non-stop transatlantic flight. Throughout most of the 1950s, the Canberra could fly at a higher altitude than any other aircraft in the world and in 1957 a Canberra established a world altitude record of 70310 feet (21,430 m). The Canberra had the ability to evade the early jet interceptor aircraft and offered significant performance advancement over contemporary piston-engined bombers such as the Avro Lincoln and the Boeing B-50.

Canberra PR3 WE151

By 1950 the Canberra design was showing its adaptability with the design of the Canberra PR3 to specification PR31/46. The prototype, VX181 flew for the first time with a designated crew of two on 19 March 1950. Only 35 PR3s were built; compared with the B2 the fuselage was stretched by 14 inches to accommodate an additional fuel tank and a camera and flare bay. This fuel tank contained sufficient fuel to extend the aircraft's range by almost 1,000 miles. It had the same Rolls-Royce Avon RA3 engines as in the Canberra B2 and apart from the PR3's increased range, performance was very similar to the B2. The Canberra PR3 had aerodynamic problems; vibration issues were largely responsible for a two-year delay to the PR3 entering service. The first examples of the PR3 did not reach 540 Sqn. until December 1952. Even then, the performance was less than advertised, with an endurance only just exceeding four hours when flown to its practical ceiling of 48000 feet.

During this Canberra development period the Royal Air Force and the United States Air Force had secret discussions to solve the problem of photographic intelligence-gathering behind the Iron Curtain and over the Soviet Union. In fact, the UK and the US had agreed to 'a full and frank interchange of all classified military information and intelligence,' except for a few declared technologies. This Top Secret 1950 Burns-Templar Agreement of 20 January 1950 led to the sharing of all strategic target material between the RAF and the USAF. The agreement was named after the heads of the respective US/UK delegation, Maj. Gen. James H. Burns, Assistant to the Secretary of Defense and Lt. Gen. Sir Gerald Templer, Vice Chief of the British Imperial General Staff. The agreement also fostered co-operation in the gathering of strategic intelligence on the Soviet Union and its Allies. A summit meeting between Prime Minister Attlee and President Truman took place at Washington on 4 December 1950. During four days of talks they discussed the sharing of risks and rewards in this sensitive business. On returning to Great Britain from the conference with President Truman, Prime Minister Atlee arranged with the Air Ministry for USAF reconnaissance aircraft to be accommodated at Sculthorpe Royal Air Force Base in East Anglia and for a select group of RAF pilots to train in them in the United States. This authorisation was done through the highest political level and not through military decision makers at command level. This plan was agreed between the United States and the United Kingdom by the highest political authorities and was undertaken with their full and complete knowledge.

Sculthorpe, originally a grass airfield, had been built just before the war as a relief landing ground for RAF West Raynham. Four Strategic Air Command RB-45C air refuelable reconnaissance bombers detached from the 323rd Strategic Reconnaissance Squadron (SRS) arrived at Sculthorpe in early March 1951. The RB-45C could fly at a maximum speed of Mach 0.72 up to 37000 or 38000 feet, only 33 RB-45Cs were built. An outcome of the agreement came in August 1951 when RAF Bomber Command set up a Special Duty Flight to train on USAF RB-45C aircraft for deep penetration flights behind the Iron Curtain. The RB-45C had been deployed operationally in Korea. On 4 December 1950, Soviet MiG–15s shot down one of the USAF's Det A's RB–45Cs, on a routine mission along the Yalu River. The

RB-45C

Fitting flight refuelling gear to the RB-45C

KB-29 refuelling an RB45C

loss highlighted the vulnerability of the unarmed RB–45s and undoubtedly helped increase tensions in the region.

In 1951 Col. Stacy D. Naftel returned from Japan to Lockbourne Air Force Base, Columbus, Ohio, with the 91st SRW and subsequently was assigned to an RB-45C detachment at Sculthorpe, working with the RB-45C equipped RAF Special Duty Flight. The RB-45C was a conversion of a conventional interim nuclear jet bomber the B-45 and was equipped for daytime imaging and for radarscope photography. When it arrived at Sculthorpe the 91st became fully engaged in undertaking daylight photographic sorties over Western Europe using Boeing KB-29P in-flight refuelling tankers to extend their mission time to an average of eleven hours. The latter could be done at night. Indeed, it was under the cover of darkness that the Special Duty Flight subsequently flew over the Soviet Union in April 1952 and again in April 1954. Even so, flying at only 45,000 feet, these sorties were vulnerable to Soviet air defences, especially as Soviet radar coverage and night interception capability rapidly improved. With its four turbo-jet engines the RB-45C was able to fly higher and faster than the de Havilland Mosquito. It also had the considerable advantage of being equipped with AN/APS-24 radar, an invaluable source of information which would later be used in the production of specialised maps for the British V-Force.

In August 1951, the Royal Air Force commenced initial training on RB-45C Tornado aircraft at Barksdale Air Force Base, Louisiana and further training at Lockbourne Air Force Base, Ohio. The nine RAF crews and doctor flew to Barksdale in a C-97 Stratofreighter in their heavy RAF uniforms on a 90 day detachment. Unusually these crews were posted in and were not volunteers leading to one member dropping out, there were two pilots and a navigator for each RB-45C. When they left England early in the morning it was chilly. When they landed at Barksdale at nine o'clock in the evening it was ninety degrees, the humidity was 99 percent and a thunderstorm and a tornado had just come across the end of the airfield. The RAF flyers soon got used to their new Louisiana environment and quickly made friends and acquaintances among the American air crews before moving on to Langley AFB, Virginia, for introduction to the more advanced RB-45C version. On 2 September they flew up to Lockbourne AFB near Columbus, Ohio, home of the 91st Strategic Reconnaissance Wing operating the only three squadrons of the RB-45C. 323 Squadron was in residence, the other one was in England (19 Tactical Reconnaissance Squadron), and the other in Japan at the time.

In second month of flight training at Lockbourne, one of the pilots made a very heavy landing one night. The aeroplane was written off but the crew was unhurt. The dramatic result of was this incident was that Lockbourne's base commander along with the Royal Air Force commander and the pilot concerned were flown to Omaha ,Nebraska , Headquarters of the Strategic Air Command to be interviewed personally by the Commander in Chief of Strategic air Command, General Curtis E. LeMay the CINCSAC. He did not like people who destroyed his aeroplanes. His anger was directed mainly at the RAF pilot who departed for home from the United States. He was immediately replaced with another Royal Air Force pilot that had already been seconded to a U.S. Air Force B-45 unit. Conversion was completed and on 1 December 1951 the RAF crews returned to Sculthorpe where they became an additional second flight stationed at the base with the resident SAC RB-45C squadron detachment.

The cover story was that the Royal Air Force was considering acquiring a number of RB-45Cs on loan and wanted to conduct air-refuelling trials. B-29s had been provided to the RAF under Mutual Defence as the Washington B.1, so this seemed a reasonable explanation. Each RAF crew now consisted of a pilot, a radar navigator and a flight engineer. The flight engineer sat in the seat normally occupied by an American co-pilot, behind the pilot. None of the aircraft carried defensive armament, so there were no gunners on the crews. It was at Bomber Command at High Wycombe near London that the air routes were drawn up. It was there Air Chief Marshal Sir Ralph Cochrane, Vice-Chief of the Air Staff, planned any issues regarding the loan of the aircraft from the USAF. At this stage SAC or anybody else on the American side had any real input into the British planning. In 1952, four US Air Force RB-45Cs were selected

North American RB-45C at RAF Sculthorpe

Fitting the RB-45C with a film magazine

Tail of a Royal Air Force RB-45C of Detachment Four at RAF Sculthorpe/West Raynham

Royal Air Force RB-45C refuelled over the Baltic near Copenhagen by a KB-29, dawn, 17 April 1952 (Images M.Mixson)

for a highly secretive RAF project to planned overflight missions deep inside the Soviet Union. The RB-45s belonged to the 322nd Strategic Reconnaissance Squadron deployed to Sculthorpe from Lockbourne at the time. Three of the aircraft flew the first RAF mission overnight 17-18 April 1952 led by Squadron Leader John Crampton DFC AFC and Bar. After a trial night-time flight, flown by Crampton's crew, to the east of Berlin on 21 March, flown to measure the state of Soviet air defence, the first overflight mission was approved and the route as briefed. Before the mission two USAF RB-45s were flown to West Raynham and repainted with RAF fin flashes and wing and fuselage roundels. All American details were deleted.

The plan was for the aircraft to follow three routes all to be flown simultaneously at night, leaving Sculthorpe in rapid succession they headed for the Skagerrak to rendezvous with the KB-29 tankers over Denmark. Taking on the maximum fuel they were to climb at maximum continuous power at Mach 0.68 to the highest altitude the night temperature would allow. The "targets" were Soviet air bases missile sites and similar areas of strategic importance, for Crompton's RB-45C there were 126 air intelligence targets. They were to take 35mm photos of the aircraft's radar display when the targets were located and identified. Timing was critical because NATO intelligence agencies would be listening for the Soviet air defence reaction to the deep penetration mission. The aircraft flew under radio silence and without navigation lights.

The three aircraft entered the Soviet Union simultaneously at three different locations in the northern, central, and southern areas of the Western Soviet Union. Flying at about 35000 feet, the RB-45s proceeded on separate tracks one to the Baltic states, Poland, and the GDR, one to Belorussia as far as Orel and the third to the Ukraine and the Black Sea coast. As each RB-45C crossed the border into the Baltic States in the north, Belorussia in the centre, and the Ukraine in the south flying as far as Rostov-on-Don (the mission Crampton flew) the Soviet air defence system sprang into action and United States and British intelligence listened in. Over the Ukraine they flew at 36000 feet at speed of mach 0.68. For all of the fighters that scrambled into

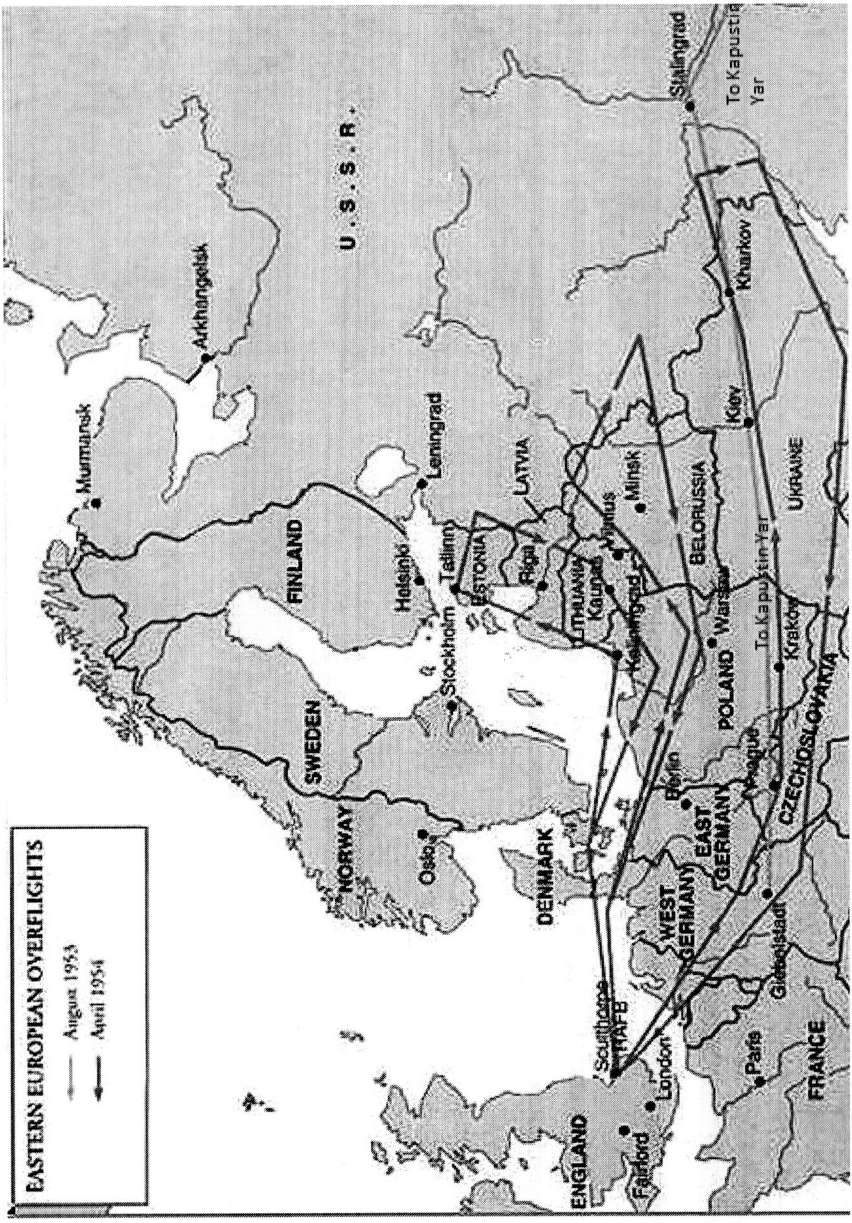
EASTERN EUROPEAN OVERFLIGHTS
August 1953
April 1954
U.S.S.R.
Murmansk
Arkhangelsk
Leningrad
FINLAND
Helsinki
Tallinn
ESTONIA
LATVIA
Riga
LITHUANIA
Kaunas
Minsk
BELORUSSIA
Kiev
Kharkov
Stalingrad
To Kapustin Yar
UKRAINE
Warsaw
To Kapustin Yar
Krakow
POLAND
Stockholm
SWEDEN
NORWAY
Oslo
DENMARK
EAST GERMANY
Prague
CZECHOSLOVAKIA
WEST GERMANY
Giebelstadt
Paris
FRANCE
Sculthorpe RAFB
London
Fairford
ENGLAND

the night sky, however, none found the British in the dark and they all returned safely to base.

The only real problem with the first overflights was the British weather. About twenty minutes before the first aircraft, flown by Flight Lieutenant Blair over the Baltic States, was due to arrive at Sculthorpe; fog rolled in from the North Sea and the aircraft was diverted to RAF Marston. Crampton was able to land at Sculthorpe during a break in the fog, after ten hours and twenty minutes in the air. The third RB-45C, flown by Flight Lieutenant Cremer, had to make a precautionary landing in Copenhagen due to engine trouble caused by icing up of the fuel filters. The crew took off again and landed at Prestwick. Then a Canberra from RAF Wyton flew the film to Central Reconnaissance Establishment. The RB-45Cs were then stripped of their British markings USAF markings painted back on the airframe but a ghost of the roundels and fin flash could be made out on the airframes.

After flying the RB-45Cs to the United States on 9 May 1952 the RAF crews travelled to Strategic Air Command's headquarters in Omaha, Nebraska, where they met General LeMay who complemented them on the success of the mission. Strategic Air Command in Omaha had decided to have the aircraft return home to the United States without first repainting them. While there were four RB-45Cs, the RAF only had three full crews to fly them. They were short a pilot for the fourth crew. Mixson flew one of them back with a British engineer in the co-pilot’s seat and Rex Sanders as radar navigator. It was a long and tiring ten-hour flight for the pilot, since the engineer couldn't help fly the plane. Snow was blowing at Lockbourne when they arrived. There were some surprised looks by the ground crew when they taxied in; the RB-45C’s resplendent in the colours of the Royal Air Force.

The information British brought back was crucial for determining the Soviet Air Forces’ order of battle. All three missions photographed and collected radar images of Soviet Long-Range Aviation (LRA) as well as nearby air defence bases. These would be bases which would need to be destroyed first at the onset of any US/USSR conflict. In the event of war - which in the 1950s seemed likely - SAC had to destroy the USSR's Long Range Air Force at the outset to prevent it from striking targets in Western Europe and the United States. The "Special Duty Flight" disbanded shortly thereafter. But in October it was reformed at Sculthorpe. Training for a second mission began in early December.

In October 1952 Col Mixson the 323rd Squadron commanding officer had sent three RB-45s to Sculthorpe Royal Air Force, Base England for the other special operation. This was a similar operation to the first one; this mission was termed "Jiu Jitsu" in Bomber Command. The aircraft left Lockbourne during October 1952 for Goose Bay, Labrador The first assignment upon arrival at Sculthorpe was to qualify two Royal Air Force pilots on the RB-45C and then check out another RAF pilot completely on the RB-45C. The two pilots were exchange officers assigned to the 914 Strategic Reconnaissance Wing Lockbourne and had had a fair number of hours on the RB-45C. (RAF pilots and radar navigators often flew on missions in USAF RB-45Cs). The third pilot had no time or experience on this aircraft. He was however a well-qualified Canberra pilot Flying Officer MacAlistair Furze. This pilot impressed the Americans with his keenness and sharpness and after seven training flights was fully qualified to fly the RB-45C including day and night refuelling and emergency procedures. The RAF detachment at Sculthorpe was recorded in the airmen's logbooks as Detachment Four. From November until December 1952 the RAF aircrews took over when the Americans stood down. They are known to have flown in RB-45Cs, 8029, 8023, 8036 and 8041.Though the December 1952 mission has been reported as cancelled there is evidence to support the view otherwise, the Americans declaring the mission a success! Did they fly it? The RB-45Cs had disappeared at the time to West Raynham only to reappear once again with Royal Air Force markings and crews. Then John Crampton led the Special Duty Flight of four RB-45Cs back across the Atlantic Ocean, landing at Lockbourne AFB in Ohio as snow was falling. Through the gloom, base maintenance personnel who approached the aircraft stared in disbelief at the US Air Force bombers still decked out in British markings.

Later another RAF mission was flown overnight on 28-29 April 1954 once again using aircraft deployed from Sculthorpe and once again led again by Crampton. Bomber Command again planned the operation which again showed three routes north, central and a much longer southern route that required different in-flight refuelling locations principally over Western Germany and Denmark. Intelligence assured them that there would be no flak and little aerial opposition with possibly some surface to air missile opposition; these flights were once again carried out at night. More importantly than the reconnaissance mission was the fact that it was being tracked again by NATO electronic services which was a primary concern.

The aircraft took-off on the night of 28 April and headed for northern Denmark for their first rendezvous with the KB-29 tankers. With a slow climb they flew over Western Germany, east by southeast at an altitude of 30000 feet outbound, they climbed and zig-zagged south-eastwards, photographing their targets until they were to the south-south-west of Moscow where they turned for the home run, still photographing, until they had to dog leg south towards Kiev to photograph more targets. This part of the mission covered more than thirty targets. As they headed for Kiev they were met with flashes in the sky which they thought were lightning storms but as they got over the city they were met with a barrage path of flak. The solution was to clear out using maximum throttle. It was later learned through intelligence that there were fighters searching for them with orders to ram. They had been tracked very accurately and the pilot requested the navigator a course to steer to Furstenfeldbruck, their refuelling rendezvous in West Germany and declared an alternative landing ground in an emergency. Problems with flight refuelling over Western Germany meant a landing at Furstenfeldbruck. They then flew home to Sculthorpe without further incident. It was there the other two RB -45Cs were waiting for they too had made successful incident free flights. On this intelligence gathering mission, all three RB-45s returned undamaged with the radar images. The information gained obtained on these overflights was used as target materials to improve Strategic Air Command and Bomber Command's location coordinates and other noted characteristics of the Soviet military targets. The intelligence collected by the RAF RB-45C flights was radarscope pictures of the plots along three routes, principally the Soviet bomber bases. Ultimately the intelligence and knowledge gathered on the Jiu Jitsu missions was used to plan and guide attacking bombers of Strategic Air Command and Bomber Command in the event of a nuclear conflict

After the mission the crews felt tribute had be paid to Mr Llewelyn, Bomber Command's chief scientific officer who played a practical role by supervising the radar installation in the aircraft and improved the quality of the radar images and even introduced a technical innovation that gave the images a stereoscopic effect. These successful long-range penetrations of Soviet airspace by RAF-operated RB-45s provided ample evidence of the Soviet Union's inability to detect and destroy intruders at that time. The Royal Air Force RB-45 sorties provided invaluable intelligence in the context of target selection, weapon selection and route planning for both Strategic Air Command and Bomber Command. Using the results of the RB-45s' radar photography, terrain analysis studies were made and from these it became possible to refine the techniques of radar prediction for the later V bombers and USAF heavy bombers.

The aeroplane Spotters around Sculthorpe were very active and informed the magazine, "Air Pictorial" that they had spotted eight Royal Air Force RB-45Cs flying around the area in this time frame. Initially the British Air Ministry denied the claim but finally admitted to one flying on trials with British markings. The Soviet defences had been alerted and tracked the aircraft but had misidentified them as Boeing B-47s.

After the Korean Armistice, the British and American governments remained partners in the Intelligence Programme and shared the intelligence acquired from it at least until April 1955, when Anthony Eden replaced Winston Churchill as Prime Minister. The last confirmed intelligence overflight mounted from Great Britain occurred in March of that year conducted from Sculthorpe by three US Air Force RB-45Cs led by Major John B. Anderson. The aircraft on this night time mission followed routes and overflew targets nearly identical to those of the earlier RAF night-time RB-45C flights. This mission was unusual in that the primary aim was not reconnaissance but to excite the Soviet air defences in order that an updated record of their existence be made.

In 1952 the Royal Air Force, had re-designed the Canberra bomber for high-altitude reconnaissance work, this was the Canberra PR3. The Royal Air Force was now using the Canberra to its maximum. Sometime during the second half of 1953, the RAF employed a high-altitude Canberra on a daring overflight of the Soviet Union to photograph the missile test range at Kapustin Yar, near Stalingrad. This site was selected because it was remote, which enhanced security and was thought to be far inside the country to discourage reconnaissance flights. It had attracted the attention of British Intelligence in 1952. This was where the Soviets were testing rockets and guided missiles using German scientists. This flight was approved by the British Prime Minister; the primary mission was flown in late August 1953 from Giebelstadt in West Germany, close to the East German border. Although initially flying above 45000 feet as a "Lone Ranger" and later above this altitude, the Canberra was continually tracked in daylight by Soviet radar as it flew over East Germany, Czechoslovakia, Poland and the Ukraine In the face of an integrated air defence system on fully alert, the Canberra aircraft, operating at above 48000 feet and remained untouched. But the Canberra was intercepted at altitude; the Soviet fighters did not have the altitude performance to destroy the aircraft. One MiG pilot who saw it shimmering in the sky did fire but could not get close to the target to make any effective hits. Much of the Canberra tail was made of plywood which was used to cover a radar system which was never fitted. It was common in early Canberra flights for this plywood to come adrift. Though the Soviets and learned authorities claim hits it is possible that this was the flaw that made the Canberra land in Iran.

The Canberra quickly photographed the target area and immediately turned southeast over the Caspian Sea towards Iran where it eventually landed. It is probable that initially there were two Canberras in this operation, each covering the flight path to check for contrailing at altitude. Many sources have tried to identify the Canberra but there is still a measure of doubt as to its serial or

Squadron. Sources indicate that due to technical problems with the camera the prints were not up to standard and were not issued to the Americans. Other sources indicate that the prints went to the CIA and the United States Air Force who wanted more, declaring that President Eisenhower was very pleased with the results. The RAF Squadron ORBs cannot confirm times or dates with any accuracy the times of the flight and some contemporary CIA intelligence report the mission as being undertaken by a de Havilland Comet Mk1! It was also stated in the same report that the British were going to go back!

Rumours about this flight reached Washington during the summer of that year but official confirmation by the United Kingdom did not come until February 1954. While on a six-week tour of Europe to study aerial reconnaissance problems for the US Air Force's Scientific Advisory Board, James Baker was briefed by RAF intelligence officials and Security Intelligence Services on the Canberra overflight of the Soviet Union. On 22 and 23 March 1954, he reported on it to the full Scientific Advisory Board at Langley AFB, Virginia. Baker also chaired the next meeting of the Air Force's Intelligence Systems Panel in late April 1954 but could not tell its members about the British overflight of Kapustin Yar because they were not cleared for this information. The panel did however discuss the modifications for high-altitude flight being made to the US Canberra, the B-57.

The Kapustin Yar mission and the RB-45C flights of April 1955 had been influenced by a memorandum from Allen W. Dulles, Director of the Central Intelligence Agency (CIA). He was convinced that a continuous aerial reconnaissance be made of the Soviet Union. The CIA was aware of the British overflights and their intelligence value. Dulles believed that the Martin B-57 Canberra could be modified for such a role and ideal for the mission with its ability to fly at 65000 feet. The Americans were well aware of the British photographic reconnaissance Canberra and its use by the Royal Air Force. In 1954 the Royal air Force flew an English Electric Canberra PR7 a distance of 156000 miles over 25 days flying 300 flying hours. It flew around the United Kingdom for seven days a week and on its busiest day it was airborne for eighteen and quarter hours.

There also existed the Olympus Canberra B.2, WD952. This aircraft was powered by two Bristol Olympus B01.99 engines replacing the Rolls Royce Avons. These engines gave the Canberra a performance of over 63000 feet, a world record. This altitude record had been exceeded unofficially several times by the same aircraft before the record-breaking flight. Test flights began on 5 August 1952 under the direction of Wing Commander W.F. Gibb on behalf of Bristol engines. His flight observer was F. M. Piper. But to save weight the observer was not carried on the world altitude flight.

On 31 August 1953, 540 (PR) Squadron recorded Canberra WJ573 flying on a trial at 50000 feet. The trial was photo trial with a Williamson F.49 12" air survey camera controlled by the navigator but no photographs were taken. The sortie was two hours twenty five minutes. WJ573 flew survey missions, camera trials and on twenty first of August flew to Alhorn from Wyton, on Exercise "Momentum." 540 (PR) Squadron was part of Bomber Command Strategic Photograph Force.

The Canberra hit the world headlines again in August 1955 when the new Canberra PR7, WT528, broke three records during the course of a double Atlantic crossing in one day and W. F. Gibb broke his own altitude record in the Olympus test-bed aircraft out of Filton.

The trial "Project Robin," involved the modification of B.2 Canberra, WH726. The aircraft was detached from 58 Squadron on 1 March 1954 and flown to the United States; this aircraft had been exchanged by the squadron for Canberra PR3, WH144. The crew returned on 10 April 1954 after a successful joint Anglo-American trial, the trial originally having been planned for two weeks. There it was fitted with a very long focal length camera colloquially known as the 'bomb camera'. This camera employed internally a series of mirrors to achieve a focal length of 240-inches and was fitted into a 10-feet long cylinder mounted in the aircraft's bomb bay. The camera was specially built for LOng-Range Oblique Photography (LOROP). It was especially designed by James Baker at the Boston University Optical Research Laboratory for aircraft which could fly at high altitude and obtain useful images. The camera pointed out of a port-facing window in the forward fuselage of the aircraft which would

WH726 camera installation

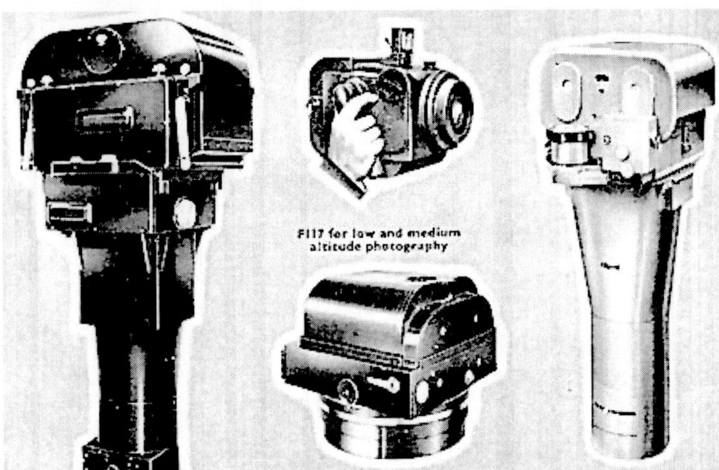

Williamson aeroplane Cameras 1955

then be flown along the border to take photographs of territory to the east. This LOROP camera permitted long range oblique photography to a distance of some 80 miles from altitude. Flying near the Soviet border, it allowed the Canberra to photograph installations well inside the country.

The Canberra was selected for the Robin project because it was the only aircraft capable of achieving the high altitude required to enable photography of targets well inside Soviet-controlled territory. The camera was reported to be so powerful that during a test flight over the English Channel off the coast of Dover, clear photographs were taken of St Paul's Cathedral, 75 miles away in central London. The first Robin sortie was flown on 23 April 1954, between Lubeck and Brunswick, Germany and flew along the East German border photographing long range targets with the camera. A near identical camera, Sharp Cut, was fitted to the Martin RB-57A and RB-57B reconnaissance bombers. LOROP missions were also flown by Boeing RB-47s along the coast of Siberia.

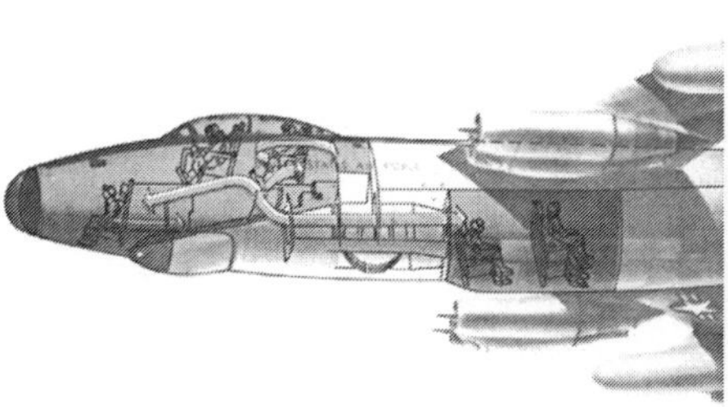

RB-47

Sharp Cut

Martin RB-57A Canberra in flight (SN 52-1447) of the 363rd Tactical Reconnaissance Group

The Martin Company had obtained a licence for the English Electric Canberra, the licence being agreed on 3 April 1951. To assist Martin in production, five subcontractors were contracted to produce about 60% of the Canberra by airframe weight. Kaiser Metals were to build the two wing panels and nacelles, as well as the rotating bomb bay doors. Hudson Motors furnished the aft fuselage section and the tail components, Cleveland Pneumatic Tool Co supplied the main and nose landing gear. Other sub-contracted items included the canopy and nose cap, tip tanks, fuel cells, forgings and castings, ejection seats, hydraulics and electrical equipment. The engine was an American adaptation of the Armstrong Siddeley Co Ltd Sapphire engine having 7,200lbst. This was a more powerful engine than the 6500lbst Rolls Royce Avon that powered existing Canberras but the extra thrust would be needed for the anticipated added weight of the B-57. Wright Aeronautical Corp paid $499800 for the manufacturing rights to build the Sapphire as the J65 engine. Buick Motors Division of General Motors Corporation sub-contracted and initially produced the engine for the B-57s.

Even with the Canberra and its reconnaissance versions there was still the need for an aircraft that would fly even higher. Dulles had received strong support from President Eisenhower for this aircraft which became Project Aquatone. The Americans were aware of a German reconnaissance rocket glider, the DFS228, which had a very high altitude performance. This aircraft was indeed of revolutionary design being nothing more than a rocket propelled sailplane. It was built to a 1941 Luftwaffe specification for an extremely high altitude reconnaissance aircraft which would use a rocket motor for take-off and resort to soaring flight to obtain its range. Much experienced in designing high altitude sailplanes, the D.F.S. 228 was designed by Felix Kracht. In 1939 Kracht's team had designed a sailplane which had flown to 38000' with a pilot using oxygen and they had concluded that at such limits the aircraft needed a pressure cabin. The prototype D.F.S. 228 was registered D-IBFQ and it was built in three sections, nose pressure cabin, fuselage centre section and a tail cone. The wing was all-wood with wooden ribs and plywood covering. The wooden centre section was designed with twin skids, camera bay, fuel tanks and rocket motor. The D.F.S. 228 had a length of 34’7”, a wingspan of 57’6” and weighed 9270 lbs. In the initial prototype the pilot sat in a cartridge operated ejection seat for flight tests at low altitudes. In later versions the pilot lay on a couch in the prone position in a Plexiglas nose which was attached to the rear bulkhead, while the wooden structure was insulated by a layer of aluminium foil between the inner and outer shells. For pilot entry the nose could slide about three feet forward, taking the pilot into the pressure cabin. Pressurisation could only be maintained up to 26000’ and above this altitude compressed air bottles had to be used. The DFS 228 could soar to an altitude of 75000 feet equipped with two Zeiss infra-red cameras. This airframe had been passed by the British to the Americans around 1946 but its fate is obscure but it did give the Americans an insight into the possibility of deploying a high altitude powered sailplane for reconnaissance work.

D.F.S. 228 atop a Dornier Mother Plane

D.F.S. 228 in flight

D.F.S. 228 preparing to land

On 3 March 1953 a formal specification was finally completed for a high altitude reconnaissance aircraft. The specification was drawn up by J H Carter, Assistant Director, Development and Planning. He saw that Russia should be overflown with a high performance manned aircraft, have a single pilot and have a suite of sensors and cameras weighing not more than 500lbs. It should have a radius of action around 1000 miles and be flown at extreme high altitude.

This specification was released to three small aircraft manufacturers. All three companies, Bell, Fairchild, and Martin, received six-month $200,000 study contracts on 1 July 1953. The new project was identified as MX-2147 and under the name BALD EAGLE. Only Bell and Fairchild were asked to design new aircraft to meet the specification. Martin was to design a modified B-57 for the specification. The design proposals were interrupted by a design from Lockheed.

Lockheed saw a production of twenty airframes each hand built with production taking from six to eight years. Lockheed made the production cost at between 150 and 300 million dollars. They recommended R.A. Bailey take over the project working in close co-operation with the company and with the President of the National Security council. The ultimate result of this programme was a joint CIA-Air Force programme, first known as AQUATONE by the CIA that resulted in the development and deployment of the U-2 aircraft, which remains in operation today.

The initial design which Lockheed submitted used the modified fuselage of the F-104 Starfighter it was known under the company designation of CL-282. More modifications took place and the aircraft was fitted with cockpit pressurisation and the fuel was to be carried in four wing tanks and one fuselage tank making a total of 925 gallons. The powerplant was to be a General Electric J73-GE-3 non-afterburning turbojet engine with a sea level static thrust of 9,300 lbs. Due to other considerations this initial design was rejected which left Lockheed to pursue other funding channels. Lockheed then proposed to have the CL-282 aircraft in the air eight months after receiving the instructions to proceed.

By 1954, the deployment of Token and other advanced Soviet radar systems had made it virtually impossible for intelligence-gathering aircraft to enter Soviet airspace undetected. To resolve this problem the Americans had already initiated a highly classified programme called Black Night, which was to result in the aircraft that would revolutionise strategic reconnaissance: the Lockheed U-2.ln December 1954 the Perkin-Elmer Corporation was requested to take on the production of the photographic equipment for the U-2 project which had been designed by Dr. James Baker. The original approach was to Mr. Richard Perkin, President of the company, who agreed to undertake the work. Dr. Roderick M. Scott was also knowledgeable of the program since he, as Chief Scientist of Perkin-Elmer, had previously worked on the optics problems with Dr. Baker. The contract for optical equipment was finally signed on 5 May 1955 was "Agency-sterile" but not "Government-sterile." It called for 36 A-1 cameras, 27 A-2's, 6 B's and 6 C's, with a target price of $5085000 ($4750000 cost plus$340000 profit), re-determinable at the time 75% of the cost had been expended. A 24-inch lens was standardized for the A configuration (rather than both 24-inch and 36-inch lenses) and it was agreed that the marginal value of the 12-inch split vertical cameras in the original specifications of the A-1 and A-2 did not warrant their inclusion.

A-2 Camera

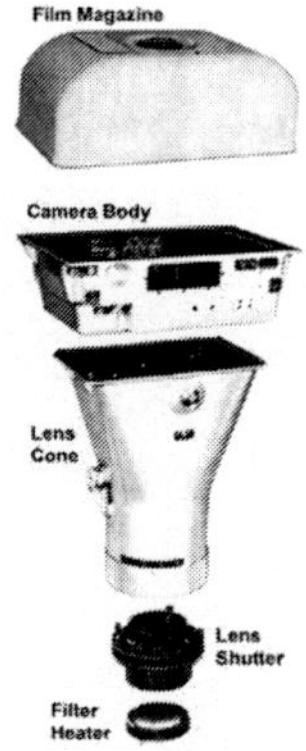

A-2 Camera Set

The A-2 camera set was first deployed in May 1956

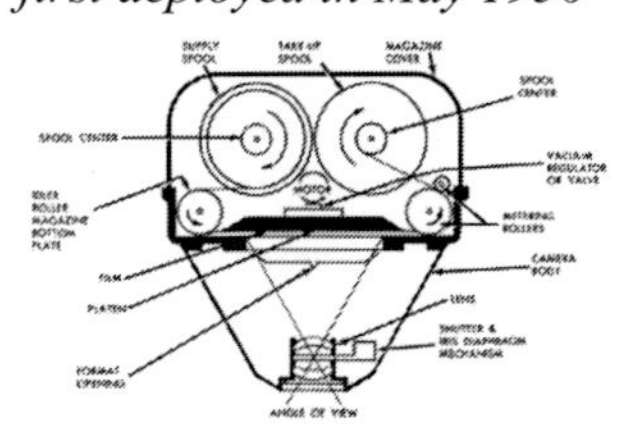

Camera feed mechanism

Installing the camera suite behind the cockpit, notice the hatch and pulley

The A-2 camera configuration was first deployed in May 1956 and was used exclusively for the first year of operations. The A-1 was not flown operationally until October 1957 and it was also used with good results in typhoon hunting missions in Japan. The B camera was slow in delivery and functioned, poorly during the combat readiness tests in July 1956 due mainly to shutter trouble. After reworking and further testing, however, the B camera became the workhorse and was used almost exclusively in the U-2 from the summer of 1958 through to 1966 with good results. The first C camera was tested in December 1956 and in January 1957 had one effective mission but it was never used operationally due to complex optical problems inherent in the design and was later shelved. Eastman Kodak received the contract to provide and develop film. The main problem was the CIA using Air Force contract numbers which came under scrutiny.

On 9 December 1954, after a visit from the Air Force Secretary for Research and Design, Lockheed received the order for the aircraft which became the Lockheed U-2. The formal contract, No SP-1913, was signed on 2 March 1955 and called for the delivery of the first U-2 in July 1955 and the last in November 1956. The U-2 was now designed to use the Pratt & Whitney (P&W) J57/P-31 engine, which developed 13000 pounds of thrust and weighed 3820 pounds giving it a power-to-weight ratio of 3.4: 1. When the U-2 first took to the air, however, these engines were not available because the entire production was needed to power specially configured Canberra RB-57Ds for the Air Force. The first U-2s therefore used P&W J57/P-37

001 the first Lockheed "Article" 4August 1955

Articles at the Ranch

Unloading from a Globemaster

Above Lockheed U-2s in flight and on the left a U-2 with its designer Kelly Johnson

engines, which were 276 pounds heavier and delivered only 10,200 pounds of thrust at sea level.

By July 1955, less than eight months after Lockheed had received the official approval to begin the project, the first U-2 aircraft was delivered for test. E. H. Land of Polaroid had developed the camera system. On 1 August the second set of taxi trials were run on U-2 No 1. Results were satisfactory but on a high speed taxi run the aircraft inadvertently left the ground by 30 feet and flew 1200 feet. The transition to flight was very smooth but not noticed by the Pilot. A hard landing resulted when the pilot cut power at low speed; the tyres blew on landing due to excess braking and caught fire. Additional taxi tests were then made on 2 August with satisfactory results and on 5 August a first flight of approximately thirty minutes was successfully and smoothly accomplished. Further low level tests were run on 6 August and on Monday, 8 August, the· Project Director and a Headquarters party along with the designer happily observed the U-2 perform at 35000 feet. On 16 August the U-2 went to 51000 feet, on 25 August to 57000 and on 1 September it reached 60000 feet. Ultimately U-2 pilots routinely flew missions at altitudes above 70000 feet, for durations exceeding nine hours, requiring the pilot to wear a full pressure suit and breathe 100% oxygen. When on operations the Lockheed U-2 spy plane was held off the power unit and glided to a lower altitude. In the flight profile it was designed to climb rapidly to a very high altitude, the pilot would then take a series of stereoscopic photographs. The U-2 was notoriously difficult to fly. Pilots called the U-2 “Dragon Lady” because of its unforgiving handling characteristics at altitude.

The British had agreed, on the 6 March 1956, to U-2 operations taking place from RAF Lakenheath. Detachment A was deployed to RAF Lakenheath during the period 29 April to 4 May 1956. Before deploying to Lakenheath the Detachment was initially based at Mildenhall. The unit was known publicly as the 1st Weather Reconnaissance Squadron, Provisional (WRSP-1). The "provisional" designation gave the U-2 detachments greater security because provisional Air Force units did not have to report to higher headquarters. To the pilots and Lockheed personnel it was simply

Det. A and although technically a CIA operation almost all logistics and maintenance support was provided by the Air Force and Lockheed. By 4 May, all of the detachment's personnel and equipment, including two aircraft, had arrived at RAF Lakenheath. The entire U-2 group was in place by 7 May, ten pilots were allocated to the Detachment but only six were available and on the 15 June the Detachment of four aircraft with the six pilots moved to Wiesbaden. It is possible that two U-2 aircraft remained in the United Kingdom for local use while the balance went to Germany.

At Lakenheath, as part of the weather study, the U-2s obtained a small sample of turbulence data from NACA VGH recorders during research flights at attitudes of 55000 feet over England and Western Europe, during the summer of 1956. This indicated substantial reductions in the number and intensity of gusts with increasing altitude. A later analysis of these results indicated that for the higher altitudes of 50000 to 75000 feet, turbulence was both less frequent and less severe than for the lower altitudes 20000 to 50000 feet. Turbulence appeared to be present at the higher altitudes of 60000 to 75000 feet less than 1 percent of the time. Moderately heavy turbulence appeared to exist on occasion at altitudes of about 50000 feet in certain areas.

The first Lockheed U-2 operational mission took place on 20 June 1956, with an overflight of Poland. Then on 4 July 1956, after overflights over Eastern European countries, the first U-2 targeted on the Soviet Union, photographed Leningrad's naval shipyards, as well as several major military airfields. These were five of the seven high priority targets for the USAF. The following day, another mission overflew Moscow as well as a number of airfields in an attempt to determine the threat from Bison heavy bombers. Powered by jet engines rather than the turboprops of Russia's other long-range bomber the Bear, the Bison appeared to be the Soviet Union's equivalent of the Boeing B-52 which was only then going into production. Pictures of the Bison taken at the Moscow May Day air show in 1954 had an enormous impact on the US intelligence community. Unlike several other Soviet post-war aircraft, the Bison was not a copy of US or British designs but represented a native Soviet design capability that surprised US intelligence experts.

At about 9am, September 17, 1956, a Lockheed U-2, serial number 56-6679, the sixth U-2 built lost part of its right wing shortly after taking off from Wiesbaden, Germany. The aircraft disintegrated in flight, killing the pilot. The fuselage disappeared towards the town of Sembach after the left wing had broken off. The exact cause was never determined. The designer believed it was caused by overpressure in the wing tanks during a steep climb but it was also noted that the U-2 might have been caught in the jet wash from a flight of four Canadair Sabres fighters that had just passed by. Though the Canadian pilots saw the aircraft break up high above them. The U-2 airframe was not stressed to withstand severe air turbulence. The Canadians termed the U-2s as, "Aircraft Zulu types."

The 4 July mission gave the United States and her Allies a better understanding of Soviet armaments and Soviet intentions. Three additional flights followed, on 9 July and 10. Also, on 10 July the Soviet Union, whose radars proved more capable of detecting the flights than expected by the CIA, filed their first protest note concerning the aircraft intrusions into Soviet airspace. Five operational missions proved that many of the guesses on Soviet important subjects were seriously wrong. By September 1957 only 17 deep-penetration missions had been flown over the Soviet Union, five of them in July 1956 and seven in August 1957. Most were flown by Detachment B, based in Adana. The new Detachment B in Adana was ready for operations in September 1956 and it was better positioned to provide coverage of the Middle East and the southern Soviet Union. Detachment B began flying missions on 11 September 1956 and soon became the primary detachment for Middle East overflights, conducting nine out of the 10 such missions flown in October.

The missions to Murmansk could be mounted by a detachment, based at Giebelstadt, West Germany. There the aircraft was not painted and they were unmarked except for a tail number and "NACA" on the tail but later they were seen in black. The aircraft were used both in daylight and in darkness. Once airborne, the U-2 would turn and head out over East Germany and the U-2 would climb

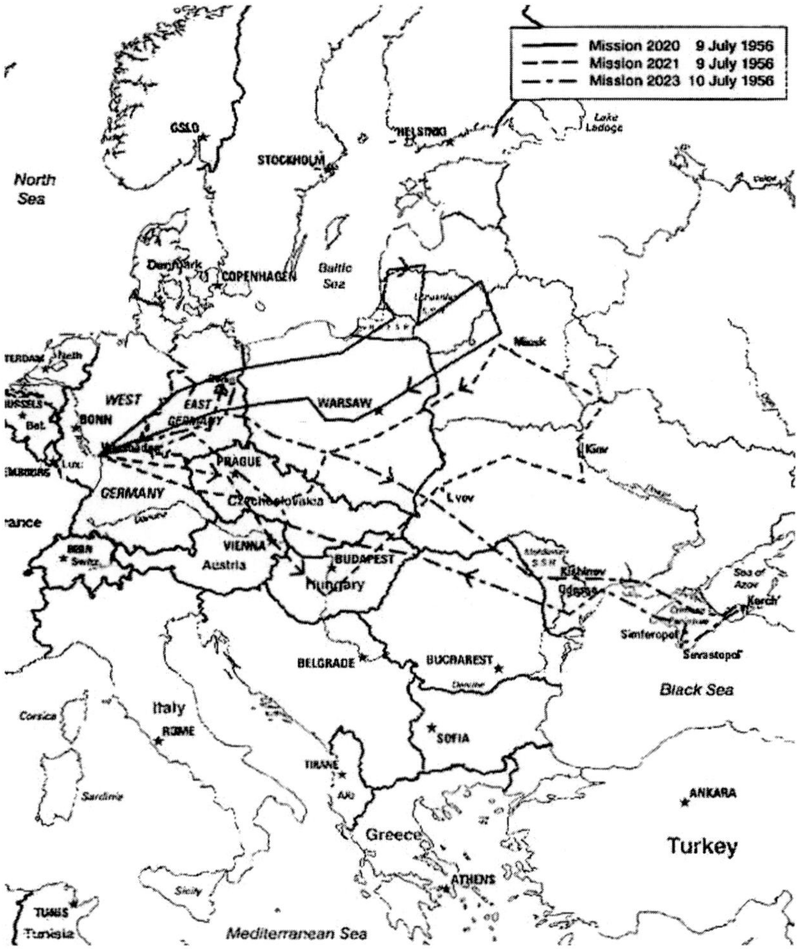

U-2 detachment at Giebelstadt operational sorties

right off of the accessible radar height coverage, which was 75000 feet. During 1956-57, the U-2 detachment at Giebelstadt had mounted only four overflights. The first two were over Eastern Europe: one over Bulgaria on 10 December 1956, flown by Carmine Vito and the other over Albania on 25 April 1957. Then a long period of inactivity followed, ending with a third mission on 11 October 1957 flown by

Jake Kratt which conducted electronic surveillance of Soviet naval manoeuvers in the Barents Sea. The flight was nine hours fifty three minutes and flown 3900 nautical miles. Although the final missions of the U-2 achieved excellent results, it had already been decided that Western Europe was not a satisfactory location for overflights of the Soviet Union and had ceased operations on 20 September 1957.

There is no exact record of when President Eisenhower gave his approval for the Murmansk missions but it is believed to have been in late September 1957. The aircraft had been modified with wing slipper tanks each with a capacity of 100 gallons. On 5 and 6 November 1957, twoU-2s took off from Giebelstadt each day and were flown via Plattsburg, N. Y., two to Edwards Air Force Base for Detachment G use, and two to Del Rio, Texas, to the SAC U-2 Wing. By 15 November all of Detachment A had departed from Giebelstadt and on that day the communications link with Giebelstadt was closed and the facilities returned to the United States Air Force. During the detachments 17 month period of operations, seven pilots had flown a total of 23 missions, six over the Soviet Union, five over Eastern Europe and most of the remaining 12 missions over the Mediterranean area. The Soviet missile programme had evolved through the German V-2 and the Soviet equivalent of long-range missiles capable of traveling 700-1000 nautical miles or more. As these missiles were being tested, evidence began to suggest a new test range was being developed by the Soviets near Novokazalinsk and Dzhusaly in the Kazakh SSR. On 5 August 1957, a CIA U-2 reconnaissance aircraft searching along the Chkalov-Tashkent rail line in the Kzyl-Orda Oblast' in Kazakhstan photographed - in the distance - what was later identified as the Tyuratam missile test range head. It was 21 days later when the Soviets announced they had successfully launched an ICBM, and two days after that announcement when another U-2 flew directly over the site providing definitive photography of all its features.

As a result of Lockheed U-2 reconnaissance the guesses and estimates which formed the basis for United States national policy could now be seen as projections from the wrong way of thinking and that, as a consequence, United States defence policy could indeed be

Tyuratam missile test range

Pilot wearing an MA-2 helmet

worthless. As a consequence the Americans felt that the danger to their international relations appeared to be far greater than if they did not carry out the AQUATONE operations. The Americans had laid out sufficient ground work to assure that the interpretation of their activities was as an intelligence operation rather than as a reconnaissance operation prelude to war.

When the U-2 was designed they were looking for the ultimate in high-altitude performance. To accomplish this, they had to devise a means to store large amounts of fuel within the airframe. The solution was to use what is known as a "wet" wing: all the cavities within the inner two-thirds of each U-2 wing were made leak proof and filled with fuel. By employing the wet-wing, the designer was not able to provide the U-2 pilot with the traditional full-empty fuel gauge, because the fuel had to be drained simultaneously from both wings to preserve aircraft balance. The U-2's wings were simply bolted to the fuselage formers and had no continuous main spar. The U-2 used the bolted-on wings in order to reduce weight and gain room for its intelligence payload, the fuel capacity was 1535 gallons. Lockheed had estimated that the wing had a life of 5000 hours. On the U-2's instrument panel was a fuel counter that was set manually by the person responsible for fuelling the aircraft. This counter was set to the precise number of gallons pumped into the aircraft. The fuel from the wings was fed by gravity to a central sump located ahead of and below the cockpit. As each gallon of fuel was fed from this sump to the engine, a metering device sent an electric pulse that caused the counter to be reduced by one digit. It was critical that the pilot keep the wings level because, as fuel was expended, one wing would sometimes feed the fuel quicker than the other and disturb the U-2's balance. To regain balance the driver had to activate pumps to move fuel from one wing to the other.

Before each flight, the navigation unit prepared a flight plan on an 8.5-by-ll-inch green card that listed each turning point in the flight and gave an estimated time of arrival at each point and an estimate of fuel usage based on the amount put into the aircraft by the ground crew. The pilot, known as the, "driver," was responsible for writing on his green card the time of arrival at each turning point and the reading of the fuel counter. The driver also carried a strip map of the area over which he was to navigate. The individual U-2s were called, “article”, each aircraft having its own "article number." On operations the aircraft became known as KWEXTRA-00 (the two-digit number identified the precise aircraft; these numbers were not related to the three-digit article numbers assigned by the Lockheed factory). The pilots were referred to as KWGLITTER-00 (the two-digit number identified the precise pilot). Even if a message or document about overflight activities fell into unfriendly hands, the contents would simply refer to code words or at worst to "articles" and "drivers." For flying at high altitude a complex life-support system was developed, which was the first partially pressurized "spacesuit" for keeping humans alive for lengthy periods at ultrahigh altitudes.

MC-3 suit (worn underneath was a standard flying coverall)

1966-Kelly Johnson with Gary Powers

The U-2 cockpit was pressurised to create an interior air pressure at an altitude of 28,000 feet. The system was designed so that if the interior cockpit pressure fell below the 28000-feet level, the pilot's suit would automatically inflate. In either case, he could obtain oxygen only through his helmet. The early models of these MC-2 and MC-3 partial-pressure suits were very uncomfortable for the pilots. To prevent loss of pressure, the heavy coveralls had to fit tightly at the wrists and ankles (in the early models of these suits, the feet were not included in the pressurization scheme). The pilot had to wear gloves and a heavy helmet that tended to chafe his neck and shoulders and was prone to fogging. Problems with the pilot life-support system were believed to have been the cause of several early crashes of the U-2. At the end of April 1960, there had been 23 U-2 overflights of the Soviet Union - all successful.U-2 overflights of the Soviet Union ended on 1 May 1960, with the destruction of F. Gary Powers's aircraft by an estimated SA-2 Guideline missile near Sverdlovsk.

Royal Air Force pilots were also involved in flying this remarkable aircraft. The Royal Air Force regarded the Lockheed U-2 as a joint UK/USA intelligence programme. The British become fully involved in the U-2 project in September 1956, when the United States supplied them with photography from U-2 missions. To handle U-2 material, the British created a new control system, which later merged with the US control system. By 1957 co-operation between the United Kingdom and the United States had expanded to include frequent consultation between the requirements and photo-interpretation organizations of both countries. A year later, in November 1958 four RAF officers arrived at Detachment B at Adana, in the Middle East, beginning the United Kingdom's participation in U-2 operations. The British brought with them about a dozen technicians to work with the project and RAF personnel for Detachment B used civilian British passports describing them as civilian employees of the London Meteorological Office. They were not allowed to wear Royal Air Force uniform locally or in the air but they also had with them a doctor. They could not record their flights in their service logs, only when they left the project. The Americans

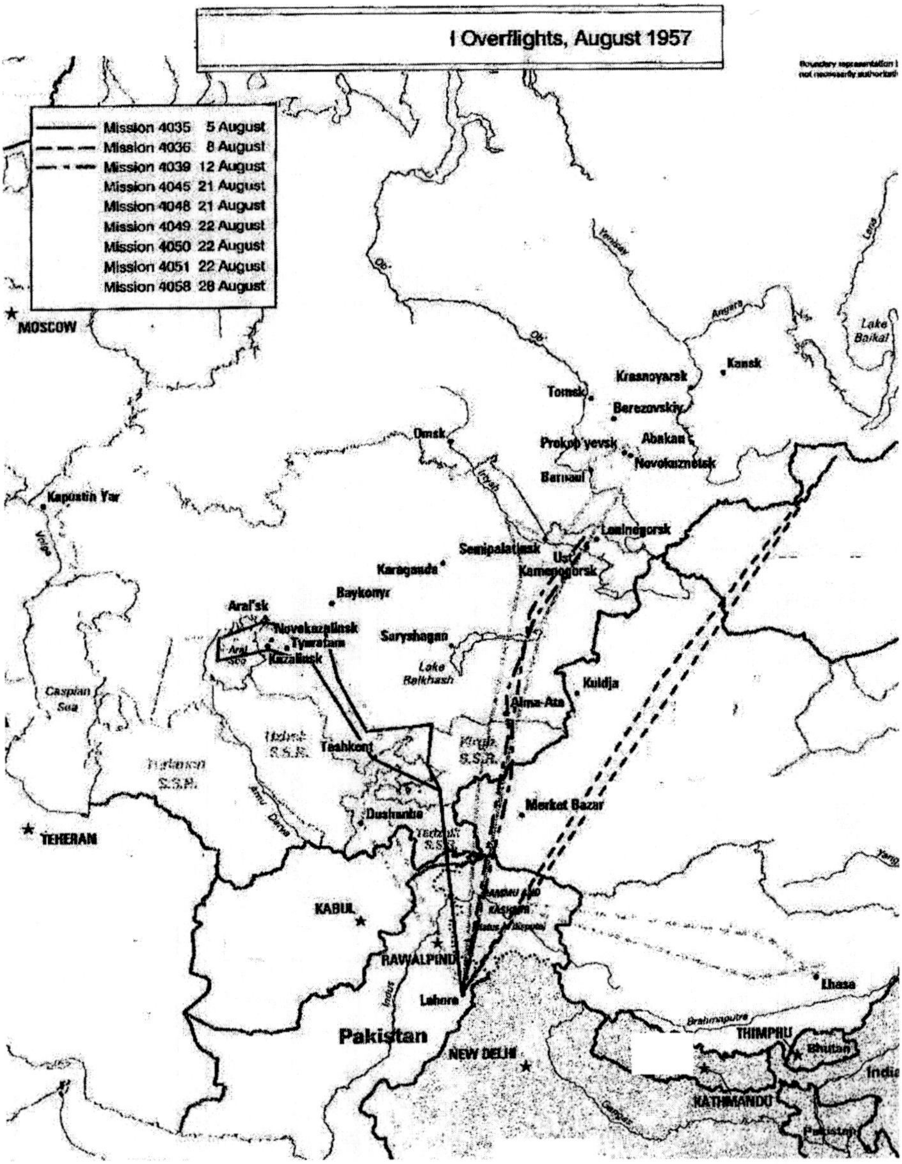

Soft Touch Missions 1957

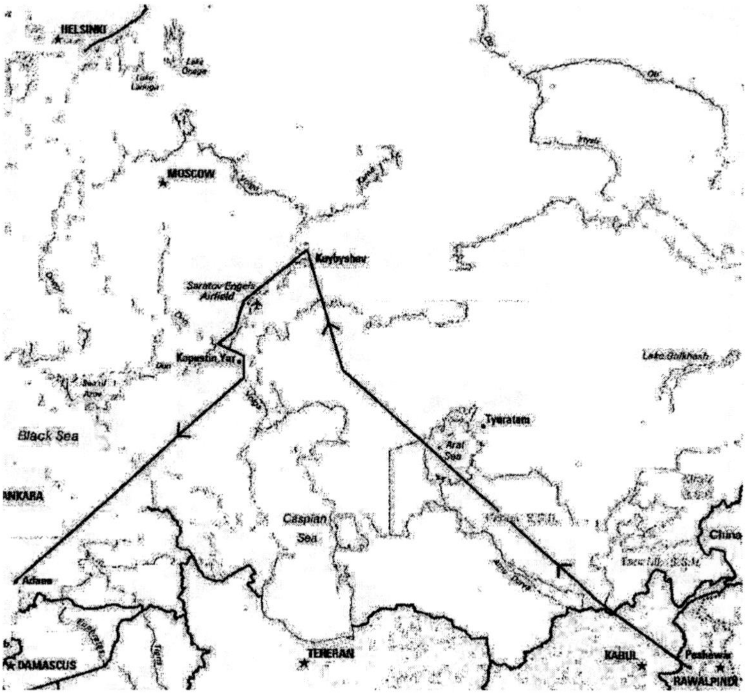

Track of the Royal Air Force U-2 mission to Kapustin Yar

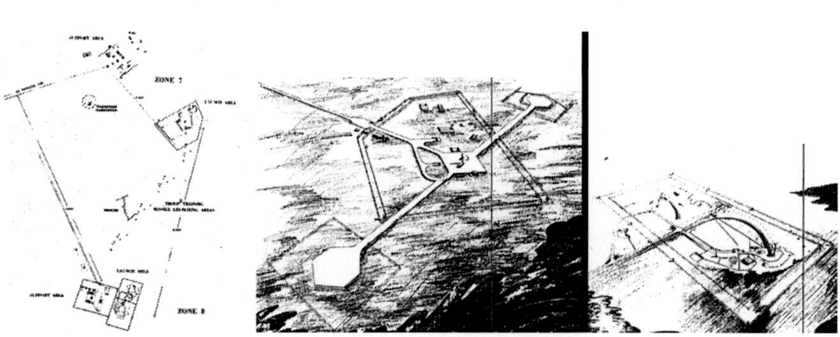

Kapustin Yar test areas 1957
Details from article plots

allocated a Lockheed T-33 and an additional Lockheed U-2 to Adana for British use.

One of the consequences of the 1956 overflights and the Soviet note of protest was that U-2 flights over the Soviet Union were banned by President Eisenhower. The idea of using British pilots in the U-2 program first arose in the spring of 1957, when the Americans began searching for ways to reduce the political risks of overflights and thus obtain more frequent authorization for missions over the Soviet Union. One of the proposals was to use non-US pilots-possibly British-to increase the possibility of plausible denial in the event of a loss. On the British side, participation in U-2 flights was a logical extension of the close co-operation that already existed between the two countries in the intelligence field. At a meeting with key Central Intelligence Agency, Defense Department, and State Department officials on 6 May 1957, President Eisenhower approved the concept of British participation in the U-2 Project. This was a fulfilment of the close co-operation between the United State and the United Kingdom which had already existed between the two countries in the intelligence field since the late fifties and early 1960's. 16 June 1958 Project KEEPER was jointly agreed between the British and the Americans. (The name was later changed to Project OLDSTER due to conflict discovered with a British cryptonym). Further possible operational bases for the KEEPER missions were not necessarily restricted to Adana, but to Giebelstadt, Germany; Kinloss, Scotland; and Cyprus. By 27 August 1958 Prime Minister Harold Macmillan had approved British participation in the project, provided missions were flown by civilian pilots in aircraft without RAF markings and no operational flights were to be made without his specific permission. President Eisenhower approved British participation the same day, subject to the American Secretary of State's concurrence. Later this arrangement proved its value when Royal Air Force pilots conducted two highly successful missions over Soviet missile testing facilities, at a time when President Eisenhower had not authorized an overflight of the Soviet Union for almost six months. Most flights were by the RAF pilots in Detachment B at Adana; however, others took place over the Eastern Mediterranean, where the United Kingdom carried out missions when its pilots took part in some overflights. During December 1958 British pilots flew their first operational mission over Middle East targets. The British flew a total of 28 missions with Detachment B (4 weather missions over England, 2 photo reconnaissance missions over the USSR from Peshawar and the balance over the Middle East).

Further on the British and Americans met on several occasions to discuss the proposal in general terms. At first the CIA did not push the proposal too hard because at the same meeting in which he approved British participation, President Eisenhower had consented to the resumption of U-2 missions over the Soviet Union, resulting in 10 overflights during the summer and autumn of 1957. But when these flights ceased in October, the thought of British participation became more attractive. By early 1958, the Americans were pressing the British to begin training pilots in the U-2 even though no final political decision on their participation had been made. At the Bermuda Conference, March 1957, the British Government on its own initiative, had offered to permit operations under AQUATONE to be conducted from bases in the United Kingdom, thus reversing their earlier negative decision. On 7 February 1958, the CIA invited the British Assistant Chief of Air Staff for Intelligence, to select a group of Royal Air Force pilots for U-2 training. In June 1958, British Air Ministry representatives came to project headquarters to work out an agreement on plans and procedures for the joint project. The two sides decided to establish a small RAF contingent that would be integrated into and supported by Detachment B at Adana. The British missions would be operationally controlled by CIA project headquarters not the USAF. Missions from Adana could be flown to Albania and as far as Tibet and Southern China.

Soon afterward four British pilots were prepared for training in Texas. One of these pilots died in a training accident in July 1958. This meant that a new team of RAF pilots had to be selected for training. Due to the addition of RAF officers to the programme, Project AQUATONE received a new codename, CHALICE, 1 April 1958. The CHALICE/OLDSTER Operational Plan, which was worked out by the British and Americans jointly, was signed on 28

October 1958.The British involvement with operations more than doubled the cost of U-2 operations. The British also had an operations officer posted into the project office from 28 June 1958. This officer was instructed to treat any information gained as privileged and would be expected to behave as a patriotic American in these cases rather than as a British subject. By the end of November 1958, three RAF pilots and a flight surgeon had joined Detachment B at Adana. Formal approval by the political leaders of the United Kingdom and the United States had come several months earlier. On 27 August 1958, Prime Minister Harold Macmillan gave his approval to British participation in the project as long as he had the right to approve or disapprove all operational flights by RAF pilots. On the same day, President Eisenhower gave his approval in principle for the joint project. In total there were eleven Royal Air Force pilots trained to fly the Lockheed U-2.

By November 1958 arrangements had been made for the title to the U-2 aircraft to be transferred on paper to the British Government. In a final exchange of letters between President Eisenhower and Prime Minister Macmillan in December, the President summarized the lines of authority for the joint program: *"British missions are carried out on your authority and are your responsibility just as our activities are authorized and controlled here in accordance with the procedures I have established. In this sense, it could be said that we are carrying out two complementary programs rather than a joint one."*

In Britain, the cover story for the RAF participation in the U-2 programme was that British fliers were being trained to fly high-altitude weather-sampling missions for the Meteorological Office. To support this cover, a U-2 was ferried from Adana to RAF Watton, England, in early May 1959 and used to fly weather missions on 7 and 8 May before returning to Adana. Two more weather-sampling flights took place over England on 5 and 6 October 1959. The other United Kingdom base considered for U-2 aircraft operations in the Great Britain for meteorology and reconnaissance was RAF Kinloss. This was because of terminal weather, availability of hangar space and the proximity to the Northern targets which were of interest to the intelligence agencies. In addition, there was the lack of air traffic in the area and its northern location eased the concern for additional security. In October 1969 a U-2 flew from North Base to Kinloss, Scotland. Later two RAF pilots ferried U-2s from Upper Heyford, UK direct to North Base. The flight lasted 13 hours 55 minutes. With pre-breathing time added, plus a 30-minute hold on the runway waiting for the weather to clear for take-off, the U-2s pilots spent well over 16 hours in their pressure suits, twice as long as usual.

For almost a year, the RAF pilots of Detachment B had been ready to fly over the Soviet Union but the British Prime Minister Harold Macmillan had not previously authorized any such missions because of his own visit to the Soviet Union, several international meetings and other state visits. As a result British U-2 missions had been confined to the Middle East. Now that the Prime Minister's approval had been obtained, Detachment B conducted a special operation with an RAF Squadron Leader pilot, who left Peshawar on 6 December 1959 and overflew Kuybyshev, Saratov Engels Airfield and the Kapustin Yar Missile Test Range before landing back at Adana. The mission photography was excellent, but it did not provide intelligence on Soviet ICBMs, which were tested at Tyuratam - the name means “arrow burial ground” - not Kapustin Yar. The Soviet Union had successfully launched the world’s first artificial satellite from Tyuratam on 4 October 1957. Since the 8 March 1957, Kapustin Yar had become a top intelligence target for the Americans, taking priority over all U-2 missions.

Then another U-2 took to the sky on a mission over the Soviet Union, called “Soft Touch.” The intelligence briefs had found that railway lines were an asset to U-2 flights. If they followed railway lines they would take them right to an SS-6 ICBM test site. As in December, the pilot was British and the mission had been ordered by Prime Minister Macmillan. On 5 February 1960, a Detachment B U-2C with an RAF pilot at the controls left Peshawar, Pakistan, to conduct an overflight. The plane overflew the Tyuratam Missile Test Range, headed northwest to Kazan and then turned south, photographing long stretches of the Soviet rail network. The excellent photography from this mission did not reveal a single missile site but analysts did discover a new Soviet bomber, dubbed the BACKFIN at Kazan. The success of the two British missions, along with the absence of Soviet protests, made the President more willing to consider a resumption of US overflights and he agreed to allow one mission to be flown during the month of March 1960.

Because of complications in getting permission from Pakistan to use the airfield at Peshawar the mission could not be staged in March and President Eisenhower agreed to extend his deadline until 10 April 1960. One day before the expiration of this deadline, a U-2 took off from Peshawar on the last successful overflight of the Soviet Union, Operation SQUARE DEAL. As had been the case during the previous two British overflights, a second U-2 flew a diversionary mission along the Soviet-Iranian border. After leaving Peshawar, mission 4155 headed first for Saryshagan, where it obtained the first pictures of two new Soviet radars, the HEN HOUSE and HEN ROOST installations. The U-2 then flew to the nuclear testing site at Semipalatinsk. Returning to the Saryshagan area, it crisscrossed the railroad network there and then proceeded to Tyuratarn, where it photographed a new two-pad, road-served launch area that suggested a new Soviet missile was in the offing. But this time the Soviet radar tracked the U-2 from the moment it took off to the minute it landed. This knowledge was ignored by the intelligence services and should have been a warning what was to come.

The pilot selected for the next operation, GRAND SLAM was Francis Gary Powers, the most experienced U-2 pilot in the program. Powers had joined the project in May 1956 and had flown 27 operational missions in the U-2, including one each over the Soviet Union and China as well as six along the Soviet border. Powers started his take off roll at 0159Z on 1 May 1960. Once airborne, Powers guided his aircraft toward Afghanistan. Following standard operating procedure, Powers clicked his radio switch when he reached penetration altitude of 66000 feet, which signalled the operations unit at Peshawar that everything aboard the aircraft was working and the mission would proceed as planned. Powers and all U-2 pilots maintained strict radio silence during penetration missions. Powers' first target was the Tyuratam Missile Test Range after which he headed for Chelyabinsk, just south of Sverdlovsk. The planned route would take him over Kyshtym, Sverdlovsk, and northwest to Kirov, north over Yur'ya and Plesetsk then to Severodvinsk, Northwest to Kandalaksha north to Murmansk and finally, west to Bodo Norway. At least 13 MiGs tried to intercept him but all failed. Powers never made it past Sverdlovsk. Four and a half hours into the mission, an SA-2 surface-to-air missile detonated close to and just behind his aircraft and disabled it 70500 feet above the Sverdlovsk. Powers managed to bail out of the wrecked U-2.

Lockheed U-2 at Bodo

The United States then released a cover story on Wednesday, 11 May 1960: the President read a statement to the press in which he publicly assumed full responsibility for the U-2 mission but he left open the question of future overflights, even though four days earlier he had approved the recommendation of his key foreign policy advisers to terminate all provocative intelligence operations against the Soviet Union. The loss of Gary Powers' U-2 ultimately resulted in the end of Detachment B at Adana. As soon as they learned that Powers was alive in Soviet hands, it immediately evacuated the OLDSTER pilots from Adana to protect the secret of their involvement in the project. Project officials hoped that flights might eventually resume from Adana, but President Eisenhower's order ending overflights of the Soviet Union made this very unlikely. After the suspension of overflight missions in May 1960, the need for British participation lessened but this involvement still continued under JACKSON which replaced OLDSTER (11 October 1960), RAF aircrews being deployed elsewhere. The United Kingdom's U-2 target list had focused on the factories and airfields responsible for building and basing Russia's strategic bomber force.

Francis Gary Powers with a Lockheed U-2 "A driver with his article." GM

After the end of Soviet overflight missions in May 1960, RAF pilots henceforth flew only training or ferry missions, although their use for operational missions was planned on several occasions. The closing down of Detachment B marked the end of Britain's direct involvement in U-2 operational overflights of the Soviet Union. A four-man unit of RAF U-2 pilots was stationed at Detachment G, Edwards AFB, until the end of the CIA U-2 program in 1974 but RAF pilots never again conducted an overflight in an Agency U-2, the need for British participation lessened. Though at a meeting in December 1966 the Americans favoured continuance of the British JACKSON unit and its participation with the Middle East and Africa being named as the likely areas where the British could obtain approval for operations. At the end of 1966 there were two Royal Air Force pilots, a flight planner and a flight surgeon at Edwards Air Force base with the JACKSON unit, all due for rotation and replacement during 1967. In July 1974 the overseas detachment which used JACKSON aircrew had its status changed and aircraft were turned over to Strategic Air Command on 1 August 1974. There was now no need for IDEALIST or JACKSON aircrew but JACKSON personnel were encouraged to stay with the project and retain their U-2 aircrew proficiency. IDEALIST was the controlling interest in Washington. The programme on the RAF side was run by the Assistant Chief of Air Staff, Operations in the Ministry of Defence and the Joint Intelligence

Committee was aware of the situation. In London, JACKSON/OLDSTER was certainly known to the Defence Committee at Cabinet level.

In mid-1963, there was set in motion Project WHALE TALE to examine the possibility of adapting the U-2 aircraft for operations from an aircraft carrier. It was also felt that to render the U-2 politically usable, modification of a few of the aircraft to permit them to operate on an aircraft carrier would help to avoid the exposure of friendly governments to political and diplomatic pressures. Design proposal for such an aircraft had been made in 1957. The Navy attempted on several occasions between 1957 and 1960 to obtain a joint agreement between CIA and the United States Air Force to the effect that a carrier capability for the U-2 should be developed. These attempts met with little success due primarily to the fact that the CIA was able to land the U-2 at selected ground bases.

The first test of the U-2's capability for carrier operations took place in August 1963 from the USS *Kitty Hawk* operating in the Pacific Ocean off San Diego, California. A U-2C, which had been loaded aboard the carrier at North Island, Naval Base took off from the flight deck with a full load of fuel and was airborne within 321 feet. No assistance from catapults was necessary. Although the take-off was very successful the attempted landing was not. The aircraft bounced, hit hard on one wing rip and then just barely managed to become airborne again before reaching the end of the deck. *(Some sources credit the RAE Farnborough with involvement in this operation and with curing the landing problems, a British pilot was provided who gave certain recommendations while the aircraft was approaching the carrier round down).* The U-2 airframe was then altered which involved strengthening the landing gear, installing an arresting hook at the rear of the fuselage and fitting "spoilers" on the wings to cancel the aerodynamic lift once the aircraft was over the flight deck. U-2 aircraft thus modified were designated U-2G. The only serious accident during the carrier pilot training programme occurred on 26 April 1965 when a U-2 crashed and burned near Edwards Air Force Base and the pilot sustained fatal injuries. The mission was to practice simulated carrier landings and the accident

USS Kitty Hawk on builder's trials

USS Ranger, Pacific, 1966

U-2 deployment on the USS America and the USS Kitty Hawk

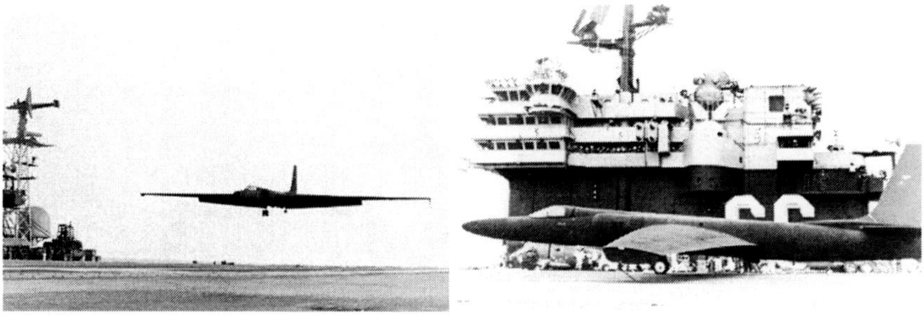

U-2 on the USS America

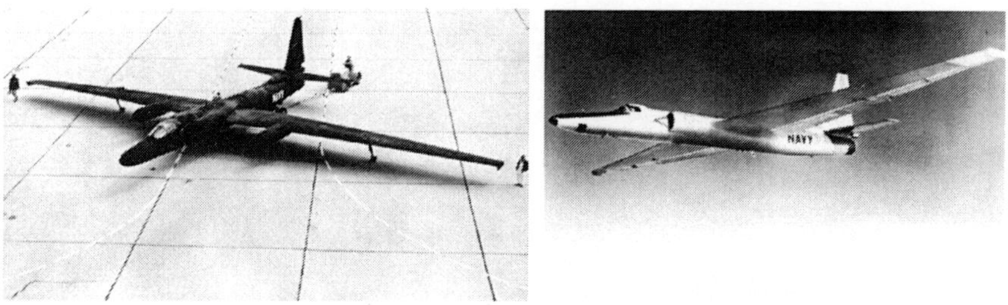

United States Navy Lockheed U-2 sea surveillance aircraft

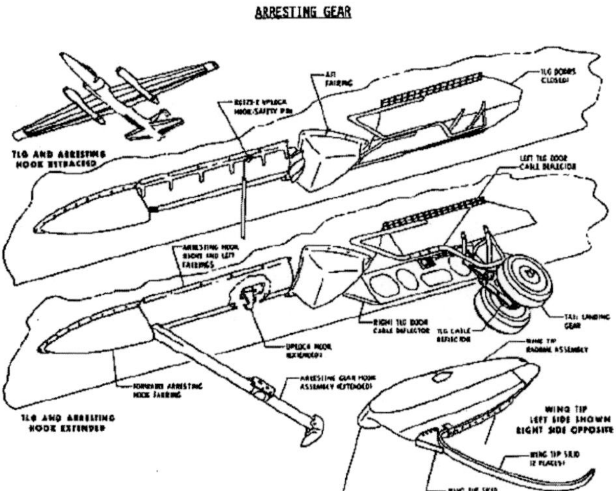

Lockheed U-2 carrier arresting gear

board findings indicated most probable cause to be low altitude, wing-low stall resulting in a spin from which the pilot could not recover. Before the actual carrier trials several pilots had been checked out in the Navy's T-2A Buckeye jet trainer and made practice landings on the training carrier USS *Lexington*. By the 9 and 10 March 1964, three pilots and an RAF Squadron Leader qualified for carrier operations in the U-2 without further incident. At this time France was testing atomic weapons in the Pacific and the on 19 May a U-2G took off from the USS *Ranger* and overflew the French atomic testing area in Operation FISH HAWK. As soon as the aircraft returned to the *Ranger*, the film was developed in the carrier's photo lab and the photo-interpreter then read out the film to see if the photography met the requirements for resolution and quality. A second U-2 flight carried out a similar mission on 22 May. The photography provided all the detail needed to identify the preparations for the nuclear test that occurred later that year. The final report on the aircraft carrier/U-2 combination declared that the combination constituted a naturally compatible and potent intelligence tool.

As of July 1967 four out of the original thirty pilots recruited in 1955-56 were· still with Detachment G, having served with the program for eleven years. In June 1963, one additional pilot was recruited and in June 1964 two more were recruited, all three from the U.S. Air Force. In November 1964, one U.S. Navy pilot was added and one of the pilots of JACKSON resigned his commission in the Royal Air Force and was hired as a contract pilot in his status as a resident alien. As of the end of 1967 there were four carrier-configured U-2's left in the CIA inventory.

Later in 1969, a new U-2, the U-2R was tested on an aircraft carrier. The U-2R was 40 percent larger than the earlier U-2. It had twice the range and could carry a payload four times as large. The Navy aircraft had an arresting hook. The outer six feet of each wing could fold back to facilitate handling aboard ship. The aircraft bore the fictitious Navy markings N812X. The first test flight of this new U-2 from an aircraft carrier took place off the deck of the Kitty Hawk-class USS *America* on 21 November 1969 with trials continuing to the 23 November. Things were progressing well but the initial landing attempt had to be cancelled when it was discovered that the ground crew had forgotten to remove the locking pin from the tail hook assembly. However, every subsequent flight was a success. Two RAF pilots were carrier qualified a few days later as were three other pilots.

The Navy wasn't finished with the U-2. Impressed by the operational performance of the Lockheed U-2R, the United States Navy ordered examples for its own use. In a separate programme in 1973-74, two U-2R aircraft were modified to the U-2EPX configuration for evaluation by the US Navy for the ocean surveillance role. During the evaluation the airplanes were fitted with a derivative of the AN/ ALQ-110 Big Look surveillance system, a modified AN/ APS-116 forward-looking radar (useful for detecting surface ships and periscopes or snorkels of submerged submarines) and an infrared detection unit. The radar, fitted in the U-2's sensor or "Q" bay, had an antenna protruding below the fuselage in an inflatable radome.

The United States Air Force called the Lockheed U-2, “Project Dragon Lady,” but after United States Navy fleet trials no Lockheed U-2 variant ever entered naval service with the fleet.

7.

MDAP

By the spring of 1945 the Allies were in control of Germany. That defeated nation had been split into four occupied zones by France, the United Kingdom, the United States of America and the Soviet Union. Even the capital, Berlin, was divided into four zones. After 1945 the Soviets had occupied their European areas and worked with brutal efficiency to subvert elections that had been mandated by the wartime agreements. They imposed Communist-dominated regimes while using diplomacy and subterfuge to confuse the West and spur the pace of Western demobilization. Soviet expansionism in such areas as Greece, Czechoslovakia, Poland and Iran warned the former allied nations what was to come.

On 12 March 1947 President Harry S. Truman made a special address before a joint session of the United States Congress. In the statement Truman recognised his British Allies were no longer in an economic position to provide aid to Turkey. Truman also advocated aid to Turkey's neighbour Greece. He made it clear that the violence used by the Soviet Union in Poland, Rumania, Bulgaria and other countries was a clear violation of the Yalta Agreement of 1945. He believed that the United States must support the free people of the world. He also believed that United States help should be made primarily through economic and financial aid which was essential to economic stability and orderly political processes. Truman proposed to ask the Congress to provide authority for assistance to Greece and Turkey in the amount of $400000000 for the period ending 30 June 1948. He felt that if he did not take this action he would jeopardise the welfare of the United States.

In addition to the Truman Doctrine the United States introduced the Marshall Plan. The Marshall Plan (officially the European Recovery Program, ERP) was passed in 1948 to give foreign aid to Western Europe. The United States transferred over $13 billion in economic recovery programs to Western European economies. It operated for four years beginning on 3 April 1948. The Marshall Plan, in addition to financial packages, required a reduction of national barriers, a dropping of many regulations and encouraged an increase in productivity, as well as the adoption of modern business practises.

The largest recipient of Marshall Plan money was the United Kingdom (receiving about 26% of the total), The next highest contributions went to France (18%) and West Germany (11%). Some eighteen European countries received Plan benefits. Although offered participation, the Soviet Union refused Plan benefits and also blocked benefits to Iron Curtain nations, such as Hungary and Poland. In 1951 the Marshall Plan was largely replaced by the Mutual Security Act.

On 4 March 1947, France and the United Kingdom signed a mutual assistance pact in Dunkirk. This treaty of friendship and co-operation treaty was openly targeted at Germany in order to forestall any new future aggression on its part. The French Government also sought to guard against what it still considered a potential threat from across the Rhine River.

The London Conference of Allied Foreign Ministers later took place in December 1947. This led to informal discussions between Britain's Foreign Minister Ernest Bevin and U. S. Secretary of State, George Marshall about the idea of developing a defensive pact in Europe. Subsequently, Bevin began to develop his concept of a "Western Union," wherein he pictured a defensive pact between Britain, France, and the Benelux countries based on the Treaty of Dunkirk. This in effect served a dual purpose by guaranteeing France's security and establishing a formula for a transatlantic defensive pact against the Soviet Union. He also conceptualized Germany as a member of this pact, because of his awareness that the real threat was the Soviet Union.

Ernest Bevin believed that all the free countries of Europe had to form a Western European defensive pact to maintain peace and that it needed to be "backed by the Americas and the Dominions." Bevin stated that this system would be comprised of Italy, Portugal, Scandinavia, the Low Countries, France, and Greece, and if circumstances permitted, would include Germany and Spain. Ernest Bevin had the strong support of Georges Bidault of France. On 22 January 1948, Ernest Bevin, British Foreign Secretary, delivered a

French Navy Avro Lancaster's of the Western Union flown from North Africa

speech to the House of Commons in which he condemned the Soviet threat and asserted his determination to further the United Kingdom's co-operation with France and the Benelux countries through a Western Union that would expand the Dunkirk Treaty. The impetus for the Western Union included in the Brussels Treaty was the collapse of the Republic of Czechoslovakia by March 1948: the Prague coup of 25 February 1948, when the communists forcibly seized power in Czechoslovakia and the mysterious death of Jan Masaryk, the pro-Western Foreign Minister, only heightened international tension and the dangers arising from what became the Cold War.

The Soviets threatened Finland, Norway, Italy, Germany and other European areas. Europe's uneasiness spurred Bevin to urgently submit his proposal to conclude an Atlantic Security Pact for the United States. On 17 March 1948 the Brussels Treaty was signed and favourably received by President Truman of the United States and quickly made known its preference for a regional pact which would exceed mere military matters. The five countries which signed the Brussels Treaty established the Western Union, designed to guard against any armed aggression in Europe (i.e. not including the overseas territories), no longer just from Germany but against any of its members. At the same time, Denmark, Norway and Sweden discussed the idea of military cooperation within a Scandinavian defence union. Inspired by Finland's experience, but remaining divided about their neutral status, these countries wanted to protect themselves against any possible Soviet pressure and considered calling on the United States to provide them with the armaments required to deter any attack. But the regional plan failed once and for all in 1949 when the Americans announced their unequivocal refusal to arm a neutral alliance.

Five days after the signing of the Brussels Pact, the first inter-governmental meeting was held between the United States, the United Kingdom, and Canada on 22 March 1948. The Brussels Treaty was scheduled to remain in force for 50 years and provided for the organisation of co-operation among the five signatories in the military, economic, social and cultural spheres. A united Military High Command of Western Union, a kind of joint HQ, was created. However, the Brussels Treaty was soon left weakened of its newly expanded authority after the signing of a succession of treaties establishing the Organisation for European Economic Cooperation (April 1948), the North Atlantic Treaty Organisation (April 1949), the Council of Europe (May 1949) and the European Coal and Steel Community (April 1951). But although the Brussels Treaty failed to create a customs union, it did partially meet the concerns of the Americans, who considered that it reinforced the position and willingness of the five member countries, all keen to receive economic and military aid from the United States.

Thus by 1948, as far as the Soviets were concerned, there was a great gulf that separated their thinking as Communists from non-Communists and particularly from the Americans. Initially the Americans felt that Stalin viewed the world somewhat in the same light as them and that Stalin's hostility and distrust, which were evident in the wartime conferences, was due to the neglect that Soviet Russia had suffered at the hands of other countries for years after the Revolution. What the Americans did not understand was that Stalin's enmity was based on profound ideological convictions. The existence of a gap between the Soviet Union and the United States, a gap that could not be bridged, was never fully perceived by the Americans. Stalin had been challenged in Greece by the British and in Iran. The only way Soviet Russia could expand was behind the Iron Curtain and in Germany. Although President Roosevelt often misjudging Stalin and his intentions, it is less often recalled that the President felt he had to make every effort to preserve U.S.-Soviet co-operation, simply because he believed that once the war ended the American people would not tolerate a large military force and the permanent overseas involvement that confrontation with the Soviets would require. Even after Soviet intentions aroused suspicions in the later Truman administration, intense public pressures for rapid demobilization of U.S. forces undercut, so American officials felt, U.S. efforts to challenge Soviet moves in Eastern Europe and Iran. The five European nations, which signed the Brussels Treaty quickly realised that they could not repel an attack from the USSR on their own.

The Soviets had blockaded Berlin in July 1948 which had been ended in May 1949. That beleaguered city being supplied by air through the air corridors. The raising of the blockade clearly demonstrated that strong Western solidarity could prevent a tense situation from escalating into a military conflict. Out of this the United States was keen to sign a military alliance with its European allies in defence against aggression from the Soviet Union. On 4 April 1949, twelve Foreign Ministers gathered in Washington to sign the North Atlantic Treaty, thereby establishing the North Atlantic Treaty Organisation (NATO), which incorporated Ernest Bevin's Western Union. In addition to the five signatory states to the Brussels Treaty,

MDAP aircraft supplied to the United Kingdom

WZ966 Boeing RB-29 Superfortress known as the Boeing Washington of 192 Sqn in 1958 over Norfolk

Lockheed Neptune used by Royal Air Force Coastal Command till the introduction of the Avro Shackleton – maintained by Scottish Aviation at Prestwick

Lockheed Neptune of Coastal Command

Grumman Avenger given to the Royal Navy pending the introduction of the Fairey Gannet, many passed on to France and the Netherlands

Douglas Skyraider used by the Royal Navy for airborne early warning. Twelve converted by Scottish Aviation as target tugs for the Swedish company Svensk Flygtjanst AB, four used for electronic warfare, SE-EBF and SE-EBK, SE-EBL, SE-EBM

MDAP Sabres in Royal Air Force service, many passed on to other nations.

the United States, Canada, Denmark, Iceland, Italy, Norway and Portugal also joined NATO. Two events - the explosion of the Soviet Union's first atomic bomb in September 1949 and the start of the Korean War in June 1950 - accelerated the creation of NATO's integrated military structure. At the same time, the United States insisted on the inclusion of Federal German troops. By 1955, after the failure of the European Defence Community (EDC), the Federal Republic of Germany officially joined NATO. This guaranteed that southern Norway would not be attacked, though this did not stop Norway withdrawing its Brigade from Germany in 1953.

The original members of NATO were: Belgium, Canada, Denmark, France, Iceland, Italy, Luxembourg, the Netherlands, Norway, Portugal, the United Kingdom, and the United States. Two other countries, Greece and Turkey, joined NATO in 1952. During the first three years of its existence, NATO evolved its governing political structure and its machinery for military collaboration and set up an integrated command structure headed by the Supreme Allied Commander, Europe (SACEUR). In 1950, the United States General and World War II hero Dwight D. Eisenhower became the first Supreme Commander of Allied Forces in Europe (SACEUR). The following year, the Supreme Headquarters of Allied Powers in Europe (SHAPE) was established near Paris then in 1967, it was moved to its permanent location in Casteau, near Mons, Belgium.

Separate aid programmes were authorized by the United States Congress immediately after World War II and had been brought together and given a common legislative basis in the Mutual Defense Assistance Act of 1949. This law was supplemented by the Mutual Security Act of 1951 and the first of an annual series of similarly titled statutes. It set up a Mutual Security Agency to supervise both military and economic aid to alleviate poverty, defined the responsibilities of the United States Secretary of Defence and other officials in connection with the program, and specified the conditions under which foreign nations were eligible. An administrative mechanism to supervise the Mutual Defense Assistance Program (MDAP) soon took shape. A team of US advisers, usually styled the "Military Assistance Advisory Group" (MAAG), was allocated to each recipient country. Each group was headed by an officer nominated by the Joint Chiefs of Staff. These groups, in cooperation with military authorities of their host nations, supervised the distribution and use of United States aid and prepared recommendations concerning further required assistance. On the basis of these recommendations, the Joint Chiefs of Staff annually prepared force bases to guide the overall programme. The programme listed the numbers of units for which the United States would furnish support, in the form of military material and training assistance.

The Joint Chiefs of Staff also defined general policies to govern the scale of equipment to be supplied to recipient national forces. The JCS recommendations, after approval by the Secretary of Defense, were transmitted to the Service Departments, which prepared the detailed lists of military hardware which were to be supplied each nation and the schedules for the training to be given foreign military nationals under the MDA program. Between 1950 and 1953, 79.3% of the budget was allocated to Europe, 9% to the Near East and Africa, 11.6% to Asia and the Pacific and 0.1% to Latin America. At the beginning of 1953 the Mutual Defense Assistance Program was in its fourth fiscal year. Appropriations had totalled more than $14 billion, of which almost 80 percent had been allocated to Western Europe—a reflection of the importance of NATO to United States policy and strategy.

By August 1952 the MDAP budget was broken down into priorities caused by the situation in Korea. At the suggestion of General Ridgway, the Joint Chiefs of Staff had adopted an amended allocation version in August 1954. It specified that US military equipment would be allocated in the following order:

First priority: United States and allied forces engaged in active combat operations short of general war.

Second priority: United States forces deployed or being maintained in readiness for immediate combat operations on the outbreak of hostilities; forces designated for defence of the continental United States and Canada.

Third priority: United States forces maintained in a state of operational readiness for deployment by D plus 30 days; forces of

other NATO countries, and those of West Germany, scheduled for deployment by D plus 30; forces of the Republic of Korea, Japan, Nationalist China, Pakistan, Yugoslavia; Spanish air defence forces; UN forces deployed in the Far East Command.
Fourth priority: United States forces designated for deployment between D plus 30 days and D plus 6 months; all MDA programs not included in previous priority classes.
Fifth priority: other United States forces.
It was specified, however, that the word priority was to be interpreted to mean an indication of relative importance; it was not to be used in an exclusive and final sense. At a meeting held in Lisbon in February 1952 the North Atlantic Council set its sights on a force of nearly 100 divisions, backed up with appropriate naval and air forces, to be reached over a period of several years. These forces were to be contributed by the twelve original members, since Greece and Turkey had not yet been admitted to NATO.

The Soviet Union organized the German Democratic Republic (East Germany) in its occupation zone and created an army, navy, and air force in the guise of police forces. The Western Powers, in turn, laid plans to rearm the Federal Republic of Germany (Western Germany), which had been created by fusion of the US, British, and French occupation zones. At Lisbon, the North Atlantic Council approved force goals for West Germany of an army of six divisions and an air force of 579 aircraft by the end of 1953, both of which were expected to double in size within a year, plus a navy of 229 vessels by 1954. At the end of 1952 the re-armament goals set at the Lisbon meeting had been substantially achieved insofar as they involved ground and naval forces. But there was a shortage of approximately 10 percent in the number of aircraft, (3,661 as compared with a goal of 4,067) and of 15 percent in the number of divisions, expected to be available (45 divisions instead of 53 2/3) to SACEUR.

A NATO decision on German rearmament had been stalled for more than two years due to conflicts with France which finally agreed to allow German rearmament within NATO in 1954. The long delay in rearmament made it ever more difficult to build the Luftwaffe. Six thousand Luftwaffe pilots had survived World War II but as time passed their skills quickly faded. When the Luftwaffe began recruiting for pilots again in 1955-56 only 160 wartime veterans were available and pronounced fully fit for service as jet pilots. From 1950 to 1955 the West German government maintained a shadow defence ministry and military staff. The German defence authorities made little effort to build up an adequate air staff. In November 1954, on the eve of rearmament, the Luftwaffe Group in the shadow defence ministry had 28 staff sections in its organization table. Of these, six sections, including the very important organization, personnel and communications sections, had no section leader. Despite personnel shortages on the German side German and American officers worked closely together. In 1954, the Germans signed a formal agreement with the U.S. and NATO nations and were committed to rearmament. A cadre German force, to provide the foundation for the Bundeswehr was to be recruited and enter service in 1955. In May 1955, Germany signed the Treaty of Paris and became a member of NATO.

NATO and the German government planned a three-year build-up phase to create an air force of 6 fighter-bomber wings (75 planes per wing), 8 day fighter wings, 2 all-weather interceptor wings (36 planes per wing), 2 reconnaissance wings (54 planes per wing) and two transport wings (48 planes per wing) – for a total of 1,322 aircraft for combat operations. In addition, the training command of the new Luftwaffe would have approximately 300 aircraft, to include Piper light trainers, Harvard IV primary trainers and T–33 jet trainers. The Bundesluftwaffe combat forces would occupy 16 air bases (one wing per base) and four training bases. Most of the equipment would be American (F–84F Thunderjet fighters and F-86 Sabre fighters/reconnaissance C–47 Dakota transports) although the Bundesluftwaffe also planned to obtain 227 British Hawker Hunter fighters to equip their day fighter squadrons; these were not delivered though planned through MDAP. The USAF and RAF drew up plans to turn over air bases to the Germans and deliver aircraft and equipment (radars, plane parts etc.) over a three to four-year period and to assist in their training and support until it was a mature force. Although Germany had been able to field its first fighter squadrons in

1957, the NATO air rearmament plan was several years behind schedule. Instead of the 1300 combat and transport aircraft the GAF was to have three years after the start of rearmament, Germany had only 350 F–84 Thunderjets and F–86 Sabre fighters and 50 transports in 1959. By 1961 the Luftwaffe had 80,000 personnel and 7 of the 16 planned-for wings. In 1963, five years behind the NATO schedule, the Bundesluftwaffe reached the size and force structure that the German government had agreed to in 1954: 92,000 men and 17 operational wings.

The choice of suitable day fighter aircraft was one of the lesser problems facing the new Luftwaffe. The best available type in production at the time was clearly the Canadian-built Canadair Sabre Mk6. 225 brand new examples of Sabre Mk6 were ordered from Canadair in December, 1956(Costing $75 million). These would be complemented by 75 surplus Sabre Mk5s drawn from the Canadian Air Division as the RCAF upgraded its twelve Air Division squadrons to the Sabre Mk6.

The Mark 5s were flown to Renfrew/Prestwick where they were overhauled by Scottish Aviation for the Luftwaffe and then were ferried by Canadian pilots to Waffenschule 10 (WS 10), the Sabre operational conversion unit at Oldenburg in Northern Germany. The Canadian pilots were ferried from Grostenquin by Beech C-45. On one occasion in September 1957 a C-45 with four pilots going to Renfrew to ferry back GAF Sabres went unserviceable and had to return to Grostenquin station. The Sabre Mk6s were shipped to Germany by sea and reassembled at Oberphaffenhoffen by Dornier. The Sabre Mk6 became operational with JG71 on 6 June 1959 and were fully operational by 1963. The last West German Sabres were phased out in 1974.

Under the terms of the Mutual Aid agreement, Canada also undertook to train 360 pilots to jet fighter standards on the Sabre for the New Luftwaffe. For example in 1957 four of the pilots from 422 Squadron were tasked to ferry four of the Scottish Aviation refurbished Sabre 5s from Renfrew to Oldenburg for WS 10. At Renfrew the pilots were allocated four Sabre Mark 5s, newly painted with the iron cross insignia on the glossy fuselage sides readied for the ferry flight. They flew from Renfrew to the RAF air base at Manston in southeast England and from there the Sabres were flown to West Germany. At Oldenburg the RCAF had set up the Canadian Advisory Group, this was the Canadian instructional cadre for the Canadair Sabre Mk6.The main task was to bring the Wing and the German pilots up to NATO operational status by training them as element and section leads and in jet fighter tactics and in air to air weapon operations. 73 Wing was under the command of Oberst (Colonel) Fritz Schroter, assisted by Oberstleutnant (Lieutenant Colonel) "Jolle" Josten, the Wing Operations Officer, both very experienced World War II fighter pilots, the Wing consisted of two Staffels. About 30 percent of the pilots were of officer rank, while the rest were of several non-commissioned ranks, the equivalent of our corporals, sergeants, and warrant officers. It was the non-commissioned pilots that did the majority of the flying, as many of the officers were left managing the numerous details of the administrative side of the air base. On the maintenance side, the Wing was assisted by two Canadian civilian technical representatives from Canadair and Orenda Engines. Later in 1964, the Wing was converted to the fighter bomber role and was renamed to JABO (Fighter Bomber Wing) 42 and was re-equipped with the Fiat G-91 aircraft. In 1971 the aircraft was changed again to the RF4E Phantom and the Wing re-designated JABO 35.

After the 1952 United States presidential elections President Truman was replaced by President Eisenhower. With a review of military budgets there was a prospective Air Force shortfall. That Service was hardest hit by the reductions in the FY 1954 budget—now promised only 794 and 885 aircraft for 1953 and 1954, respectively and foresaw an actual decline to 871 in 1956. Then a US aircraft contribution of 1628 was approved for 1954 but the overall total was reduced to 6728 aircraft. Only in naval forces did the Council anticipate that the earlier 1954 goal would be substantially achieved. On 13 October 1954 it was proposed that Germany have an air arm of 30 (to be increased later to 200) aircraft and an air force with 1,326 aircraft, 600 fighter-bombers, 108 fighter reconnaissance, 450 day-fighters, 72 all-weather fighters, and 96 transports.

The Mutual Defense Assistance Act of 1948, enacted into law on 6 October 1949 authorized the Government of the United States to extend aid, either by outright grant or on a reimbursable basis to certain friendly nations whose security must be maintained in the interests of preserving world peace. As a result each year the United States Air Force budget allocated resources to MDAP. The following were allocated to the United Kingdom:-

1950	Total	1951	Total
B-29	70	B-29	65
		P2V-5	52

(106 Spitfires to Greece, Canada Re-Imbursable F-86 Government Funded Project, {GFP}, Programme)

1952	Total	1953	Total
B-29	84	B-29	83
RB-29	3	RB-29	3
P2V-5	3	P2V-5	6 (8 by June 1953)
(Four AD-4W allocated nation not traced)		F-86E	24 (24 by June 1953)
		(USAF Canadair Sabre F-86E 60 {26 by June})	

1954	(Sept '53)	(June '54)	Total
B-29	56	69	51
P2V-5	51	50	10
F-86	289	409	95
RB-29	3	3	-

1955	(Sept '54)	(June '55)
B-29	9	9
P2V-5	50	51
F-86E	399	370
Hawker Hunter	0	68

1956	(June '55)	(June '56)
B-29	84	-
P2V-5	52	-

F-86E (Ship Sets)	370	(18)
RB-29	60	-
Hawker Hunter	-	233

1957

No deliveries, aircraft temporary diverted to the USAF

1958	Total	(June '58)
B-29	84	84
P2V-5	52	52
F-86E	60	60
F-86E (GFP)	173	69
RB-29	3	3
Hawker Hunter	432	513

NOTE: GFP- Government Funded Project

1960	Total
B-29	84
P2V-5	52
F-86E	60
F-86E (GFP)	10
RB-29	3

Grant Aid: CF-100 53 Hawker Hunter 531

(1960 totals carried forward to 1963)

In addition to aircraft and spares, the United States supplied to the United Kingdom, radio and radar, including spares and aircraft support equipment. The Royal Navy also received early warning aircraft such as the Douglas AD-4W and anti-submarine Grumman Avengers. The Royal Navy's three inch anti-aircraft armament was funded through MDAP. To other NATO nations the United States MDAP aid, supplied small arms and munitions in addition to aircraft and aeronautical supplies. By 1964 the Mutual Defense Aid Program became known as the Mutual Aid Program (MAP).

Appendix

1. Spotters Notebook
2. Number Crunching
3. Evaluation of the Me-262
4. Select Patents Frank Whittle
5. MiG-15
6. Canadair T-33 Silver Star
7. Avro CF-100
8. Obituary
9. North American B-45
10. Published U-2 Flights Gary Powers
11. First Jet Pilot Roster, 616 Meteor Squadron, 21 July 1944

12 Canadair Sabre in the Congo

13 Supplement Structural Diagrams

1.

SPOTTER'S NOTEBOOK
Select Canadair Sabre Aircraft Movements

Mk.2	19274, 19337 19359	Prestwick	Turkish A.F.	Feb.1955
Mk.2	19121, 19126, 19127, 19128	Prestwick	Greece	Feb. 1955
Mk.5	23168, 23151, 23226	Stanstead	R.C.A.F.	June 1955
Mk.2	19108, 19102,	Filton	(Engine Overhaul)	March 1956
Mk.4	19646, 19623, 19706	Speke		June 1957
Mk.4	19457, 19759, 19849	Dunsfold		Sept. 1957
Mk.4	19529, 19725 Speke to Dunsfold			Dec. 1957
Mk.5	BB138, BB139, BB142, BB143, BB151, BB152, BB166 (ex RCAF 23179) BB175	Renfrew		Feb. 1958
Mk.5	BB144	Prestwick		June 1958
Mk.5	BB164, BB147	Renfrew		May 1958
Mk.5	BB140	Renfrew		June 1958
Mk.4	51-9642 (XB768), 51-9771 (XD769), 51-9772 (XD770), 51-9707 (XD706)	Dunsfold		Dec. 1958
Mk.5	23219 College of Aeronautics			1961
Mk.5	23062	Blackbush		1955
Mk.5	23038	Prestwick		1958
Mk.5	23022	Prestwick		1959
Mk.5	23166	Prestwick		1957
Mk.4	19471	Prestwick		1956
Mk.6	23392	Prestwick		1963
Mk.2	19104 Greek Air Force	Ringway		1955
Mk.4	19484	Ringway		1956
Mk.4	19680	Speke		1954
Mk.6	23613, 23625, 23486, 23374, 23554, 23662, 23374, 23572	Langar		1958
Mk.6	23653	Prestwick		1959
Mk.6	23640	Prestwick		1963
Mk.6	23522	Prestwick		1964
Mk.4	19612	Speke		1956
Mk.6	23374	Prestwick		1958

Mk.4	19659, 19702		Speke	1954
Mk.2	19285		Ringway	1955
Mk.6	23653		Prestwick	1958
Mk.6	23553		RNAS Sanderling	1960
Mk.6	23666		Langar	1958
Mk.2	19349	Greek Air Force	Ringway	1954
Mk.2	19151		Odiham	1953
Mk.6	23665		Prestwick	1960
Mk6	23510		RNAS Sanderling	1969
Mk.4	19587		Stanstead	1957
Mk.4	19460		Speke	1954
Mk.2	19450		Ringway	1953
Mk.2	19254		Ringway	1954

Ex-RCAF Sabre Mk5 at Cranfield College of Aeronautics

2.

Number Crunching

(a)

RAF/USAF/MDAP Sabres dumped at the Staravia scrapyard at Church Crookham, logged on 11th Sept 1964

19486, 19522, 19540, 19772, 19771, 19642, 19478, 19728, 19764, 19707, 19590, 19472, 19883, 19734, 19529, 19495, 19517, 19557 19699, 19880. (Spotted Iain C. MacKay)

(b)

North American F-86F-30-NA Sabre
at Scottish Aviation Prestwick,
Initial MDAP contract work, USAF Europe,
Spotted, Iain C. MacKay, June 1956.
All were from the USAF 50th FBW, Hahn AFB, West Germany.

52-4615: (MSN 191-311) 1953: USAF 417th FBS (50th FBW). To MASDC from Scottish Aviation Ltd, Prestwick Airport, UK Apr 21, 1956. Departed Jul 10, 1957. To Pacific Airmotive, Chino, CA, Returned to service with 3525th CCTW, Williams AFB, AZ. 1965: USAF 4520th CCTW. Apr 9, 1965: Crashed north of Nellis AFB, NV due to engine failure
52-4650: (MSN 191-346) 1953: USAF 10th FBS (50th FBW). Transferred to the South Korean AF. Transferred to the Imperial Iranian AF. Transferred to the Ethiopian AF as 278. 1996: Hulk recovered from Ethiopia and slated for restoration
52-4609: (MSN 191-305) USAF 50th FBW. To MASDC from Scottish Aviation Ltd, Prestwick Airport, UK Jul 7, 1956. Departed Jul 3, 1957. To Pacific Airmotive, Chino, CA, Returned to service with 3525th CCTW, Williams AFB, AZ.1961: USAF 4510th CCTW. Aug 3, 1961: Written off at Gila Bend, AZ
52-5370: (MSN 193-99) 50th FBW, Hahn AB, West Germany. To MASDC May 27, 1956. Departed Mar 8, 1957. To Pacific Airmotive Corp, Chino, CA. Returned to service with 3525th Combat Crew Training Wing, Williams AFB, AZ. Back to MASDC Jun 26, 1961. To reclamation Sep 20, 1963
52-4674: (MSN 191-370) USAF 417th FBS (50th FBW). Transferred to Philippine AF.
52-4596 : (MSN 191-292) 1955: USAF 50th FBW. To MASDC from Scottish Aviation Ltd, Prestwick Airport, UK Apr 21, 1956. Departed Jul 19, 1957. To Pacific Airmotive, Chino, CA, Returned to service with 3525th CCTW, Williams AFB, AZ 1961: USAF 4510th CCTW. May 8, 1961: Written off at Luke AFB, AZ

52-4597: (MSN 191-293) USAF 417th FBS (50th FBW). To MASDC from Scottish Aviation Ltd, Prestwick Airport, UK Jul 6, 1956. Departed Jul 16, 1957. To Pacific Airmotive, Chino, CA, Returned to service with 3525th CCTW, Williams AFB, AZ. 1962: USAF 4510th CCTW. Mar 7, 1962: Crashed near Gila Bend, AZ. Pilot was killed
52-4477: (MSN 191-173) USA 357th FIS. To MASDC from Scottish Aviation Ltd, Prestwick, Scotland Mar 26, 1956. Departed Jun 24, 1957. To Pacific Airmotive Corp (PAC), Chino, CA. Returned to service with 4530th Combat Crew Training Wing at Williams AFB. Back to MASDC. Departed May 6, 1960. To North American Corp, Inglewood, CA. To MAP (Argentinan AF_ Aug 18, 1960
52-4479: (MSN 191-175) USAF 357th FIS. 8/1955: To MASDC from Scottish Aviation Ltd, Prestwick, Scotland Mar 26, 1956 Departed Jun 21, 1957. To Pacific Airmotive Corp, Chino, CA. Returned to service with 4530th Combat Crew Training Wing, Williams AFB, AZ. Back to MASDC Jun 12, 1959. Departed May 5, 1960. To North American Corp, Inglewood, CA. 1960: Transferred Aug 18, 1960 to the Argentine AF as C-102. 1st Grupo (IV Brigada Aerea). 8/25/1983: Written off at Mendoza.
52-4480: (MSN 191-176) to MASDC from Scottish Aviation LTD, c, Scotland Mar 26, 1956. Departed Jun 19, 1957. To Pacific Airmotive Corp, Chino, CA. Returned to service with 4530th Combat Crew Training Wing, Williams AFB, AZ. Back to MASDC. Departed May 10, 1960. To North American Corp, Inglewood, CA. To MAP (Argentinian AF) 2 Sep 1960
52-4483: (MSN 191-179) to MASDC from Scottish Aviation Ltd, Prestwick Airport, UK Mar 26, 1956. Departed Jun 25, 1957. To Pacific Airmotive Corp, Chino, CA, Returned to service with 3525th Combat Crew Training Wing, Williams AFB, AZ. Back to MASDC as FC282 Jul 8, 1966. To excess Apr 13, 1972
52-4659: (MSN 191-355) USAF 50th FBW. To MASDC Jul 7, 1956 from Scottish Aviation Ltd, Prestwick Airport, UK. Departed Jul 5, 1957. To Pacific Airmotive, Chino, CA. To reclamation May 22, 1958
52-4676: (MSN 191-372) 1953: USAF 417th FBS (50th FBW). To MASDC from Scottish Aviation Ltd, Prestwick Airport, UK May 27,

1956. Departed Dec 1, 1956. To Pacific Airmotive, Chino, CA, Returned to service with 3525th CCTW, Williams AFB, AZ. Transferred to Philippine AF
52-5363 (MSN 193-92) USAF 48th FBW. USAF 50th FBW. To MASDC Apr 21, 1956 from Scottish Aviation Ltd, Prestwick, Scotland. Departed May 28, 1957. To Pacific Airmotive Corp, Chino, CA Returned to service with 3535th Combat Crew Training Wing, Williams AFB, AZ

3.

Evaluation of the Me-262
(Project NAD-29)
1 February 1947

Roy W. Adams

INTRODUCTION

A considerable amount of research and experimental work has been carried out during the war on jet propulsion in general. This method of propulsion has the advantages of potentially higher speeds, greater rate of climb, and higher ceiling, but is inefficient at moderate speeds and does not, at least in its present state of development, have endurance comparable with that of a conventionally engined aircraft of similar structural characteristics end fuel capacity. At high speeds, the efficiency of a jet-propulsion unit is increased and a greater range will therefore be obtained but the already low endurance is then further reduced. This inherent lack of endurance is the principal disadvantage of the jet-propelled aircraft when used as an interceptor fighter, as obviously, to be successful, the airplane must have sufficient time in the air to intercept formations of enemy aircraft travelling at high speeds and frequently changing course. An attempt to overcome this disadvantage while still maintaining the high, speeds required was undertaken by Germany and the culmination of their efforts resulted in the Messerschmitt Me-262.

This airplane was the first German jet-propelled aircraft to go into production and was used in operations on a small scale beginning in the summer of I944 until the termination of the European war.

DESCRIPTION

General The ME-262 is a twin-jet, single-place, low-wing monoplane. It can be used as a fighter, a fighter bomber, or a reconnaissance-type airplane.

Fuselage

The fuselage is slim and pointed with a flat belly, and for a single-place aircraft is exceptionally roomy; the large stowage capacity has been dictated by the heavy fuel requirements of the two jet-propulsion units. It is of semi-monococque construction and steel is employed in the fabrication of the pointed nose portion including the thin outer skin. The rear portion of the fuselage is made from duralumin. The entire fuselage is of substantially triangular cross section, approaching a circular section at the nose. The tail is very slim, the maximum width at a point 18 in. forward of the horizontal stabiliser leading edge being only 2 ft. 1 in

Wing

The thin single-spar wing has a span of 41 ft, with the leading edge swept back approximately 12 degrees. The trailing edge, outboard of the power units, is also slightly swept back; inboard of the power units, the trailing edge is swept forward.

Automatic slots extend along the entire leading edge of the wing, both inboard and outboard of the power units. They are of steel construction throughout and mounted on steel brackets. Flaps of modified Handley-Page type are incorporated inboard and outboard of the power units.

Tail Unit

For ease of construction, the fin is made in two halves and belted together. The narrow-chord rudder has an over-all height of 6 ft. 11 in. It extends from the top of the fin to the bottom of the fuselage. The 12 ft. 4in.-span tail plane is set fairly high and has pronounced sweepback on the leading edge.

Cockpit

The cockpit is enclosed in a streamlined canopy that is hinged on one side and held in place by a lever-operated bolt on the other. In emergency the entire cover can be jettisoned mechanically.

Landing Gear

The landing gear is of the tricycle type, the main wheels retracting inward into the bottom of the fuselage immediately behind the main spar. The nose wheel retracts in a vertical position into the space beneath the armament Installation in the nose. Hydraulic retraction is employed for the nose wheel as well as for the main wheels, All three wheels are equipped with hydraulic brakes, the nose-wheel brake being hand-operated and the main-wheel brakes foot- operated.

Fuel Capacity

There is a fuel tank forward of the cockpit with a capacity of 196 gal, and one behind the cockpit having the same capacity. Beneath the pilot there is a reserve tank of approximately 50gal. Oil capacity is two gallons. Fuel is pumped by electric immersion pumps. All fuel tanks are self-sealing.

Armament

The standard armament of the ME-262 was four MK 108/30mm cannon firing simultaneously and converging at 500 yards. These guns are grouped in the nose of the fuselage and as their over-all length is only 3ft 6 in, a very compact installation was achieved with no external projections. For flight testing, the cannon were removed and the ports left open.

There two external bomb racks faired into the underside of the fuselage, the forward end of the racks located at a point approximately in line with the loading edge of the power units. They have a maximum carrying capacity of 500 lb each.

The pilot's armour protection consists of a 16 mm bulkhead in front and rear of the cockpit. Also for frontal protection there is a wind shield, 3-1/2 in. in thickness.

Communication and Radio Equipment

The radio used in the Me-262 conformed to the usual type of equipment, for Gorman aircraft fulfilling similar functions. A few two-place trainer versions were modified with radar and adapted as experimental night fighters.

Factual Data

Dimensions

Span	41ft.
Length	34ft 9 in
Height	11ft 4 in
Chord of wing at root	8 ft. 4 in
Chord of wing at tip	2 ft. 10 in

Weights

Basic weight	8514 lb
Maximum take-off	15620 lb

Power Plants

The Me-262 is powered by two Jumo 004 turbojet propulsion units. This unit has a sea level (15°C) static thrust at 8700 rpm of 1980 lb. It is of the axial-flow type with an eight-stage compressor at the leading end. The weight of each unit is approximately 1500 lb.

The units are located low beneath the wing so that there is no interruption of the main spar.

Performance

Normal take-off	111 – 124 mph
Normal cruising	465 mph
Normal stall	112 – 125 mph

Final approach 155 mph

Maximum flight duration at low altitudes is 45 to 50 min at high altitudes it ranges from 60 to 90 min.

Pressure Altitude Feet	Still Air Temperature C	rpm	Tail Pipe Temperature °C	True Air Speed	Weight 13,100lb ft./min
4,000	11	8400	595	524	XXXXXX
20,200	-12	8200	600	516	
20,200	-12	8650	735	568	1500
35,300	-45	8220	610	509	
35,300	-45	8650	700	546	

Pilot's Observations

<u>Purpose</u>
To forward pilot's comments on handling characteristics of Me-262.

<u>Factual Data</u>

Introduction

The Me-262 is a German jet fighter bomber powered by two Jumo 004 axial-flow jet engines rated at 1980lb thrust (each) at 8700 rpm.

Two airplanes, Nos. T-2-7111 and T-2-4012 were used in this test programme. General maintenance was very difficult on both airplanes. Number T-2-711 was flown, 12 flights for a total of 10 hr and 40 min, and No, T-2-14012 was flown eight times for a total of I4 hr and 40 min. Four engine changes were necessary on No. T-2-4012 and five on No. T-2-7111. Power failure in flight resulted in abandonment of the airplane and complete, destruction of No. T-2-7111. Tests were discontinued on No. T-2-14012 after two single-engine landings resulting from engine failure in flight, because the value of further flights was not believed to be worth the risk and trouble of maintaining the airplane.

2. Weight and Center of Gravity Information

Flights were made with a take-off gross weight of 13500 lb at 22.3% M.A.C. (full main tanks only, 474 gal).

3. Flight Characteristics

a. Cockpit layout

The cockpit is somewhat cramped and it is difficult to turn in the seat to obtain vision to the rear. The location of the instruments and controls is satisfactory except that the throttles and starting controls are located too far aft for easy manipulation.

b. Brakes and ground handling

The brakes were very poor, which made ground handling difficult.

c. Take-off and initial climb

All take-offs were running take-offs, due to the poor brakes. The ground roll was slightly longer than ordinarily required. The nose wheel could be lifted off at about 100 mph IAS, and the take-off was made at about 120 mph in a nose-high attitude.

d. Climb

No unusual characteristics were noted in the climbs.

e. Handling and control at various speeds

The handling characteristics were poor at all speeds above 350 mph. The airplane would not make a very satisfactory gun platform because of a tendency to hunt directionally, which resulted in snaking at speeds above 400 mph IAS.

f. Trim and stability

Changes in trim due to operation of the landing gear and flaps ware excessive. The relatively large trim changes with changes in power were also objectionable. Longitudinal trim was accomplished by changing the angle of incidence of the stabilizer, which was somewhat slower in operation than the usual trim tab.

No tests were made to check the asymmetric power handling characteristics but several engine failures resulted in single-engine landings being made without difficulty. The minimum control speed for operation on one engine appeared to be 160 mph and above 180 mph; the single-engine performance was quite good.

g. Stalls and stall warning

Several straight-ahead power stalls were made.

The stalls were clean and straight with no tendency to drop a wing. A stall warning, consisting of buffeting of the airplane and controls, occurred at a speed approximately 5 mph above the stall. Indicated stalling speed in the clean configuration was 130 mph, and in the landing configuration approximately 120 mph.

h. Noise and vibration

The noise level was higher than that of a P-80, although still not objectionable. Wind noise around the canopy contributed greatly to the noise level

i. Vision

Vision was rather poor due to the design of the canopy. Many braces obstructed the line of vision and distortion was apparent when locking upward. Vision to the rear was poor because of the difficulty of turning in the neat to look aft.

Approach and landing

Preparations for landing required some care because of the large trim changes encountered when lowering the flaps and landing gear. Approach was normal at 150 mph IAS, with good forward visibility. The landing occurred at approximately 120 mph in a very nose-high attitude (because of the slots). The resulting ground roll was straight with no tendency to swing. The ground roll was long because of the poor brakes.

4. General Functioning

Power plant and associated equipment

a. Except for excessive trouble which developed with the engines, maintenance by a trained crew with all necessary spares readily available might be considered comparable to that required on the P-80A. However the engines appeared most unreliable and required frequent replacements. The brakes never functioned satisfactorily, as compared to those installed on our own aircraft, and required excessive maintenance.

b. Hydraulic, pneumatic and electrical systems

No trouble with the operation of the hydraulic or electrical systems was experienced, With the lift unit inoperative, there is no hydraulic pressure and the landing gear and flaps must be lowered by use of a pneumatic emergency system.

This unit was used successfully although considerable time was required to bleed the hydraulic lines before another flight could be made. The jettisonable canopy also worked perfectly, in the instance in which it was used, although it would have been better if the release were located on the floor instead of at shoulder level, so that the pilot could lower his head when releasing the canopy. When leaving the plane the pilot jumped, at a speed of approximately 150 mph, from the right side – apparently just clearing the lower surface of the stabiliser.

CONCLUSIONS

Despite a difference in gross weight of nearly 2000 lb, the Me-262 No, T-2-711 was superior to the average P-80A in acceleration and speed, and approximately the same in climb performance. The handling characteristics of the Me-262 airplanes tested were very poor. However, it is believed that, with the exception of the directional hunting or yawing, they would have been considerably improved if the aileron and elevator servo tab had been connected. The Me-262 apparently has a higher critical Mach number from a drag standpoint than any current AAF fighters.

APPENDIX

Reference should be made to the following documents:-

"Me-262 Pilot Handbook" Report No. F30 -1111- ND

"Me-262 Maintenance Handbook" Report No. TK-1131- N6

Analysis Div., AMC, Wright-Patterson Air Force Base, 0.
EVALUATION OF THE ME-262, by Roy W. Adams.
Technical Report. Feb 47. 7p. incl. illus. Rept. No.F-TR-1133-ND. Project no. NAD-29.
UNCLASSIFIED
DIVISION: Aircraft & Flight Equipment (1)
SECTION: Aircraft Design (2)
DISTRIBUTION: Copies obtainable from ASTIA-DSC.

4.

Select Patents
Frank Whittle
Date Range 1931 – 1952

1. GB347206 (A) Improvements relating to the propulsion of aircraft and other vehicles.
2. GB347766 (A) Improvements relating to centrifugal compressors and pumps
3. GB375104 (A) Improvements relating to the supercharging of aircraft internal combustion engines (Joint Patent)
4. GB456976 (A) Improvements relating to centrifugal compressors
5. CH188758 (A) Kraftanlage zum Antrieb von Flugzeugen
6. FR807926 (A) Perfectionnements aux □ystems de propulsion des aéronefs
7. GB461887 (A) Improvements relating to internal combustion turbines.
8. GB471368 (A) Improvements relating to the propulsion of aircraft.
9. FR818703 (A) Perfectionnements apportés aux dispositifs pour la propulsion d'aéronefs
10. CH195823 (A) Einrichtung zum Antrieb von Flugzeugen durch Reaktionswirkung.
11. US2113102 (A) (A) Electrical torque transmission
12. US2168726 (A) Propulsion of aircraft and gas turbines

13. GB511278 (A) Improvements relating to turbines and compressors
14. GB512064 (A) Improvements relating to the propulsion of aircraft
15. US2378372 (A) Turbine and compressor
16. GB577132 (A) Improvements relating to the control of fluid-flow in conduits connected in parallel
17. GB577971 (A) Improvements relating to aircraft propulsion systems and power units.
18. GB582978 (A) Improvements in gas turbines.
19. GB583022 (A) Improvements relating to internal combustion turbines and the like.
20. GB583111 (A) Improvements relating to apparatus and systems for the production of a flow of energised gas, for example for the propulsion of aircraft.
21. GB588084 (A) Combustion engine with ammonia injection.
22. GB593403 (A) Power plant for the propulsion of aircraft.
23. GB629143 (A) Improvements in or relating to aircraft power unit installations
24. GB641062 (A) Improvements in or relating to the manufacture of metals
25. US2601194 (A) Multiunit gas turbine power plant for aircraft propulsion (Applicant POWER JETS RES & DEV LTD)
26. GB677835 (A) Improvements relating to rotary compressors (Applicant POWER JETS RES & DEV LTD)

5.

USAF MiG 15

A team of five top USAF test pilots evaluated the Red interceptor against the North American F-86 Sabre in a series of flight tests which covered the range from round-the-field flights to simulated combat. Results of the tests still are being studied; but here are the first pilot reports:

- The Sabre was preferred over the MiG as a combat weapon.
- Lack of automaticity on the MiG kept the pilot busy and diverted his attention from alert flying.
- The MiG is slower in flat-out level flight.
- Stall warning is insufficient in the MiG.
- The MiG cockpit is uncomfortable and on the small side.
- Heating and ventilating systems are poor.

MiG History - This particular fighter had been built in 1951 and was the same model used in combat in Korea.

Ro Kum Snk, senior lieutenant, North Korean air force, flew the Russian-built craft to Kimpo Air Base on 21 September 1953; the following day the swept- wing interceptor was on its way to Kadena Air Force Base, Okinawa. Testing over the course of 11 days revealed that overall the aircraft was a reasonably good fighting machine, but lacked the sophistication of American aircraft like the F-86. During testing it was discovered that the fastest the MiG could fly was 0.98 Mach before becoming uncontrollable, a situation that nearly caused the aircraft to crash. While the MiG-15 enjoyed a better climb rate and a higher operational ceiling than the F-86, it suffered from problems with oscillation, poor pressurization, un-expected pitch-up at high speeds, unrecoverable spins, no warning of impending stalls and a particularly dangerous emergency fuel pump that could cause the aircraft to explode if improperly activated. Despite the MiG's shortcomings, evaluators determined that the MiG-15 and F-86 were nearly equal in performance. Pilot experience and training proved to be the most important determining factor between the two aircraft.

United States Air Force MiG-15

6.

Canadair T-33 Silver Star

A variant of Lockheed's F-80 "Shooting Star" the T33A was the most widely used tandem two-seat advanced trainer in the world. The prototype T-33 flew for the first time on 22 March 1948.The parent company, Lockheed, had manufactured a total of 5,691 T-33A and T-33B trainers when the last was delivered in August

1959. The aircraft was supplied to the air arms of some twenty-five countries and manufactured 655 examples in Canada by Canadair as the CL-30 Silver Star T-33AN. The Silver Star Mks.2 and 3 differed from the U.S. manufactured T-33A in being powered by a Rolls-Royce Nene 10 turbojet. Canadair was given a contract in September 1951 to manufacture the T-33 in Canada with the first flight being in December 1952. T-33's were used as trainers with the RCAF in the 1950's and 60's. Canada donated T-33s to Bolivia, France, Greece, Portugal and Turkey under the Mutual Aid Program.
Engine: 5100 lb (2315 kg) thrust Rolls-Royce Nene 10 turbojet Maximum speed: Mach .787, 600 mph (960 km/h) Empty weight: 8440 lb (3832 kg) Loaded weight: 18400 lb (8217 kg) Span: 37 ft 7 in (11.48 m) without tip tanks Length: 37 ft 9 in (11.49 m) Height: 11 ft 8 in (3.6 m) Wing area: 238 sq ft (22.11 sq m)

7.

AVRO CF-IOO MR. 4B (1961)

By 1961 served with four R.C.A.F. squadrons based in Europe, the CF-I00 mk. 4B was to be withdrawn from service in 1962. The initial production CF-I00 Mk. 4A had 6,500 Ib.s.t. Orenda 9 turbojets and was the first model fitted with APG-40 radar. Production was completed in 1956 with the 510 CF-I00 Mk. 4. Nationality: Canadian. Type : Two-seat All-weather Fighter. Power Plants: Two 7,275 Ib.s.t. Orenda II turbojets. Armament : Eight 0·5-in. guns and (wingtip pods) 104 2·75-in. rockets. Weights: Empty, 24,408 lb.; normal loaded, 35,500 lb. Performance: Max. speed, 650 m.p.h. at 10,000 ft. (Mach 0 ·89); initial climb, 8,000 ft . / min.; ceiling, 50,000 ft.; combat radius (standard tankage) , 650mls. Dimensions : Span, 53 ft. 7 in.; length, 54 ft. 2 in.; height, 14 ft. 6 in.; wing area, 540 sq. ft.

AVRO CF-IOO Mk. 5 (1961)

Equipping nine home-based R.C.A.F. squadrons and two Belgian squadrons, the CF-I00 Mk. 5 is lighter than its predecessor and has increased wing span to improve high altitude performance. Fifty-three were supplied to Belgium through MDAP but most R.C.A.F. fighters of this type were Mk. 4Bs brought up to the later standards.
Nationality: Canadian. Type: Two-seat All-weather Fighter. Power Plants: Two 7,272 Ib.st Orenda II turbojets. Armament: One hundred and four 2·75 - in. rockets in wingtip pods. Weights: Empty, 23,100 lb.; normal loaded, 33,600 lb.; max., 36,000 lb. Performance: Max. speed, 650 m.p.h. at 10,000 ft. (Mach 0·89); initial climb, 8,500 ft. / min.; ceiling, 54,000 ft; range (max. fuel), 2,000 + mls. Dimensions: Span, 60 ft. 10 in; length, 54 ft. 2 in.; height, 14 ft. 6 in.; wing area, 591 sq. ft.

8.

OBITUARY

Anthony (Tony) Gunter-Smith (15 Jan 1924 - 1 Dec 2014)
In loving memory of the late Anthony (Tony) Gunther-Smith
who sadly passed away on 1st December 2014
GUNTER-SMITH Anthony Benjamin (Tony) Died peacefully on
1st December 2014 aged 90 years.
Loving Husband of Mary and Widower of the late Brenda.
Father, Stepfather, Grandfather, Uncle and
Brother to a loving family. Ace Pilot and Flying Instructor,
R.A.F, R.C.A.F and Oxford Aviation Kidlington.
Requiem Mass to be held at the Church of
The Good Shepherd Woodthorpe on Thursday 11th December at
2.00pm followed by Cremation at Wilford Hill.

9.

NORTH AMERICAN NA-153
B-45A

Few new features separated the B-45C from the B-45A. The B-45C was equipped for air refuelling and fitted from the start with wing tip tanks. The air refuelling arrangement consisted of a boom receptacle located on the top of the fuselage, about midway, and of a single-point refuelling receptacle on the left side aft of the bomb bays. The B-45C was often flown with 1200 gallon wing tip tanks; when full, each fuel tank weighed some 7500 pounds. The RB-45C also looked like the B-45A, except for a small bump on the tip of the aircraft's nose, where a forward oblique camera was enclosed. The RB-45C in addition featured a water injection system for increased take-off thrust that utilized two 214-gallon droppable tanks suspended beneath the nacelles by means of assisted take-off suspension hooks. If preferable, the RB-45C could make use of 2 droppable assisted take-off rockets located on the underside of the nacelles. The RB-45C included sweeping internal changes. Five stations were provided and these stations could mount ten different types of cameras. However, the crew could not move to the aft camera compartment when the RB-45C was flying; in-flight access to the bomb bays was possible, but only if the bomb bays were empty, the bomb-bay doors were closed and the pressurized compartments were depressurized. The B-45 Tornado was

NACELLE AFT LOWER DOOR

8027

81
BE-0

capable of carrying the 12000lb Tallboy and the 22000lb Grand Slam. A special modification to the bomb bay made the Tornado nuclear capable, this was the Backbreaker modification.

The B/RB-45s were not officially committed to the Korean War but three TAC B/RB-45s reached the Far East in the autumn of 1950. The small detachment, TAC personnel and civilian technical representatives included, departed for Japan in late September for the express purpose of measuring the reconnaissance capability of a configuration which had not yet been given the most telling of all tests, that of actual combat. Arrival of the RB-45s was well timed, as the RB-29s of the 91st Strategic Reconnaissance Squadron were no longer able to perform with impunity the special missions ordered by Far East Air Forces or the targeting and bomb-damage assessment photography desired by its Bomber Command. Eager to maintain its reconnaissance capability in the face of the Soviet-built MiG jets, Bomber Command on 31 January 1951 took control of the RB-45 detachment and attached it to the 91st Squadron. The RB-45 crews managed to outrun and outmanoeuvre the MiGs for several months. Yet, on 9 April 1951, one of the too few RB-45s barely escaped a numerically far superior enemy. In the ensuing months, while the RB-29s were no longer allowed to enter north-western Korea, even with escort, the RB-45s could still go into the MiG-infested area if they had jet fighter escort. However, after another harrowing experience on 9 November 1951, the RB-45s also were restricted by Far East Air Forces from entering the sensitive areas of north-western Korea in daylight. In January 1952, the 91st Squadron was directed to convert to night operations but testing soon showed that the squadron's RB-45s could not be used for night photography because the aircraft buffeted too badly when its forward bomb bay was opened to drop flash bombs. In any case deficiencies confirmed soon after the RB-45s had reached Japan, 43 plus the many commitments levied on the 33 aircraft, had foretold the eventual end of the RB-45's Korean experience.

North American began working on the B-45C design on 22 September 1947 two months after the AAF had endorsed the aircraft's production. Design of the RB-45C was initiated in January 1949 when the entire B-45 programme was significantly reduced. The additional production of two B-45C's and 49 RB-45Cs (Manufacturer's Model NA-162), under contract since 17 June 1948, was cancelled either in late 1948 or early 1949. Although money was a factor, the Air Force's belief that a reconnaissance version of the B-47 would be superior to the best RB-45 confirmed the cancellation. Production of the B-45C was completed on 13 April 1950, that of the RB-45C in October 1951, when the last aircraft were delivered. The B/RB-45C phase-out followed the B-45A pattern. In mid-1959, only one RB-45C remained in the United States Air Force inventory.

The Air Force started taking delivery of the B-45C in May 1949 and of the RB-45C in June 1950. Even though a few of the aircraft were deployed overseas in late 1950, no B/RB-45C unit reached an initial operational capability (IOC) before 1951. The RB-45Cs were earmarked for SAC, primarily. The command's inventory reached a peak of 38 aircraft in 1951, some B-45s being included in this total. However, no B/RB-45 aircraft remained on the SAC rolls in 1953. Yet, this did not spell the RB-45's end.

On 29 July 1952 an SAC RB-45C and a Boeing KB-29B tanker of the 91st Strategic Reconnaissance Wing flying RB-45C (Serial Number 48-042), a SAC aircraft commanded by Maj. Louis H. Carrington, made the first nonstop, trans-Pacific flight from Elmendorf AFB, Alaska, to Yokota AB, Japan. This flight, made possible by two KB-29 inflight refuelling, earned Major Carrington and his 2-man crew the Mackay Trophy for 1952.

TECHNICAL AND BASIC MISSION PERFORMANCE DATA
B/RB-45C AIRCRAFT

Manufacturer (Airframe): North American Aviation, Inc., Inglewood, Calif.

Manufacturer (Engines): The General Electric Co. Schenectady, N.Y.

Nomenclature: Light Tactical Bomber and Day or Night Photo-reconnaissance Aircraft. Popular Name: Tornado

Powerplant

No. & Model (2)J47-GE-7 or -13 and (2)J47-GE- 9 or -15

Manufacturer........General Electric

Engine Spec No .....E-581 & E-582

Type .... Axial

Length............. 144"

Diameter ....39"

Weight (dry) ... . .2525 lb

RATO

No. & Model (2) XLR13-AJ-l

Manufacturer . . . . Aerojet

Spec No S60ALD- 4000

Weight (dry) . .. 800 lb ea

General characteristics: Crew: 4 (Pilot, Co-Pilot, Bombardier-Navigator and Tail Gunner)

Length: 75 ft 4 in Wingspan: 89 ft 0 in Height: 25 ft 2 in Wing area: 1175 sq ft Aerofoil: root: NACA 66–215; tip: NACA 66–212

Empty weight: 45694 lb Gross weight: 81418 lb

Max take-off weight: 91775 lb

Performance: Maximum speed: 566 mph Cruise speed: 365 mph Range: 1,192 miles Ferry range: 2,170 mi Service ceiling: 46,000 ft Rate of climb: 5,200 ft/min Wing loading: 69.3 lb/sq ft Thrust/weight: 0.26

10.

Published U-2 Flights by Francis G. Powers

Contract commenced

14 May 1956

Flying with Detachment "B"

4 August 1957 China, TiHwa. Mongolia (abort before Irkutsk)

27 September 1956 Turkey, Greece, Sicily, Crete Rhodes, Cyprus

30 October 1956 Lebanon, Israel, Jordan, Sinai

7 November 1956 Syria, Iraq, Persian Gulf Saudi Arabia

20 January 1957 Syria, Turkish Border

20 June 1957 Syria

4 August 1957 China, Ti Hwa, Mongolia

12 October 1957 Syria

6 November 1957 Black Sea

18 January 1958 Black Sea

7 May 1958 Iran Soviet Border
21 June 1958 Egypt, Israel, Jordan, Lebanon
29 June 1958 Egypt, Israel, Lebanon
15 July 1958 Syria, Iraq, Jordan
22 July 1958 Syria, Iraq
25 July 1958 Iran, Iraq, Syria
21 August 1958 Saudi Arabia, Yemen, Aden
29 August 1958 Soviet/Iranian Border
3 April 1959 Egypt, Syria
8 April 1959 Mediterranean
10 April 1959 Mediterranean
11 April 1959 Syria, Iraq, Israel
28 July 1959 Egypt, Syria, Saudi Arabia
21 August 1959 Iran, Afghanistan Borders
12 September 1959 Iran, Afghanistan Border
18 October 1959 Iran, Afghanistan Borders
23 October 1959 ME (Aborted)
23 February 1960 Iran, Iraq, Israel, Syria
1 May 1960 Kyshtym, Sverdlovsk, Kola Peninsula (LOST)

Contract Termination
6 October 1962

11.

First Jet Pilot Roster 616 Meteor Squadron 21 July 1944

Meteor 1 D.	F/O MACKENZIE	RED 1.	1430	1515	ANTI-DIVER PATROL
A.	S/L WATTS	3.	1500	1525	DITTO
HJW.	W/C WILSON	YELLOW 1	1600	1655	DITTO
D.	F/O RODGERS	2	1640	1725	DITTO
G.	W/C MCDOWALL	MILLER 1	1530	1625	DITTO
C.	F/O CLARE	2	1725	1805	DITTO
A.	W/O WILKES	HUGO 32	1800	1830	DITTO
D.	W/C MCDOWALL	HUGO 12	1825	1910	DITTO

Anti-diver patrols were against the V-1 flying bomb

THE GLOSTER METEOR JET FIGHTER

Somewhat belatedly the Ministry of Aircraft Production has released some particulars of this Rolls-Royce jet-engined machine. The official description will be found on p. 32.

These special *Flight* drawings show it to be of the variety once described by Dr. Roxbee Cox as "ordinary aircraft with invisible airscrews."

Main dimensions are: span 43ft., length 41ft. wing area 374 sq. ft.

12

Canadair Sabre in the Congo

By early December 1962, requests had gone out by the United Nations to, among others, Greece, Italy and Pakistan to provide Sabres as fighter cover during the Congo confrontation, but these only resulted in an Italian promise to provide four Sabres without crews. By the middle December, the plan was to have four Italian Sabres with Ethiopian pilots and six Sabres with crews from the Philippines and soon afterwards some promises of Iranian participation were received. The use of F-84s was also considered, possibly flown by Turks but again this remained at the discussion stage, as was the use of Norwegian F-86s and pilots. On 15 December 1962, the Philippine Air Force was tasked by its government to set up a new fighter squadron for participation as PAFCON (Philippine Air Force Contingent) in the Congo. The new squadron was called the 9th Tactical Fighter Squadron (9th TFS) and named "Limbas" after a Philippine bird of prey. Captain Luis J. Diano was given command of PAFCON and hand-picked nine additional pilots for the contingent. It was agreed that the Filipinos would use only the Italian Sabres, since there was no longer any hope of Ethiopia providing pilots again to fly those. The Italians had delivered the promised four Sabres, plus a spare aircraft, i.e. five in all. These were Canadair Sabre Mk.4s modified with "6-3" wings, also known as F-86E(M)s. The aircraft left Italy on 8 January 1963. The Sabres had originally been paid for by the US funds under MDAP and were officially owned by the USA. They now reverted back to US control and were formally transferred to the United Nations under MDAP, being handed over at N'Djili airport Congo on 30 January 1963 by pilots of the Italian 4a Aerobrigata, two Italian C-119s brought spare parts. On 12 February the Sabres were taken over by the newly arrived Filipinos and shortly thereafter flown to Kamina, where the 9th TFS was known as UN Fighter Squadron 9, 9th Philippine Fighter Squadron or just 9 Squadron. The only Sabre deployment known elsewhere came on 2 April, when a pair of 9 Squadron aircraft were temporarily based at

Elisabethville to "show the flag" over southern Katanga .Each squadron had its own sector near Kamina for training but at times there was some dog-fighting between members of different squadrons. The Filipinos in particular would train together with the Swedes while the Iranians tended to keep to themselves. The Filipinos were unhappy with their Sabre Mk.4s. These were considered heavier and clumsier than the later F-86F with slatted wings they were used to and also inferior to the Swedish SAAB J 29.

The new arrangement, agreed in March and put into effect in late April, was that 9 Squadron and 103 Squadron each operated two of the Canadair Sabres, with the fifth aircraft used as a common spare. Each Sabre "squadron" was thus reduced to just two aircraft but in reality not even this number could be maintained. The general serviceability of the Canadair Sabres was poor and on 10 April, for example, only a single aircraft was listed as serviceable. Already at this date, two of the Sabres had only five and six hours left to their next major inspection. The whole set-up was quickly proving impractical, therefore in May 1963 the UN asked Sweden to take sole responsibility for the ONUC fighter operations. In late May preparations began to disband the remaining parts of both the Philippine and the Iranian squadrons. On 8 June 1963 the two Sabres used by 103 Squadron were ferried over to N'Djili airport in Leopoldville and this was most likely the last flight of any of the UN Sabres. The other three Sabres had been ferried over a few days earlier and they had to be cannibalized for parts to make the last two aircraft airworthy. Both Sabre squadrons formally disbanded soon afterwards and the last Filipinos left the Congo on 23 June 1963.Since the five Canadair Sabres stored at N'Djili belonged to the United Nations rather than to any specific nation, there was some discussion what to do with them. One suggestion was to use them to train Congolese pilots but this was frankly not realistic and was not adopted. On 8 August 1963, at which time the ONUC fighter force was being finally disbanded, ONUC requested permission from New York to dispose of the Sabres, which were considered a “liability". UN headquarters gave the go-ahead to scrap the aircraft on 1 December and once the guns and some instruments had been removed the Sabres were partly dismantled at N'Djili in the spring of 1964 and some key components smashed with sledgehammers. Four of the Sabres were ultimately scrapped but one was salvaged and taken to the Lovanium University in Leopoldville (now Kinshasa).

UN Fighter Squadron 9 Equipment

Serial	Type	C/N	Previous I/D	From	To	Remarks
19483	F-86E(M)	383	XB576	30 Jan 1963	Jun 1963	- Rendered non-flyable at Leopoldville spring 1964. Later scrapped.
19542	F-86E(M)	442	XB639	30 Jan 1963	Jun 1963	- Rendered non-flyable at Leopoldville spring 1964. Preserved at Lovanium University, Kinshasa.
19695	F-86E(M)	595	XB857	30 Jan 1963	Jun 1963	- Rendered non-flyable at Leopoldville spring 1964. Later scrapped.
19709	F-86E(M)	609	XD708	30 Jan 1963	Jun 1963	-Rendered non-flyable at Leopoldville spring 1964.ex-52-10179 Later scrapped.
19784	F-86E(M)	684	XB896	30 Jan 1963	Jun 1963	- Rendered non-flyable at Leopoldville spring 1964. Later scrapped.

13

Supplement Structural Diagrams

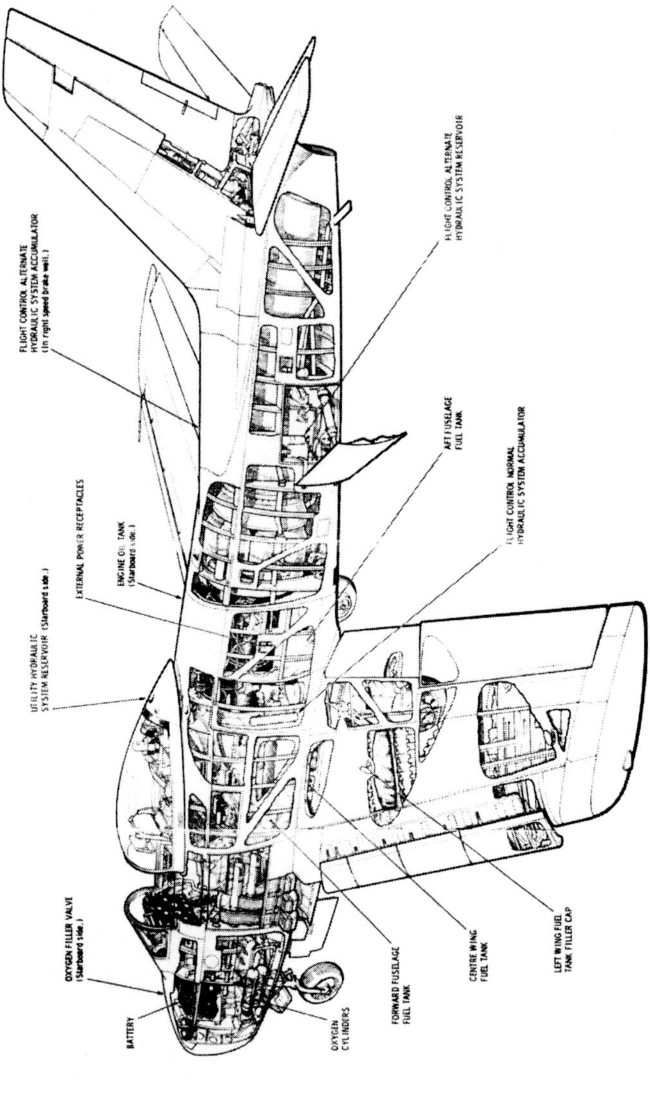

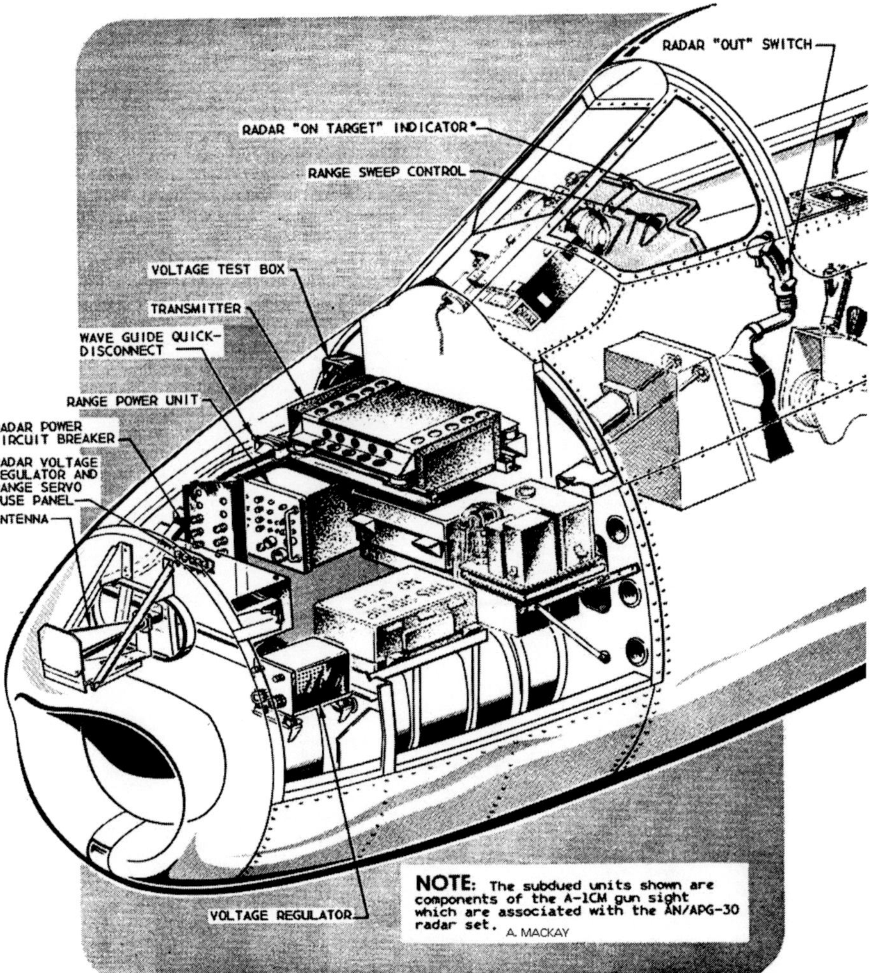

*On Airplanes F-86F-15 and subsequent, the "ON TARGET" indicator is installed in the A-4 sight head.

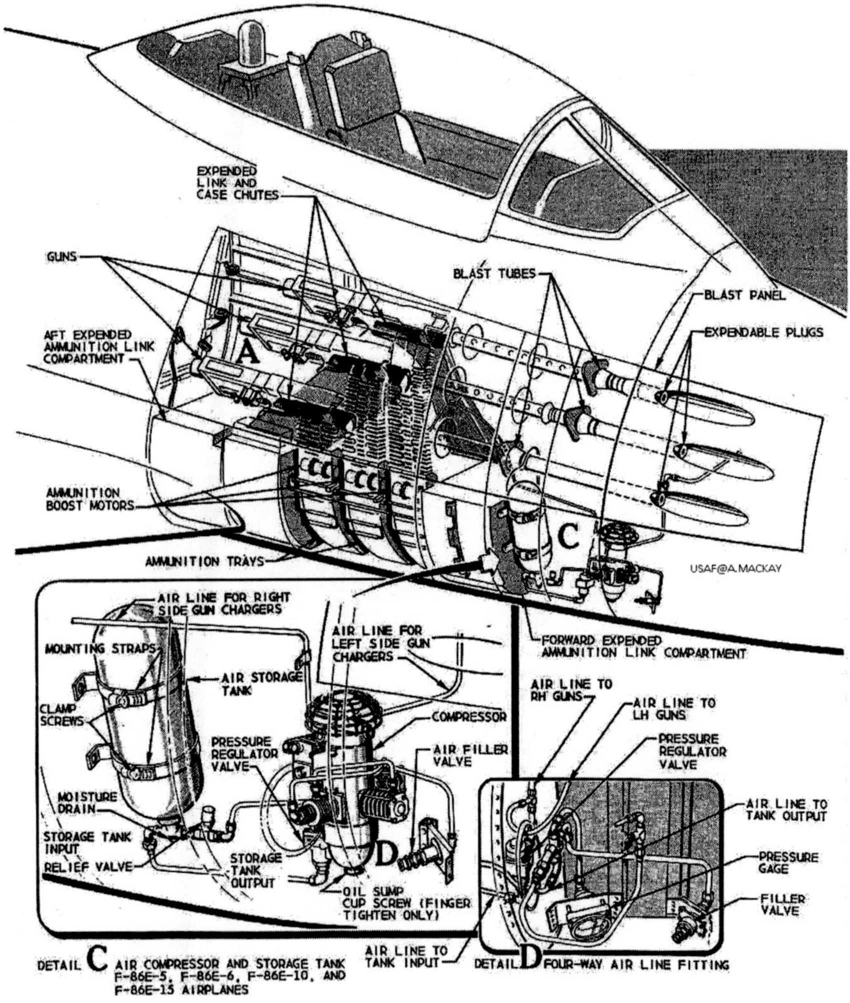
EXPENDED LINK AND CASE CHUTES
GUNS
BLAST TUBES
BLAST PANEL
EXPENDABLE PLUGS
AFT EXPENDED AMMUNITION LINK COMPARTMENT
A
AMMUNITION BOOST MOTORS
C
AMMUNITION TRAYS
USAF@A.MACKAY
AIR LINE FOR RIGHT SIDE GUN CHARGERS
AIR LINE FOR LEFT SIDE GUN CHARGERS
FORWARD EXPENDED AMMUNITION LINK COMPARTMENT
MOUNTING STRAPS
AIR STORAGE TANK
CLAMP SCREWS
COMPRESSOR
PRESSURE REGULATOR VALVE
AIR FILLER VALVE
MOISTURE DRAIN
STORAGE TANK INPUT
RELIEF VALVE
STORAGE TANK OUTPUT
D
OIL SUMP CUP SCREW (FINGER TIGHTEN ONLY)
AIR LINE TO RH GUNS
AIR LINE TO LH GUNS
PRESSURE REGULATOR VALVE
AIR LINE TO TANK OUTPUT
PRESSURE GAGE
FILLER VALVE
AIR LINE TO TANK INPUT
DETAIL C AIR COMPRESSOR AND STORAGE TANK F-86E-5, F-86E-6, F-86E-10, AND F-86E-15 AIRPLANES
DETAIL D FOUR-WAY AIR LINE FITTING

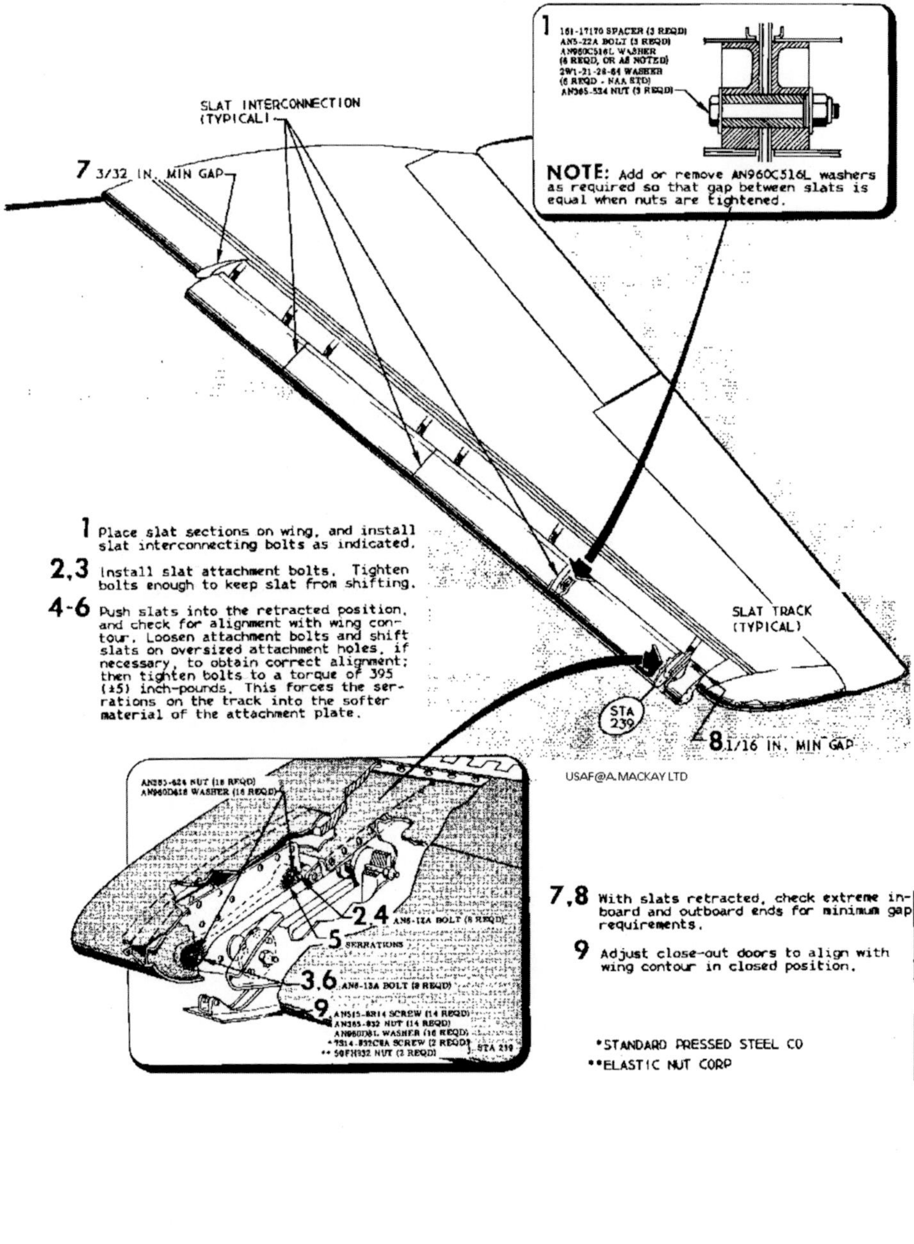

USAF@A.MACKAY LTD

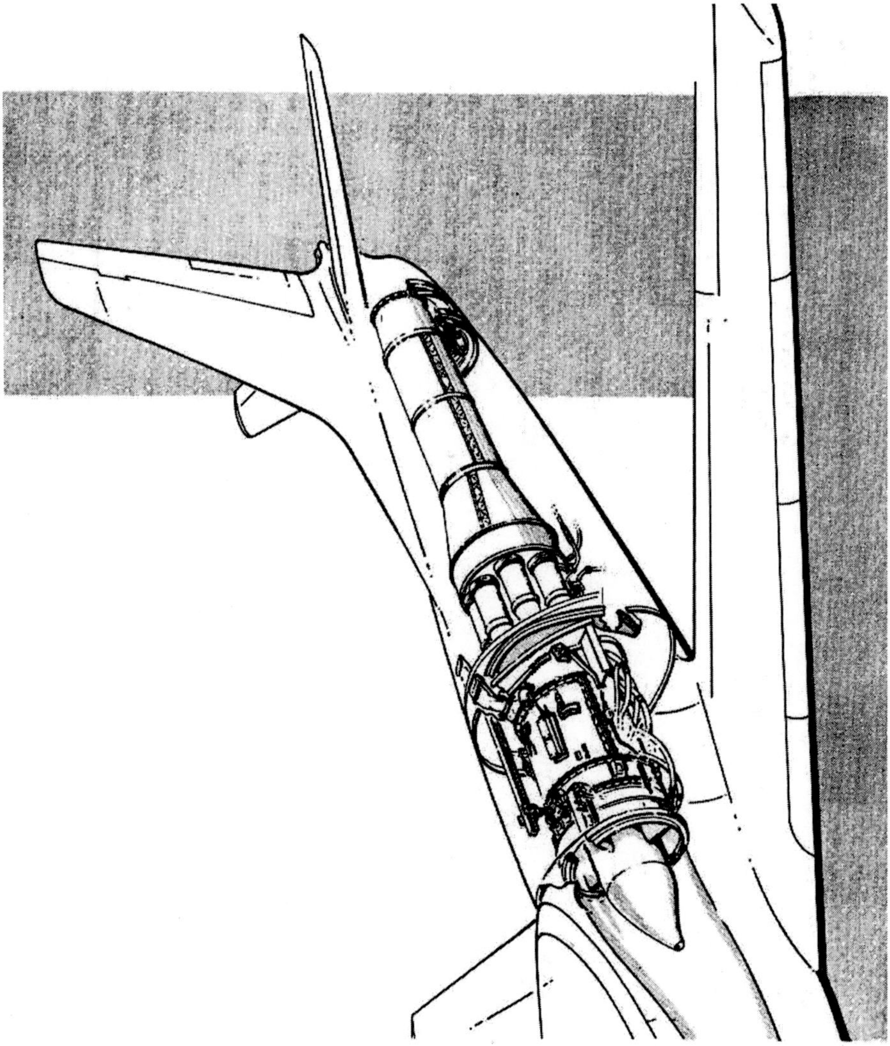

SELECT BIBLIOGRAPHY

PERIODICALS

Flight, Aeroplane, Air Pictorial, All Hands Magazine 1948, Royal Air Force Flying Review, Aeronautics, Air Force Magazine, Aeroplane Spotter, Air Enthusiast, Air International, Journal of Engineering for Gas Turbines and Power, Les Ailes, Pegase, NASA Magazine, Airfix Magazine, Aviation Classics, Aviation Week, International Air Power Review, Meccano Magazine, Aeromilitaria 2012, Studies in Intelligence, Air Power History, Aero Digest, Aviation Magazine International, Commercial Motor, Vayu Aerospace and Defence Review, June 1914, The Scotsman, Barron's National Business and Financial Weekly.

Select Bibliography

1. Central Intelligence Agency: (CIA) history: National Photographic Interpretation Center: The Years of Project HTAUTOMAT, 1956-1958, 6 Volumes, Directorate of Science and Technology Historical Services, NPIC-3, 1974 (Sanitised)
2. The Central Intelligence Agency and Overhead Reconnaissance: The U-2 and OXCART Programs, 1954-1974, History Staff Central Intelligence Agency, 1992, (Sanitised)
3. QUEST, History of Spaceflight Quarterly, Volume 17, Number 3, 2010
4. The U.S. Air Force in Korea, MiG Alley, William T. Y'Blood, Air Force History and Museums Program, 2000
5. A Need to Know, The Role of Air Force Reconnaissance in War Planning, 1945–1953, John Thomas Farquhar Lieutenant Colonel, USAF, Retired, Air University Press Maxwell Air Force Base, Alabama, February 2004
6. The Lens of Power: Aerial Reconnaissance and Diplomacy in the Airpower Century, Joe Santucci, Maxwell Air Force Base, Alabama 2013
7. C.I.A. EO 13526 3.5(c) Speech given by Mr. Richard M. Bissell 12 October 1965 (Sanitised)
8. National Reconnaissance Almanac, National Reconnaissance Office, Center for the Study of National Reconnaissance,14675 LeeRoad,Chantilly,VA,20151-1715, January 2011
9. The Canberra in the RAF, Journal 43a, Royal Air Force Historical Society, 2009
10. The Proceedings of the RAFHS Seminar on Cold War Intelligence Gathering, Journal 23, Royal Air Force Historical Society, 2001
11. Lockheed U-2, Jay Miller, Aerofax, Incorporated Austin, Texas, 1983

12. Marion Mixson Obituary, 21 May 2010, Tampa Bay Times, St Petersburg, Florida, 2010
13. Early cold war overflights, 1950-1956: symposium proceedings / Editors, R. Cargill Hall and Clayton D. Laurie. National Reconnaissance Office, U.S. Government Printing Office, Washington D.C. or National Technical Information Service (NTIS), Springfield Va. 2003
14. HR70-14, Reconnaissance, Memorandum, Allen W. Dulles, Central Intelligence Agency, 24 November 1954 (Sanitised)
15. The National Reconnaissance Office (NRO): Its Origins, Creation & Early Years, HQ, US Air Force, Washington, DC, 1997
16. United States Cryptologic History, Series VI the NSA Period 1952 – Present, Volume 5, American Cryptology during the Cold War, 1945-1989, Book I: The Struggle for Centralization, 1945-1960, Thomas R. Johnson, Center for Cryptologic History, National Security Agency, 1995 (Sanitised)
17. Heart Throb Pilot: Overflights in the European Theater, Gerald E. Cooke N/D (Sanitised)
18. Project Whale Tale, In Cumulative Documents, 346 pages, Summary of OSA Activities for week Ending 17 July 1963, Assistant Director, OSA Deputy Assistant Director, OSA et seq.
19. The Early Overflights, Air Force Magazine, 2020
20. The Air Force and the National Security Space Program 1946 - 1988, R. Cargill Hall, USAF Historical Research Center, 1988
21. Beacon Hill Report: Problems of Air Force Intelligence and Reconnaissance, Project Lincoln, Massachusetts Institute of Technology (MIT), 1952
22. The Fedden Mission to America, December 1942 - March 1943: final report. Ministry of Aircraft Production, 1943 -National Library of Australia
23. The World's First Jet Engines, Journal 53, Royal Air Force Historical Society, 2012
24. Fedden Mission to Germany, Final Report, Ministry of aircraft Production, June 1945, CIOS, 1945
25. Messerschmitt Me262, Arrow to the Future, By Walter J. Boyne, Schiffer Military/Aviation History, Atglen, PA, 1994
26. Les premiers avions à réaction Heinkel He 176 et He178 Alfred Bodemer, Pegase - No56, Decembre 1989
27. Skyfall, Michael Dobbs, Smithsonian, November 2015
28. German Gas Turbine Developments During the Period 1939-1945, BIOS Overall Report No 12 HMSO N/D
29. The UN's First "Air Force": Peacekeepers in Combat, Congo 1960–64 Walter Dorn, The Journal of Military History 77 (October 2013): 1399-1425

30. Estimated Aerodynamic Characteristics for Design of the F-86E Airplane, Engineering Department, North American Aviation NA-50-1277 26 12 1950
31. The North American F-86A Sabre, Edward Shacklady, Profile Number 20, Profile Publications, 1965
32. The Canadair Sabre, Gerhard Joos, Profile Number 186, Profile Publications, 1967
33. American Spy Plane on Exhibition in Moscow, Supplement to Soviet Weekly, Printed by the Co-operative Printing Society Limited (T.U), 7-11. Tudor Street. London, E.C.4, England
34. Remembering the Dragon Lady, The U-2 Spy Plane, Memoirs of the Men who made the Legend, Brigadier General (Rtd), Gerald E. Mcilmoyle, Linda R. Bromley, Helion and Company; Reprint edition (15 Jan. 2013)
35. Seeing Off the Bear: Anglo-American Air Power Cooperation During the Cold War, Proceedings, Joint Meeting of the Royal Air Force Historical Society and the Air Force Historical Foundation, Editor Roger G. Miller Air Force History and Museums Program United States Air Force Washington, D.C. 1995
36. UNITED STATES AIR FORCE STATISTICAL DIGESTS FISCAL YEARS 1950 to 1963 Directorate of Statistical Services Comptroller of the Air Force N/D
37. Canadair the First Fifty Years, Ron Pickler, Larry Milberry, Canav Books, 1995
38. The Air Estimates 1950-51, cmd7898, HMSO, 1950
39. Indo-Pak War, V.P.Juneja, A New Light Publication, New Delhi, 1971.
40. Jet Propulsion Progress, Leslie E. Neville & Nathaniel F. Silsbee, McGraw Hill Book Company Inc., New York and London, 1948
41. Royal Air Force In Germany 1945-1993, The Royal Air Force Historical Society Seminar, Journal 22a, Bracknell, 9 December 1998.
42. Silver Wings, Golden Valor: The USAF Remembers Korea Edited by Dr. Richard P. Hallion, Air Force History and Museums Program, Washington, D.C. 2006
43. Technical Report TR-AE-63: MIG-15 (VK-1) Pilot's Operating Manual, Air Technical Intelligence Center, Wright Patterson Air Force Base, Ohio, 26 April 1955
44. NATO, The First Five Years, 1949-1954, Lord Ismay, North Atlantic Treaty Organisation, Palais de Chaillot, Paris, France, 1st November, 1954
45. Technique et science aéronautiques, AFITA, 6, rue Cimarosa, Paris (XVJc). Kltber 37-21 C. C. P.: PARIS 3054-95, 1948
45. AF(C)-1-1, Flight Manual, Models U-2C and U-2F Aircraft N/D Changed 15 August 1968
45. Beyond Courage, Clay Blair, Arrow Books, The Anchor Press, Essex, 1957

45. RAF Fighter Command 1936-1968, Norman Franks, Patrick Stephens Limited, 1992
46. Early Russian Jet Engines, Vladimir Kotelnikov & Tony Buttler, Rolls Royce Heritage Trust, Derby, 2003
47. The Quick and the Dead, W.A. Waterton, Frederick Muller Ltd, London, 1956
48. Aviation in Scotland, J.D. Gillies & J.L. Wood, Glasgow Branch, Royal Aeronautical Society, Glasgow, 1966
49. Glasgow's Airport, Dugald Cameron, Holmes McDougall, Glasgow, 1990
50. The North American Sabre, Ray Wagner, Macdonald, London, 1963
51. The Gloster Meteor, Edward Shacklady, Macdonald, 1963
52. Canadair Sabre Mk. 1-6, Richard Ward & Gerhard Joos, Osprey Publications Ltd. 1971
53. Jet, The Story of a Pioneer, Sir Frank Whittle, K.B.E., C.B., F.R.S. Frederick Muller Ltd., 1953
54. The Collectors, Kevin Wright, Helion & Company, Warwick, 2019
55. By Any Means Necessary, William E. Burrows, Arrow Books, London 2001
56. Sculthorpe, Secrecy and Stealth, Peter B. Gunn, The History Press, Gloucester, 2015
57. Spyflights of the Cold War, Paul Lashmar, Sutton Publishing, Gloucester, 1998
58. To Save a City, The Berlin Airlift 1948-1949, Roger G. Miller, Air Force History and Museums Program, 2013
59. The Soviet Atomic Bomb, Dr Vladimir Shamberg, United States Air Force Academy, Colorado, 2001
60. War Prizes, Phil Butler, Midland Counties Publications, 1994
61. Aircraft Power Plants, Frank L. Wattendorf & H.S. Tsien & Pol Duwez, Air Material Command, Dayton, 1946
62. Air 27, Operation Records Book for all squadrons mentioned, held at the National Archives, Kew. Not all are complete, full name of the Squadron helps search.
63. Hansard, both houses.
64. Aircraft Engines of the World, Paul H. Wilkinson, Wilkinson, New York, 1945
64. Luftwaffe, Secret Jets of the Third Reich, Dan Sharp, Morton's Media Group, 2015

Merchant City Print High Street, Glasgow Scotland